FIRST NATIONAL VACCINE LAW CONFERENCE

Papers and Proceedings

LOREN MILLIKEN, MONTRECE RANSOM,
ALEXANDRA BHATTI, ANGELA SHEN, EDITORS

AMERICAN BAR ASSOCIATION
Health Law Section

Cover design by Jill Tedhams/ABA Design

Printed in the United States of America.

28 27 26 25 24 5 4 3 2 1

ISBN 978-1-63905-414-5

A catalog record for this book is available from the Library of Congress.

To Matthew Brown and his son, Alexander,
who continues to buzz with positivity.

Order of Articles

Foreword

A Proper Introduction to Vaccine Law, and a Very Necessary National Vaccine Law Conference

Brian Dean Abramson and Montrece Ransom

Introduction

Vaccine law has seemingly sprung from obscurity and into the public eye just within the past few years. As a practical matter, however, vaccine law has cycled through periods of public concern (and public amnesia) for centuries. Like many aspects of health law, the loosely connected web of statutes, regulations, and policies governing vaccine development, distribution, administration, and post-administration tracking has moved in fits and starts. Innovations and improvements in the field have often been spurred by events that are tragic, even catastrophic, to the population.[1]

Although vaccination is widely recognized as one of the greatest historical public health achievements,[2] there is something to be said for the times when no one working outside of the immediate field *thinks* very much about vaccine law. Those are the times when all is going quietly enough in this corner of the public health sphere that the concerns of the

1. Brian Dean Abramson, Dorit Reiss, Peter O. Safir & John R. Thomas, Vaccine, Vaccination, and Immunization Law, 2d ed., 1-12 (2002); Peter Barton Hutt & Richard A. Merrill, Food and Drug Law: Cases and Materials 8 (1991).

2. Alexandra Bhatti, Stacy P. Kershner & Shade O. Olowookere, *Vaccination Law Across the Life-Course*, in Montrece McNeill Ransom & Laura Magaña Valladares, eds., Public Health Law: Concepts and Case Studies 73–97 (2021).

field fall far into the background of public contemplation. Recent times, however, have been anything but quiet.

So it is that in the spring of 2022, a group of frequent correspondents in various corners of the field of vaccine law, observing the continued growth of misinformation and disinformation flowing in response to the COVID-19 pandemic, decided that it was necessary to bring stakeholders from different aspects of the field together for the first-ever National Vaccine Law Conference. In a short window of time, a singular effort produced a historic program, the proceedings of which are now before you.

Despite the increasingly popular sentiment that "the pandemic is over"—including a statement as such by the President of the United States—this rather aspirational assertion does not comport with any medical or health policy definition of the subsidence of pandemic dangers.[3] At the time of the official termination of the national emergency in the United States, "Arcturus," the latest subvariant of omicron, had been reported in nearly 30 countries, was growing its presence in the United States, and was noted to have the potential to cause a summer surge.[4] However, the declining sense of peril will only widen health disparities and exacerbate the vaccine law issues now advancing throughout America and the world.

Vaccination mandates remain in place and, in some professions and environments, must for the foreseeable future. The arguments initially deployed by opponents of vaccination against the COVID-19 vaccines have since been pressed against the vaccines that protect against childhood diseases that once populated graveyards with rows of tiny headstones. Early in 2023, a measles outbreak was reported in Ohio, with one medical professional noting that parents who had otherwise fully vaccinated their children were under-vaccinating with the measles, mumps,

3. Michelle A. Williams, *Why Biden's premature COVID ending could help it surge*, THE HILL (Sept. 23, 2022), https://thehill.com/opinion/healthcare/3658032-why-bidens-premature-covid-ending-could-help-it-surge/.

4. Rachel Nania, *What to Know About Arcturus, the Latest COVID Variant*, AARP (May 1, 2023), https://www.aarp.org/health/conditions-treatments/info-2023/arcturus-new-covid-variant.html.

and rubella (MMR) vaccine.[5] Measles, which had previously resurged in 2019,[6] has been a longstanding target of antivaccine efforts.[7]

Echoes of History

The response to any given public health emergency—and, in particular, the success of that response—shapes policies for addressing future public health outcomes. The contours of the changes thus wrought are decidedly affected by the politics of their time. For example:

> In 1813, the U.S. Congress responded to a smallpox epidemic by enacting one of the nation's first federal statutes related to general health, titled "An act to encourage vaccination." The act authorized the president to appoint an agent ". . . to preserve the genuine vaccine matter, and to furnish the same to any citizen of the United States, whenever it may be applied for. . . ." However, the act would be repealed in 1822[8] following an 1821 smallpox outbreak that was thought to have been caused by the distribution of contaminated vaccines.[9]

The repeal of the 1813 act was not the only plausible outcome of the purported contamination event. By contrast, a 1901 incidence of deaths of children in the Midwest, from infection via tetanus-contaminated doses of diphtheria antitoxin, spurred the creation of the first federal regime for ensuring drug safety, a precursor to the system that remains in place today.[10] With greater foresight and political will, the 1821 incident could well have led not to a retreat from efforts to combat smallpox through a

5 Hanna Webster, *The Ohio measles outbreak and the danger of losing herd immunity*, Pittsburgh Post-Gazette (Feb. 12, 2023), https://www.post-gazette.com/news/health/2023/02/12/ohio-measles-outbreak-mmr-vaccine/stories/202302090111.

6. Bhatti et al., *supra* note 2, at 77.

7. *See* Abramson et al., *supra* note 1, at 12-24.

8. 3 Stat. 677 (1822).

9. Abramson et al., *supra* note 1, at 1-10-11, *citing* John P. Griffin, John Posner & Geoffrey R. Barker, eds., The Textbook of Pharmaceutical Medicine, 7th ed. 465 (2013).

10. U.S. Food & Drug Admin., *Science and the Regulation of Biological Products: From a Rich History to a Challenging Future* 2 (Mar. 2002), https://www.fda.gov/media/108536/download; Ross E. DeHovitz, *The 1901 St Louis Incident: The First Modern Medical Disaster*, 133 Pediatrics 964, 965 (June 2014), https://publications.aap.org/pediatrics/article-abstract/133/6/964/76022/The-1901-St-Louis-Incident-The-First-Modern?redirectedFrom=fulltext.

federally supported vaccination program but to enhanced efforts at the federal level to ensure the safety of the vaccine itself.

Of course, in the 1820s, as today, a substantial contingent of the population opposed vaccination, and this opposition encompassed sowing doubts about both the qualities of the vaccine and the character and motivations of its proponents. Pamphlets distributed in the decades following the introduction of vaccination asserted a wide range of detriments to the practice. Some claimed that the use of cattle as the bodies within which to grow the vaccine for use in people threatened humans with contamination with the characteristics of the animal. Others deemed the prevention of disease through vaccination to be an affront to the divine prerogative to use death by disease as a form of judgment. Still others made the uncomfortably familiar assertion that the smallpox vaccine was worse than the disease itself.[11]

Courts were not immune from such misinformation. As late as 1919, the North Dakota Supreme Court held a vaccination mandate to be in violation of state law in *Rhea v. Board of Education of Devils Lake*:[12]

> A concurring opinion in that case referenced an anti-vaccination book then in circulation. Citing this book, the concurring opinion questioned the value of the practice and asserted, among other things, that vaccination was not necessary in such a sparsely populated state, where disease was less apt to spread; that the smallpox vaccination was more dangerous than the disease itself, which was "the least dangerous of the infectious diseases" and that the decline in the disease could be credited to improved sanitation rather than to vaccination.[13]

Historically, vaccination has been unique as a segment of the larger field of public health in the degree to which it draws opposition fueled by misinformation and disinformation. For the purposes of this foreword, we roughly adopt the American Psychological Association definitions of misinformation as false information haphazardly spread due to miscommunication, ambiguity, and mistaken popular beliefs, and disinformation as false information intentionally developed and disseminated in a

11. *Smallpox*, MEDICAL HERITAGE LIBRARY, https://www.medicalheritage.org/resource-sets/vaccines/smallpox/.

12. 41 N.D. 449, 171 N.W. 103 (1919).

13. ABRAMSON ET AL., *supra* note 1, at 15-5, *citing Rhea*, 41 N.D. 458–60, 171 N.W. at 107.

calculated, often targeted manner,[14] with the intent of disrupting trust in health authorities and the practices they advocate.

Our country's history and legacy of racism and discrimination in medicine and healthcare also weigh heavily here. Horrific experiments on enslaved people, forced sterilizations on Black women, and the U.S. Public Health Service Syphilis study are only examples of the historical atrocities that have led to lingering mistrust, vaccine hesitancy, and heightened susceptibility to misinformation among Black, indigenous, and people of color (BIPOC). Paraphrasing the message in the closing keynote address for the first National Vaccine Law Conference, if we are to advance vaccine equity in this country, we must be honest about the gravitational pull this history exerts today.

Areas of Vaccine Law

Vaccine law, as a field, can be divided into several distinct areas of practice. The nature of these areas tends to isolate practitioners within silos of expertise, such that a participant in one area may have little exposure to the others, even though the work of each is critical to public outcomes as a whole. Indeed, the work of vaccine law professionals in any field may broadly affect public perceptions of vaccination. One driving factor in the establishment of the National Vaccine Law Conference was to bring together practitioners in these areas in ways that had not previously been attempted, to foment an exchange of perspectives and ideas.

The key areas of law can be described along a pathway following the life cycle of the vaccine itself, each facing its native challenge and each subject to its own body of misinformation arrayed against it. The first area is regulatory. From the moment virologists or biochemists or other such researchers develop an idea of how to vaccinate against a particular disease, or how to improve the workings of a particular vaccine, their work comes within the ambit of regulatory structures. The components of a vaccine are, fundamentally, chemical substances, and the formulation of a new vaccine or vaccine ingredient must be done under carefully controlled conditions. Once formulated, the vaccine must be tested, and if the intent is for the vaccine to be distributed in the United States, the results of these tests (good or bad) must be reported to the U.S. Food and Drug Administration (FDA), which evaluates pharmaceutical products

14. *See Misinformation and disinformation*, AMERICAN PSYCHOLOGICAL ASSOCIATION (2023), https://www.apa.org/topics/journalism-facts/misinformation-disinformation.

for approval for distribution to the public.[15] Once licensed by the FDA, the manufacture and marketing of the vaccine will remain under scrutiny for so long as the product is on the market.[16]

At the same time, the inventors of this new vaccine, or their employers, will almost invariably wish to protect their valuable intellectual property rights by securing patent protections for the invention. Of course, they may at the same time discover that someone else has already come to a similar idea, and their own description of their invention must be tweaked to constitute something novel and therefore patentable. The regulatory regime governing licensure has implications for intellectual property protection.

Presuming that the manufacturer has secured both FDA licensure (or, in a public health crisis, an Emergency Use Authorization) and at least provisional patent protection,[17] it may then begin manufacturing and marketing its new product. At this point, additional public health considerations come to the fore. If the vaccine is for a rare or unusual disease, then there may be little further consideration of its public health impact. However, if the vaccine effectively counters a common malady, then it may be evaluated by the Centers for Disease Control and Prevention's (CDC's) Advisory Committee on Immunization Practices, ACIP, to determine whether it should be added to the recommended vaccination schedule and subject to a variety of additional questions that come up under these circumstances.

For vaccines that are generally addressed to a disease of concern, we proceed, then, to the broader area of public health law itself. Here, numerous legal issues and questions will arise concerning health equity and whether (and how much) public funding should be dedicated to persuading the population to receive this vaccination and, indeed, to paying for doses of the vaccine itself to be distributed and administered. At the state level, questions may arise as to whether the administration of these vaccines should be limited to physicians, as is the case with most prescription drugs, or whether they may be administered by other medical professionals, pharmacists, nurses, and the like. Issues may also arise

15. ABRAMSON ET AL., *supra* note 1, at 2-6-7.

16. *Id.* at 2-25-27.

17. While patent registration is not a legal requirement to enter the market, under normal circumstances it is economically unfeasible to proceed with the introduction to the market of a new vaccine for which intellectual property rights remain uncertain. No manufacturer wants to establish a market only to find that they cannot prevent a competitor from immediately usurping their work through an interchangeable product.

regarding access to vaccines for disabled persons who rely on others to address medical needs, for persons who are detained or incarcerated, or for minors with parents who oppose vaccination. For a new vaccine, it must be incorporated into systems design to track the vaccination status of individuals and to record any occurrences of adverse reactions.

It is also at this stage in public consideration that public health officials and state legislatures must consider whether the vaccine should be mandated for particular populations, which may range from school students to medical workers to first responders, and at the federal level, possibly to military personnel or immigrants to the United States. Even outside of the public sphere, private entities may consider whether to mandate the vaccination of their employees, subject to state and federal limitations on such requirements. Because most mandates are determined at the state level or territorial level, the United States has dozens of different structures, ranging from minimal requirements that are easy to evade or be exempted from on medical or religious bases to those that are strictly enforced and difficult to avoid.

Irrespective of whether a vaccine is mandated, consideration must also be given to the question of what happens if an individual recipient has an adverse reaction, particularly if that reaction is serious, to the point where the injured party may be entitled to compensation. Vaccine injury compensation is a unique area of tort law in the United States and many other countries that have established programs specially geared for addressing such interests, particularly concerning vaccines that are broadly mandated.

It is important to note that none of this happens in a static environment. A vaccine, once developed, may routinely and repeatedly be improved through advances in the technology of formulation and manufacture. The disease that the vaccine is designed to counter may itself evolve, requiring adjustment to the vaccine to match this evolution. The discovery of specific contraindications in the intended recipient population may necessitate the development of alternative vaccines that allow individuals contraindicated for a particular formulation to receive the benefit of the protection offered by another.

Lastly, we are presently living through a societal phenomenon under which any new vaccine that is introduced will likely face a gauntlet of skepticism, misinformation, and possibly intentional and coordinated disinformation.

The series of steps just described generally assumes normal conditions. However, as we have recently learned, during a pandemic, these steps can be thrown into substantial disarray. With respect to COVID-19 vaccines, there are simultaneously substantial regulatory challenges, intellectual property disputes, unresolved questions about future funding to ensure public access, a heavily contested array of vaccination mandates, and open questions regarding the future of adverse event compensation, all against the backdrop of the most substantial antivaccine effort to be deployed against the new vaccine, possibly since the advent of the smallpox vaccine itself. Indeed, the COVID-19 crisis early on indicated a historic failure of state governments to take measures to protect their population from the disease and has ultimately led to an unprecedented level of state action in opposition to vaccination.

Following are some of the key issues arising in each of these areas of vaccine law.

Current Regulatory Vaccine Law Issues

The licensure, production, and marketing of pharmaceutical products in the United States are regulated by the FDA, which has broad authority and a lengthy history of acting in this field. Perhaps the most pernicious myth directed toward the regulatory structure of vaccines in the United States is that the FDA and related agencies are captured entities, susceptible to being bribed or manipulated into putting unsafe products onto the market for the benefit of powerful pharmaceutical companies. One aspect of this concern is the perceived "revolving door" through which government employees move to lucrative positions in the private sector, and vice versa. Claims of impropriety are belied, however, by the fact that the FDA imposes fines and penalties amounting to hundreds of millions of dollars every year on the exact same pharmaceutical companies that manufacture the vaccines complained of. Since 2000, FDA has assessed, in total, nearly twenty billion dollars from the largest pharmaceutical companies.[18]

In fact, one of the great curiosities of the COVID-19 pandemic has been the accusation that the responsible agencies promote ineffective vaccines while dismissing the efficacy of other drugs claimed to be effective against the disease—Ivermectin, manufactured by Merck, also a major manufacturer of vaccines, and hydroxychloroquine, for which related drugs are manufactured by Sanofi and Pfizer, also noted vaccine manufacturers.

---

18. *Violation Tracker Agency Summary Page*, Good Jobs First (updated 2022), https://violationtracker.goodjobsfirst.org/prog.php?agency_sum=FDA.

In one sense, it is odd that calls for the FDA to revoke EUA status or full licensure of COVID-19 vaccines tend to arise most fervently from adherents to a political philosophy that is often anathema to the very fact of drug regulation in the first place. It is true that the FDA has occasionally erred, allowing products to enter the market that were later found to have negative effects undiscovered during clinical trials. The historical alternative to federal regulation of pharmaceutical products, however, was the proverbial wild West of snake oil salesmen concocting whatever mix they desired (often combining alcohol with any number of substances now heavily controlled or deemed illegal altogether) and selling it on streetcorners, announcing any number of ills claimed to be cured.

In fact, it is remarkable to think about how little regulated the development of the first vaccine was. Dr. Edward Jenner, having observed the apparent immunity to smallpox gained by milkmaids who had been exposed to cowpox, intentionally infected the eight-year-old son of his gardener with cowpox and then intentionally exposed the child to smallpox.[19] Jenner's clinical trial had a sample size of one, with no placebo group, no institutional review board—indeed, no governance whatsoever beyond Jenner's own self-supervision. Jenner's methodology would today be considered both ethically and scientifically unacceptable. In the looser mores of his day, however, it was sufficient to spark a scientific revolution.

Current Vaccine Intellectual Property Issues

Patent law may seem an unlikely field to have issues with vaccine-related misinformation, but in 2021, *USA Today* published a piece debunking a variety of conspiracy theories regarding patents in connection with COVID-19. One such theory asserted that patents owned by the National Institutes of Health (NIH) regarding coronavirus were used to control profits arising in connection with coronavirus-related pandemics (including the COVID-19 pandemic). Another purported that the NIH's ownership of this technology indicated the agency's involvement in the creation of the virus itself. Related to this, another theory claimed that the virus was intentionally manufactured by the United States and that reason the virus was first found in Wuhan, China, was that ownership of a product of nature being barred under U.S. patent meant that the United States had to outsource such manufacture to a lab in another country.[20]

19. ABRAMSON ET AL., *supra* note 1, at I-7.

20. Camille Caldera & Miriam Fauzia, *Fact check: 'Plandemic II' alleges false conspiracy theory involving CDC, NIH; pandemic not planned*, USA TODAY

A less conspiratorial issue is the plethora of proposals to waive patent rights as a solution to accessibility barriers attributed to intellectual property rights, including proposals to this effect emanating from the Biden administration.[21] Near the beginning of the COVID-19 pandemic, several manufacturers made patent pledges, asserting that they would not enforce their patents during the pandemic to avoid any such disruptions. Interestingly, this did nothing to dissuade Allele Biotechnology—a manufacturer of biological products but not vaccines—from suing Pfizer for infringement of Allele's protein-marking technology in the course of Pfizer's development of its COVID-19 vaccine.[22] That case was ultimately settled.

Current Issues with Equity, Funding, and Access to Vaccines

Among the most prominent aspects of the pandemic has been its disproportionate impact on racial, ethnic, and other minorities. Our collective experience in the pandemic highlighted how these inequities show up in vaccine access, distribution, and uptake as well. In July 2021, the Centers for Disease Control and Prevention (CDC) reported that of the 57 percent of COVID-19 vaccine recipients for whom race was known, 61 percent were white, 15 percent were Latinx, and just 9 percent were Black.[23] Two years later, data from the CDC shows Black Americans remain more likely to die and more likely to be hospitalized from COVID-19 than White Americans, yet rates of COVID-19 vaccination remain low among this population.[24]

(Aug. 23, 2020), https://www.usatoday.com/story/news/factcheck/2020/08/23/fact-check-plandemic-ii-alleges-false-cdc-nih-conspiracy-theory/3408658001/.

21. Emma Farge, Stephanie Ulmer-Nebahay & Philip Blenkinsop, *U.S. President Biden calls for intellectual property protection waivers after Omicron discovery*, REUTERS (Nov. 26, 2021), https://www.reuters.com/business/healthcare-pharmaceuticals/us-president-biden-calls-intellectual-property-protection-waivers-covid-19-2021-11-26/.

22. Allele Biotechnology & Pharm., Inc. v. Pfizer, Inc., No. 20-cv-01958-H-AGS (S.D. Cal., May 4, 2021).

23. *See COVID Data Tracker*, CENTERS FOR DISEASE CONTROL AND PREVENTION (June 30, 2021), https://covid.cdc.gov/covid-data-tracker/#vaccination-demographic.

24. *Hospitalization and Death by Race/Ethnicity*, CENTERS FOR DISEASE CONTROL AND PREVENTION (accessed on May 5, 2023), https://www.cdc.gov/coronavirus/2019-ncov/covid-data/investigations-discovery/hospitalization-death-by-race-ethnicity.html.

There are many known legal and policy drivers of racial inequity in access to and uptake of vaccines generally, and the COVID-19 vaccine specifically. These include structural racism, health system infrastructure, physical distribution channels, opt-in and demand-based signups, access to information and distribution platforms, misinformation, and justified medical, public health, and governmental mistrust.[25]

The COVID-19 pandemic strained healthcare systems across the country and throughout the world and highlighted these equity concerns with respect to initial efforts to vaccinate the population. Early on in the pandemic, it was also observed that people took every measure imaginable to "jump the line" and get access to vaccination before they were eligible. In January 2021 in New York, it was noted that "[a] Covid-19 vaccination site in a Latino neighborhood in New York City hard hit by the pandemic saw an overwhelming number of White people from outside the community show up to get the shot."[26] In February, two women in Florida dressed as "grannies," donning wigs, glasses, and gloves, to get vaccinated before their cohort was eligible,[27] and in March it was reported that wealthy donors to a Florida hospital were given access to vaccination before eligible members of the public.[28]

Since that initial rush to vaccinate subsided, the situation has turned on its head, with governments encountering difficulty in persuading the unvaccinated to receive vaccines, and even in persuading the initially vaccinated to receive boosters. Such efforts have been hamstrung by the politicization of the issue. A bill pending in the Idaho state legislature would make it a crime to administer an mRNA vaccine in that state (even to adults who wish to receive one and are satisfied that they are aware of

---

25. Olatunde C. Johnson & Kristen Underhill, *Vaccination Equity by Design*, 131 Yale L. J. F. 53 (2021), www.yalelawjournal.org/forum/vaccination-equity-by-design.

26. Nicquel Terry Ellis, *A vaccination site meant to serve a hard-hit Latino neighborhood in New York instead serviced more Whites from other areas*, CNN (Jan. 30, 2021), https://www.cnn.com/2021/01/30/us/new-york-vaccine-disparities/index.html.

27. *Young women in Florida dress as 'grannies' in apparent attempt to get COVID-19 vaccine, official says*, ABC7 Eyewitness News (Feb. 19, 2021), https://abc7.com/dr-raul-pino-women-dress-as-grannies-for-covid-vaccine-coronavirus-in-florida-department-of-health-orange-county/10351857/.

28. Ben Conarck, *Baptist Health silent on report saying it put donors in front of COVID vaccine line*, The Miami Herald (Mar. 5, 2021), https://www.miamiherald.com/news/coronavirus/article250012419.html.

any risks).[29] Within days after this bill was announced, a Florida county party organization voted for a ban on all COVID-19 vaccines in the state and sent that request to the governor of the state for consideration.[30] While it is doubtful that these efforts to literally criminalize the administration of the vaccines themselves will pass, we have been surprised before in recent times.

At the same time as these antivaccine efforts have continued in the political sphere, funding for COVID-19 vaccination has waned,[31] and manufacturers have announced dramatic price increases per dose.[32] In the environment of the belief that the pandemic is ending, these developments will likely dampen enthusiasm for vaccination.

Current Issues with Vaccine Passports and Vaccination Mandates

The COVID-19 pandemic shed some light on one long-standing question of constitutional law in the United States: can the federal government mandate vaccination for some portion of the civilian population? In a pair of motions to enjoin executive agency actions pending further litigation decided by the Supreme Court in early 2022, it was held that the Occupational Safety and Health Administration (OSHA) likely did not have the power to mandate the vaccination of employees of all companies employing over 100 people,[33] but that the Centers for Medicare and Medicaid Services (CMS) did have the authority to withhold funding from healthcare providers that did not have a reasonably fully vaccinated staff.[34]

---

29. HB 154 (2023); *see also* Thao Nguyen, *Idaho bill would criminalize giving mRNA vaccines—the tech used in popular COVID vaccines*, USA TODAY (Feb. 21, 2023), https://www.usatoday.com/story/news/nation/2023/02/21/idaho-mrna-covid-19-vaccines/11316055002/.

30. *Florida county Republican Party votes to ban the COVID-19 vaccine*, CBS NEWS (Feb. 21, 2023), https://www.cbsnews.com/miami/news/florida-county-republican-party-votes-to-ban-the-covid-19-vaccine/.

31. Alexander Tin, *Biden administration is preparing for the end of free COVID-19 vaccines as funds run dry*, CBS NEWS (Sept. 2, 2022), https://www.cbsnews.com/news/free-covid-19-vaccines-biden-administration-congress-funding/.

32. John Yang & Sarah Clune Hartman, *Why manufacturers are hiking COVID vaccine prices*, PBS NEWS (Jan. 14, 2023), https://www.pbs.org/newshour/show/why-manufacturers-are-hiking-covid-vaccine-prices.

33. NFIB v. OSHA, No. 21A244, 595 U.S. ____ (Jan. 13, 2022).

34. Biden v. Missouri, No. 21A240, 595 U.S. ____ (Jan. 13, 2022).

The pandemic also saw the first widespread use by U.S. states and municipalities of imposing obtaining vaccination passports as a prerequisite to access restaurants and entertainment venues. A report released in February 2023 indicated that such restrictions were evaded easily enough to have no discernible effect on vaccination rates.[35] This contrasted with the experience in European countries, where such vaccination requirements were imposed more uniformly. In France, for example, a vaccine pass requirement was imposed under which individuals over the age of 16 "were required to demonstrate they had been vaccinated against COVID-19 to enter restaurants, bars, fairs, seminars, trade schools, and public transportation."[36]

A 2021 study in *The Lancet* reported that vaccination rates generally rose in countries that introduced early COVID-19 vaccine certification systems, which were understood by their populations to be precursors to vaccination mandates. This increase was most pronounced among people under 30, with some increase among those aged 30–49. The increase began before the mandates themselves were implemented, projecting anticipation of the mandate.[37]

Peculiar to the United States, one of the most frustrating tactics encountered during the pandemic, and one oddly in contrast to efforts to coopt doses intended for historically disadvantaged minority communities, has been the direction of antivaccine messaging toward those same minority communities. There is, admittedly, a history of medical misconduct toward minorities, which opponents of vaccination have highlighted to depress minority vaccination uptake.[38] In areas where members

35. John Domen, *Restaurants, jobs asked for proof of COVID vaccine. So did it increase DC's vaccine rates?*, WTOP News (Feb. 22, 2023), https://wtop.com/dc/2023/02/study-how-effective-was-dcs-indoor-covd-19-vaccine-mandate-in-raising-vaccination-rates/.

36. Brian Dean Abramson & Ashira Vantrees, *The Global Environment of Vaccination Mandates*, 15 Medicine, Law & Society 202 (Oct. 2022), *citing Health pass becomes 'vaccine pass': Details of France' tough new Anti-pandemic bill*, France24 (Jan. 17, 2022), https://www.france24.com/en/france/20220117-health-pass-becomes-vaccine-pass-details-of-france-s-tough-new-anti-pandemic-bill.

37. M. C. Mills & T. Rüttenauer, *The Effect of Mandatory COVID-19 Certificates on Vaccine Uptake: Synthetic-Control Modelling of Six Countries*, 7 The Lancet 1, e15–22 (Oct. 6, 2022).

38. Jessica Guynn, *'We are going to have to save ourselves,' Black community fights deadly COVID vaccine conspiracy theories*, USA Today (Mar. 10, 2021), https://www.usatoday.com/story/tech/2021/03/10/covid-vaccine-facebook-youtube-instagram-black-misinformation-fight/6943180002/; Will Stone, *An Anti-Vaccine Film Targeted To Black Americans Spreads False Information*, NPR (June 8, 2021),

of these groups are successfully dissuaded from vaccination, this is then exploited to enable the communicators of these antivaccine messages to assert that vaccination passport requirements are inherently racially biased, due to the disproportionate limitations imposed on communities successfully dissuaded from vaccination.

The prevalence of vaccination mandates led to a historic level of litigation in opposition to them. By September 2022, it was reported that "[l]awsuits opposing COVID-19 vaccine mandates have surpassed the 1,000-complaint mark. The vast majority of these cases (75 percent) have been filed against employers."[39] Many U.S. states sought to impose historically novel limitations on the ability of private employers to require that their employees be vaccinated including Alabama,[40] Florida,[41] Montana,[42] North Dakota,[43] and Texas.[44] South Carolina enacted legislation specifically prohibiting a broad list of businesses from discriminating on the basis of vaccination through December 31, 2023.[45]

Three states have specifically required employers to exempt employees from COVID-19 vaccination mandates if the employee can demonstrate the presence of antibodies for the disease, these being Arkansas,[46] North Dakota,[47] and South Carolina.[48] Exemptions for persons having "COVID-19 immunity" or "natural immunity" are required by Florida,[49] Indiana,[50] and Tennessee.[51] Exemptions based on a prior COVID-19

---

https://www.npr.org/sections/health-shots/2021/06/08/1004214189/anti-vaccine-film-targeted-to-black-americans-spreads-false-information.

39. Patricia Anderson Pryor, *Challenges Against Employer COVID-19 Vaccine Mandates Show No Sign of Slowing*, National Law Review (Sept. 19, 2022), https://www.natlawreview.com/article/challenges-against-employer-covid-19-vaccine-mandates-show-no-sign-slowing.

40. S.B. 267 (Ala. 2021).

41. Fla. Exec. Order No. 21-81 § 2 (Apr. 2, 2021); S.B. 2006 (Fla. 2021); Fla. Stat. § 381.00316 (2021).

42. Mont. Exec. Order No. 7-2021 (Apr. 13, 2021).

43. H.B. 1511 (N.D. 2021).

44. S.B. 968 (Tex. 2021).

45. H. 3126 (S.C. 2021).

46. S.B. 739 (Ark., Oct. 13, 2021).

47. H.B. 1151 (N.D., Nov. 12, 2021).

48. H. 3126 (S.C., Apr. 25, 22); effective through Dec. 31, 2023.

49. S.B. 2006 (Fla. 2021); Fla. Stat. § 381.00316 (2021).

50. H.B. 1001 (Ind., Mar. 3, 2022).

51. S.B. 1982 (Tenn., May 4, 2022).

infection, without specifically referencing immunity, are provided for in Texas[52] and Utah.[53]

In May 2022, the state of Montana enacted a COVID-19-driven set of vaccination and immunity antidiscrimination statutes including an effective ban on employer vaccination mandates, specifically framed as a privacy protection that prohibited employers from requiring employees to disclose their vaccination status.[54] In December 2022, this prohibition was held unconstitutional and preempted by federal laws by the U.S. District Court for the District of Montana in *Mont. Med. Ass'n v. Knudsen*.[55]

In October 2022, CDC's ACIP voted unanimously to add COVID-19 vaccines to the recommended pediatric immunization schedule. Most healthcare providers follow ACIP guidance when making vaccine recommendations for their patients. However, ACIP recommendations for childhood vaccinations are not mandates. Under our system of federalism, it is up to each state to determine the schedule of vaccinations that all schoolchildren must receive before being admitted to school.[56] Washington D.C. is one of the very few jurisdictions in the United States to mandate them.[57] Its mandate, among the strictest in the nation, applies to children aged 12 and older, requiring the initial two-shot course and a booster for in-person school attendance. New Orleans has a similar mandate in place, for children aged five and older. Still other, larger school districts are encouraging but not mandating that children be vaccinated. As of February 2023, 21 states have laws in place that ban student COVID-19 vaccine mandates.[58]

State laws requiring students to be vaccinated are recognized as "critical components of an effective vaccine delivery system." Such laws have been upheld by the Supreme Court, even in the absence of the threat of an outbreak.[59] According to Bhatti et al., "Schools are where a large number of children congregate in close proximity, and many diseases are easily spread, so they present a unique opportunity for vaccination enforcement."[60] However, COVID-19 school entry mandates have served

52. S.B. 968 (Tex. 2021).
53. H.B. 63 (Utah, Mar. 22, 2022).
54. Mont. Code Ann. §§ 49-2-312 and -313 (2022).
55. No. CV 21-108-M-DWM (D. Mont., Dec. 9, 2022).
56. Bhatti et al., *supra* note 2, at 82.
57. *States Address School Vaccine Mandates*, NASHP (Feb. 6, 2023), https://nashp.org/states-address-school-vaccine-mandates-and-mask-mandates/.
58. *Id.*
59. Zucht v. King, 43 S. Ct. 24 (1922),
60. Bhatti et al., *supra* note 2, at 85.

to highlight the potential impact such mandates can have on health disparities. Because minority children are historically immunized at lower rates than the general population, equity advocates argue that vaccine mandates serve to disproportionately prevent minority students from attending school. A fall 2022 study supports this assertion, finding that while roughly 60 percent of student enrollment in D.C. schools is Black, only 23 percent of children 12 to 15 and 31 percent of 16- and 17-year-olds had received three shots of a COVID vaccine.[61]

Current Vaccine Injury Compensation Issues

Individuals who assert that they have been injured by one of the routinely mandated childhood vaccines in the United States must first seek compensation through the National Vaccine Injury Compensation Program. A long-standing falsehood directed against this program is that its operations are in some way shrouded in mystery. While it is little known, the details of the functioning of the program are readily available to the public, as is substantial data on its caseload and resolutions. Opponents of vaccination have been noted to "believe not simply that the court is a tough hurdle, but that its requirements are part of a government plan to mislead citizens and to conceal vaccine injuries by denying claims."[62]

Even before the pandemic, a global vaccine injury compensation program had been proposed.[63] In 2021, in response to the COVID-19 pandemic, the World Health Organization (WHO) established a global no-fault compensation program for vaccine injuries resulting from administration of COVID-19 vaccines. The program is limited to "92 low- and middle-income countries and economies eligible for support via the Gavi COVAX Advance Market Commitment" and is the first multinational vaccine injury compensation program.[64]

---

61. Douglas Blair, *As DC Plans to Ban 40% of Black Teens From School, Mayor Rejects DC COVID-19 Vaccine Numbers*, The Daily Signal (Aug. 15, 2022), https://www.dailysignal.com/2022/08/15/as-dc-plans-to-ban-40-of-black-teens-from-school-mayor-rejects-dc-covid-19-vaccine-numbers/.

62. Anna Kirkland, Vaccine Court: The Law and Politics of Injury 7 (2016).

63. John D. Winter, Cassye Cole & Jonah Wacholder, *Toward A Global Solution on Vaccine Liability and Compensation*, 74 Food & Drug L.J. 1 (2019), https://www.fdli.org/wp-content/uploads/2019/03/Winter.pdf.

64. *No-fault Compensation Programme for COVID-19 Vaccines is a World First*, WHO (Feb. 22, 2021), https://www.who.int/news/item/22-02-2021-no-fault-compensation-programme-for-covid-19-vaccines-is-a-world-first.

Within the United States, the invocation of a national health emergency was accompanied by an invocation of the Public Readiness and Emergency Preparedness Act (PREP Act),[65] providing immunity from liability for COVID-19 vaccine manufacturers and administrators. In fact, U.S. Department of Health and Human Services (HHS) Secretary Alex Azar declared a public health emergency in the United States on January 31, 2020,[66] and just days later, on February 4, 2020, Secretary Azar issued a Notice of Declaration under the PREP Act for medical countermeasures against COVID-19, specifically covering "any vaccine, used to . . . prevent, or mitigate COVID-19." Although the national health emergency has since been revoked by President Biden, the legal immunity conferred by the PREP Act declaration remains effective through October 1, 2024.[67] The PREP Act relegates asserted COVID-19 injuries to the Countermeasures Injury Compensation Program (CICP), which provides compensation "to certain persons who sustain serious physical injuries or death as a direct result of administration or use of covered countermeasures identified by the Secretary by the Secretary in declarations issued under the PREP Act."[68]

A major question looms over the eventual expiration of the PREP Act invocation. Unless COVID-19 vaccine injuries are moved to the coverage of the National Vaccine Injury Compensation Program (NVICP), manufacturers will become directly and immediately liable in civil litigation for asserted injuries.[69] This is not unheard of in the field—such liability currently inheres for vaccines not covered by the NVICP, such as those for rabies, shingles, and tuberculosis. None of those vaccines, however, are broadly mandated for any purpose in the United States,[70] nor are they used in anything approaching the sheer volume of COVID-19 vaccines, and the need for a solution to this question comes with a clear deadline.

65. 42 U.S.C. §§ 247d *et seq.*

66. Alex Azar, *Determination that a Public Health Emergency Exists*, Public Health Emergency (Jan. 31, 2020), https://www.phe.gov/emergency/news/healthactions/phe/Pages/2019-nCoV.aspx.

67. *Notice of Declaration under the Public Readiness and Emergency Preparedness Act for medical countermeasures against COVID-19*, HHS (Feb. 4, 2020), https://www.govinfo.gov/content/pkg/FR-2020-03-17/pdf/2020-05484.pdf.

68. 42 C.F.R. pt. 110, 76 Fed. Reg. 62306 (Oct. 7, 2011).

69. Jenna Green, *COVID vaccine injury claims in 2022 were stuck in limbo. What's next?*, Reuters (Dec. 30, 2022), https://www.reuters.com/legal/litigation/covid-vaccine-injury-claims-2022-were-stuck-limbo-whats-next-2022-12-30/.

70. Notably, tuberculosis vaccination is widely employed in prisons, and while prison inmates are supposed to be able to refuse vaccinations, cases abound in which inmates have been either coercively or forcefully vaccinated.

Novel Antivaccine Activism Issues

The COVID-19 pandemic has been described as the event for which anti-vaccine activists have been preparing for years. Over a decade ago, Justice Scalia observed, in *Bruesewitz v. Wyeth*,[71] that vaccines had become "victims of their own success," with their high success rate in combating disease leading the public to be "much less alarmed at the threat of those diseases, and much more concerned with the risk of injury from the vaccines themselves."[72] The fear and discontent with the government's response to the pandemic, combined with the rise of social media platforms as perfect venues for ensconcing vaccine skeptics in echo chambers of disinformation, laid fertile ground for a resurgent anti-vaccination movement to attain historic levels of social and political influence.

This has also placed us in the midst of an unprecedented level of falsification of vaccination records, not merely from individuals making fake cards purporting to show their vaccinated status but also from greedy medical professionals willing to enter false records into systems intended to protect the public health through the very accuracy of their data.

In March of 2021, an FBI public service announcement warned of "individuals selling fake COVID-19 vaccination record cards and encouraging others to print fake cards at home."[73] This announcement specified that "the unauthorized use of an official government agency's seal (such as HHS or the CDC) is a crime, and may be punishable under Title 18 United States Code, Section 1017, and other applicable laws."[74]

As early as May 2021, a California bar owner was arrested for selling counterfeit COVID-19 vaccination cards and charged with identity theft, forging government documents, and falsifying medical records.[75] A July 2021 U.S. Department of Justice report of the arrest of a "California-licensed naturopathic doctor" described "an alleged scheme to sell homeoprophylaxis immunization pellets and to falsify COVID-19 vaccination cards by making it appear that customers had received the U.S.

---

71. 562 U.S. 223 (2011).

72. *Id.* at 226.

73. *If You Make or Buy a Fake COVID-19 Vaccination Record Card, You Endanger Yourself and Those Around You, and You Are Breaking the Law*, FBI (Mar. 30, 2021), https://www.ic3.gov/Media/Y2021/PSA210330.

74. *Id.*

75. Emma Bowman, *California Man Arrested in Suspected Fake COVID-19 Vaccine Card Operation*, NPR (May 8, 2021), https://www.npr.org/2021/05/08/994967439/california-man-arrested-in-suspected-fake-covid-19-vaccine-card-operation.

Food and Drug Administration (FDA) authorized Moderna vaccine."[76] This was "the first federal criminal fraud prosecution related to homeoprophylaxis immunizations and fraudulent Centers for Disease Control and Prevention (CDC) COVID-19 vaccination record cards."[77] In August 2021, CNN reported on the ease with which university students could obtain counterfeit vaccination cards.[78]

In January 2022, Long Island nurses Julie DeVuono and Marissa Urraro were charged with a scheme to sell thousands of falsified vaccination records, alleged to have brought them more than $1.5 million. Critically, the misconduct alleged went beyond merely providing forged vaccination cards and extended to entering this false information into New York's state immunization database.[79]

The pandemic, in fact, brought even more unusual patterns of misconduct than this. In January 2021, Wisconsin pharmacist Steven Brandenberg was arrested and his license was suspended after he intentionally spoiled COVID-19 vaccine doses.[80] Brandenberg "purposefully removed a box of COVID-19 vaccine vials manufactured by Moderna—which must be stored at specific cold temperatures to remain viable—from a hospital refrigeration unit," allowing these spoiled doses to be administered to 57 patients seeking COVID-19 vaccination.[81] Under police questioning, Brandenburg eventually confessed that the act was intentional, driven by antivaccine conspiracy theories.[82] He was ultimately sentenced

---

76. Press Release, *Woman Arrested for Fake COVID-19 Immunization and Vaccination Card Scheme*, DOJ (July 14, 2021), https://www.justice.gov/opa/pr/woman-arrested-fake-covid-19-immunization-and-vaccination-card-scheme.

77. *Id.*

78. Neelam Bohra & Justin Lear, *More than 400 universities are requiring Covid-19 vaccines. But the murky threat of fake vaccination cards worries some students and experts*, CNN (Aug. 8, 2021), https://www.cnn.com/2021/08/08/us/university-vaccine-mandates-fake-vaccine-cards-trnd.

79. Amanda Holpuch, *Two Long Island nurses made more than $1.5 million in a fake vaccine card scheme, prosecutors say*, The New York Times (Jan. 29, 2022), https://www.nytimes.com/2022/01/29/us/long-island-nurses-fake-vaccine-cards.html.

80. Lexi Lonas, *Wisconsin suspends license of pharmacist suspected of intentionally spoiling COVID-19 vaccine*, The Hill (Jan. 14, 2021), https://thehill.com/homenews/news/534294-wisconsin-suspends-license-of-pharmacist-suspected-of-intentionally.

81. Press Release, *Hospital Pharmacist Sentenced for Attempt to Spoil Hundreds of COVID Vaccine Doses*, U.S. Dep't of Justice (June 8, 2021), https://www.justice.gov/opa/pr/hospital-pharmacist-sentenced-attempt-spoil-hundreds-covid-vaccine-doses.

82. Lonas, *supra* note 80.

to three years in prison, an additional three years of supervised release, and a fine of $83,800.[83]

Similarly, in December 2022, a German nurse identified as "Antje T" was prosecuted in that country for intentionally injecting elderly patients with saline instead of the COVID-19 vaccine that they believed they were receiving. She was suspected of doing so in up to 8,600 cases, although she only admitted to doing so with respect to six patients with whom she was directly caught administering the false shot. Convicted only with respect to those cases, she was stripped of her nursing license and sentenced to six months of probation. Evidence introduced in the proceeding showed that she had "shared various conspiracy theories on the internet and social media," although a court spokesperson stated that "the chamber could not determine with the necessary certainty that this set of ideas was the motive for her actions and that she then acted to sabotage a vaccination campaign."[84]

These instances are particularly chilling when considering the impact of corrupted data on public policy development. If thousands of people are registered in various databases as having been vaccinated when they are not, confidence in those records must be diminished. Where an unvaccinated person contracts the disease against which the vaccine is arrayed, a falsified record creates a misleading impression regarding the efficacy of that vaccination. Worse yet, in cases such as those arising in Wisconsin and Germany, even the recipients of the shot are unaware that they have not actually been vaccinated, meaning that they may modify their conduct with false confidence in a protection they do not actually have.

Another modern oddity arising in antivaccine rhetoric is the belief that any entity that is operating internationally in the field of vaccination is therefore doing so nefariously. Of course, infectious diseases having no regard for national boundaries means that international efforts are required to effectively address their spread. In February 2023, a rumor circulated among antivaccine activists that the Biden administration was preparing to enter into a pandemic planning treaty that would cede U.S.

83. Press Release, *supra* note 81.

84. Christian Oliver, *Anti-vaxxer nurse who injected up to 8,600 patients with saline instead of Covid vaccine walks free*, MSN *via* DAILY MAIL (Dec 1, 2022), https://www.msn.com/en-gb/news/world/anti-vaxxer-nurse-who-injected-up-to-8-600-patients-with-saline-instead-of-covid-vaccine-walks-free/ar-AA14MOrA.

sovereignty to the WHO—a legal impossibility even if attempted, but also not at all contemplated in the wording of the agreement itself.[85]

Closing Thoughts

There is no pat answer as to what happens next concerning the many unresolved public policy questions raised by the experience of the pandemic. A second National Vaccine Law Conference, promising greater reach and coverage, is already being developed. The challenges that revealed themselves during the COVID-19 pandemic are not going away, but neither are the communities of legal and health policy professionals who are dedicated to using their skills to protect as many lives as possible from the ravages of contagious disease. The field of vaccine law will continue to experience fits and starts along the way, but the way is lit, and our determined intent is to keep it so.

85. Sudiksha Kochi, *Fact check: False claim that pandemic accord gives WHO control over US pandemic policies*, USA Today (Feb. 23, 2023), https://www.usatoday.com/story/news/factcheck/2023/02/23/fact-check-false-claim-us-sovereignty-and-who-accord/11313805002/.

Preface

Montrece Ransom and Loren Milliken

It is an honor and great pleasure to bring this book project, the *First National Vaccine Law Conference: Papers and Proceedings*, to fruition. Vaccines are proven public health tools and are among the most effective means to prevent the spread of infectious diseases, and an essential tool for maintaining rates of vaccine-preventable diseases is vaccine law. The First National Vaccine Law Conference was a first-of-its-kind opportunity, held September 15–18, 2022, for lawyers, policymakers, healthcare practitioners, public health practitioners, and academics working on issues related to vaccine law and policy issues to convene and exchange ideas and to address the urgent need for an increased understanding of the interrelated operations of different aspects of vaccine, vaccination, and immunization law.

This book is the result of those conversations, and it is meant to serve two purposes. First, it provides an opportunity to recognize those who heard the call to convene. Second, this book is meant to represent the proceedings of that conference and to capture and share the thought leadership of conference organizers, speakers, and other experts in vaccine law and policy. Jointly organized by conference planners, participants, and speakers, in partnership with the National Network of Public Health Institutes and the American Bar Association and coedited by Montrece McNeill Ransom, Loren Milliken, Alexandra A. Bhatti, Emely Sanchez, and Angela K. Shen, this text contains manuscripts that reflect the spirit of the conversations and presentations featured at the First National Vaccine Law Conference.

In January 2023, the editorial team issued a call for papers for speaker submissions and a limited call for papers for independent proposals. The chapters included are those that met the norms and rigor of publication requirements. The topics covered in this book are central to current discussions of the First National Vaccine Law Conference. The Foreword, written by Brian Dean Abramson, the founder of the conference, and Montrece McNeill Ransom, the closing keynote speaker and coeditor, further frames the context of the conference and this resulting book. It offers a tour of historical and current trends in vaccine law and regulation, intellectual property, equity, funding, access, vaccine passports, and more. The chapters within the book cover a wide breadth of vaccine law issues, including vaccine hesitancy, religious exemptions, regulation, intellectual property, vaccine injury, self-administered vaccines, vaccine law and individual rights, and privacy and confidentiality laws.

The following gives a short preview of each chapter:

- Cunniff, Mevis, and Bhatti's chapter, *Policy Considerations to Address the Risk of Disease Outbreaks: Ensuring High Routine Vaccination Coverage Rates Is Critical to Protect Public Health from Preventable Diseases*, details an alarming rise in vaccine hesitancy and uses recent measles outbreaks as a cautionary tale against future vaccine-preventable outbreaks.
- Furthering the conversation on vaccine hesitancy, Price's *A Jewish Perspective on Vaccines, Acceptance, and Hesitancy* details hesitancy and resistance to vaccines within a small segment of the Jewish community and gives examples of how to approach more insular Jewish communities.
- Two chapters address the pressing issue of religious exemptions in extraordinary detail. Brown and Hughes's *Does God Want You to Be Vaccinated? The Legal Status of Religious Exemptions* and Parmet and Khalik's *Free Exercise Challenges to Vaccine Mandates: The Destabilization of the Law and Its Implications* both give an overview of pre-pandemic precedents and more recent court legal challenges to mandates.
- Malkin and Pappas's *Regulatory and Patent Drivers for Vaccines and Other Treatments for Infectious Diseases and Considerations for Balancing Innovation and Collaboration for Future Public Health Emergencies* addresses the intersection of regulatory and intellectual property (IP) and discusses the U.S. Food and Drug Administration's evolving role in policy issues relating to pharmaceutical IP.
- Meyer's *The Two Federal Vaccine Injury Compensation Programs: Successes and Failures and Proposals for Improvement* reviews the National Vaccine Injury Compensation Program (NVICP) in the U.S. Court of Federal Claims, which covers injury for the childhood and annual flu vaccines, and the Countermeasure Injury Compensation Program (CICP) in the

Department of Health and Human Services that handles COVID-19 vaccine injury claims.

- Adding to the conversation on vaccine injury, Boltyanskiy, Hoon, Palle, and Winter's *Improving Mechanisms to Compensate Individuals for Vaccine Injuries* argues that increasing the funding for and participation in global vaccine-injury compensation schemes can provide an insurance system for the general public to overcome hesitancy and skepticism toward the safety and efficacy of vaccines as well as incentives to manufacturers to innovate swiftly, particularly in the context of a global health emergency.
- Hughes, Walters, and Tuazon's *The Elusive Self-Administering Vaccine: Understanding the Legal and Regulatory Hurdles* outlines the promise and challenge of different self-administered vaccine modalities. The chapter details how a more robust suite of delivery options has the potential to maximize vaccine access equity and adherence.
- Strombom's *Steps to Stringency: California's Vaccinations Laws* provides a brief background on vaccination policy authority on the federal, state, and local levels and then provides an in-depth look at recent vaccination policy within California. The case study of California shows the progression toward more stringent vaccination laws and the pushback that occurs when public health measures limit individual choice.
- Tovino's *Patient Privacy, Health Information Confidentiality, and Vaccine Information* examines the application of illustrative privacy and confidentiality laws to a variety of activities involving vaccine information, showing when vaccine information is protected by federal and state law and when it is not.

Special appreciation is due to authors patiently revising and re-revising manuscripts to address the comments and suggestions from peer reviewers. Their expertise and attention to detail make this book a quality addition to the literature.

Chapter 1

Policy Considerations to Address the Risk of Disease Outbreaks: Ensuring High Routine Vaccination Coverage Rates Is Critical to Protect Public Health from Preventable Diseases

Luke Cunniff, Kate Mevis, and Alexandra Bhatti

Overview

Vaccination in children and adolescents can help prevent a wide array of potentially deadly diseases and promote health.[1] In the United States alone, routine childhood vaccination has been estimated to prevent approximately 42,000 early deaths, 20 million cases of disease, and $68.8 billion in societal costs—in a single birth cohort.[2] In order to combat the risk of future outbreaks, concerted interventions are needed

1. Catch up on well-child visits and recommended vaccinations. Centers for Disease Control and Prevention. https://www.cdc.gov/vaccines/parents/visit/vaccination-during-COVID-19.html. Reviewed March 15, 2022. Accessed June 8, 2022.

2. Zhou F, Shefer A, Wenger J, et al. Economic evaluation of the routine childhood immunization program in the United States, 2009. *Pediatrics*. 2014;133(4):577–85. doi: 10.1542/peds.2013-0698.

to protect routine, recommended vaccination services and sustain high vaccination coverage rates.

In a concerning trend, a rise in vaccine hesitancy (the refusal of or delay in the acceptance of vaccination despite the availability of vaccination services)[3] over the past several decades and severe disruptions to Centers for Disease Control and Prevention (CDC)-recommended vaccination during the COVID-19 pandemic have put communities at risk of vaccine-preventable disease outbreaks.[4,5] Recognizing the importance of ensuring high vaccination coverage rates (VCRs) for CDC-recommended vaccinations, the CDC released a "Call to Action" and ensuing campaign in 2021 to get kids caught up on recommended vaccines.[6,7] Of note, the Call to Action highlighted a steep drop in measles vaccine public sector doses ordered during the pandemic, suggesting a decline in vaccination.[8]

There is concern about the potential spread of infectious diseases such as measles, as most children are back in the classroom and public health systems continue to experience varying degrees of strain due to the pandemic. With a recent reemergence of vaccine-preventable disease outbreaks in the United States fueled by unvaccinated groups and global

---

3. Meeting of the Strategic Advisory Group of Experts on immunization, October 2014: Conclusions and recommendations. World Health Organization. https://www.who.int/publications/i/item/WER8950. Published December 2014. Accessed June 10, 2022.

4. Olive JK, Hotez PJ, Damania A, et al. The state of the antivaccine movement in the United States: A focused examination of nonmedical exemptions in states and counties. *PLoS Med.* 2018;15(6):e1002578. doi: 10.1371/journal.pmed.1002578.

5. Murthy BP, Zell E, Kirtland K, et al. Impact of the COVID-19 pandemic on administration of selected routine childhood and adolescent vaccination—10 U.S. Jurisdictions, March-September 2020. *MMWR Morb. Mortal. Wkly. Rep.* 2021;70(23):840–45.

6. Childhood vaccination toolkit for clinicians: Get kids caught up on routine vaccines. Centers for Disease Control and Prevention. https://www.cdc.gov/vaccines/hcp/childhood-vaccination-toolkit.html. Reviewed May 6, 2022. Accessed June 10, 2022.

7. Resources to encourage routine childhood vaccinations. Centers for Disease Control and Prevention. https://www.cdc.gov/vaccines/partners/childhood/stayingontrack.html. Reviewed May 6, 2022. Accessed June 10, 2022.

8. Help kids' safe return to school—get caught up on recommended vaccines. U.S. Department of Health and Human Services. https://www.cdc.gov/vaccines/hcp/clinical-resources/downloads/safe-return-school.pdf. Published March 2021. Accessed June 10, 2022.

progress threatened by declines in vaccination during the pandemic, health officials are on high alert.[9,10,11,12]

From Elimination to Recent Outbreaks: The Reemergence of Measles Serves as a Cautionary Tale for Declines in CDC-Recommended Vaccinations

Measles is a highly infectious viral illness that requires high VCRs to prevent outbreaks.[13] Measles virus is particularly contagious as it can live for up to two hours in an airspace after an infected person leaves an area.[14] As a result of a highly effective vaccination campaign, measles was declared eliminated (absence of continuous disease transmission for greater than 12 months) in the United States in 2000.[15] It joined the list of diseases including rubella, diphtheria, polio, and smallpox that were successfully eliminated due to effective vaccination campaigns.[16]

However, growing vaccine hesitancy is threatening progress made in achieving and maintaining high VCRs to help protect children, their

9. Dimala CA, Kadia BM, Nji MAM, et al. Factors associated with measles resurgence in the United States in the post-elimination era. *Sci. Rep.* 2021;11(51). doi: 10.1038/s41598-020-80214-3.

10. Patel M, Lee AD, Clemmons NS, et al. National update on measles cases and outbreaks—United States, January 1–October 1, 2019. *MMWR Morb. Mortal. Wkly. Rep.* 2019;68(40):893–96. doi: 10.15585/mmwr.mm6840e2.

11. Seither R, Laury J, Mugerwa-Kasujja A, et al. Vaccination coverage with selected vaccines and exemption rates among children in kindergarten—United States, 2020–21 school year. *MMWR Morb. Mortal. Wkly. Rep.* 2022;71(16):561–68. doi: 10.15585/mmwr.mm7116a1.

12. Worldwide measles deaths climb 50% from 2016 to 2019 claiming over 207,500 lives in 2019. World Health Organization. https://www.who.int/news/item/12-11-2020-worldwide-measles-deaths-climb-50-from-2016-to-2019-claiming-over-207-500-lives-in-2019. Published November 12, 2020. Accessed June 10, 2022.

13. Durrheim DN. Measles elimination—using outbreaks to identify and close immunity gaps. *N. Engl. J. Med.* 2016;375:1392–93. doi: 10.1056/NEJMe1610620.

14. Transmission of measles. Centers for Disease Control and Prevention. https://www.cdc.gov/measles/transmission.html. Reviewed November 5, 2020. Accessed June 10, 2022.

15. About measles: Measles history. Centers for Disease Control and Prevention. https://www.cdc.gov/measles/about/history.html. Reviewed November 5, 2020. Accessed June 10, 2022.

16. van Panhuis WG, Grefenstette J, Jung SY, et al. Contagious diseases in the United States from 1888 to the present. *N. Engl. J. Med.* 2013;369(22):2152–58. doi: 10.1056/NEJMms1215400.

families, and their communities from measles.[17,18,19] In 2019, the United States saw the greatest number of measles cases reported since 1992.[20] The CDC recommends kindergarten measles, mumps, and rubella (MMR) vaccine coverage rates of 95 percent or above to achieve herd immunity.[21] CDC data from the 2020–2021 school year shows that most states have fallen below that threshold (the full list of states can be found in Figure 1).[22]

Figure 1 Most States Were below the CDC-Recommended MMR Two-Dose 95 Percent Vaccine Coverage Rate (2020–2021 School Year)[23]

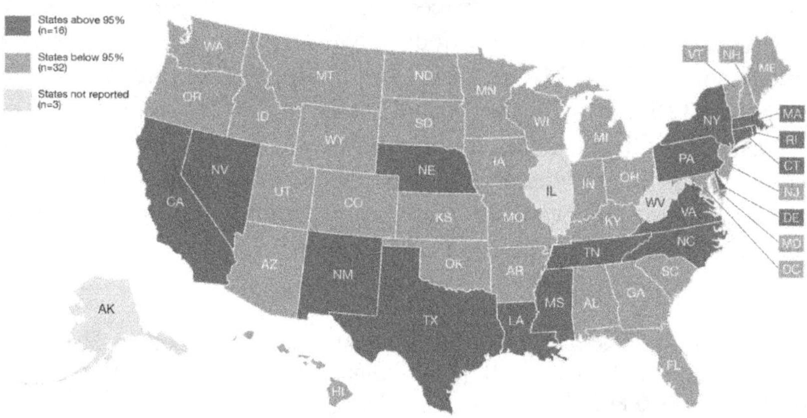

17. Dimala et al., *supra* note 9.

18. Gardner L, Dong E, Khan K, et al. Persistence of US measles risk due to vaccine hesitancy and outbreaks abroad. *The Lancet*. 2020;20(10):1114–15. doi: 10.1016/S1473-3099(20)30522-3.

19. Lo NC, Hotez PJ. Public health and economic consequences of vaccine hesitancy for measles in the United States. *JAMA Pediatr*. 2017;171(9):887–92. doi: 10.1001/jamapediatrics.2017.1695.

20. Patel et al., *supra* note 10.

21. Kindergarten immunization coverage rates 2018–19: Mumps, measles and rubella vaccine. National Conference of State Legislatures. https://www.ncsl.org/research/health/kindergarten-immunizations-coverage-rates-2018-19-mumps-measles-and-rubella-vaccine-postcard.aspx. Published January 30, 2020. Accessed June 10, 2022.

22. Seither et al., *supra* note 11.

23. Lo and Hotez, *supra* note 19.

In 2020, the number of measles cases in the United States dropped significantly, not due to an increase in vaccination but likely due in part to social distancing measures put in place during the COVID-19 pandemic. However, these same measures also led to a decrease in routine preventive services, such as vaccinations, which has experts concerned that there could be an uptick in measles cases as restrictions ease.[24,25] As exhibited by the rapid global spread of COVID-19, disease knows no borders and sustaining high VCRs is vital to prevent measles outbreaks. Details on measles outbreaks with more than ten confirmed cases over the past ten years in the United States can be found in Table 1. The data demonstrates that most infected individuals across the outbreaks were unvaccinated for measles and came from communities with low overall vaccination coverage.

24. World Health Organization, *supra* note 12.

25. Measles data and statistics: Global measles outbreaks. Centers for Disease Control and Prevention. https://www.cdc.gov/globalhealth/measles/data/global-measles-outbreaks.html. Updated April 7, 2022. Accessed June 10, 2022.

Table 1 Overview of Measles Outbreaks in the United States since 2011 (>10 Cases)

Measles Outbreak Time Period	Number of Confirmed Cases	Percentage (%) of Infected Patients Confirmed to Be Either Unvaccinated or Only Partially Vaccinated for Measles	Economic Impact of Outbreak (does not include individual direct/indirect costs)	Key Characteristics of Measles Outbreak
September 2018 to July 2019, New York, New York[26]	649[27,28]	~81%[29]	**$8.4M** on the direct response[30]	The outbreaks in communities in New York City and New York state rapidly grew and persisted due to pockets of low vaccination coverage and variable vaccine acceptance, high population density, and continuous importations of measles cases among unvaccinated persons traveling internationally.[31]
December 2018 to March 2019, Clark County, Washington[32]	71[33]	90%[34]	**~$2.3M** on the response[35]	The outbreak was concentrated in a geographic pocket of high vaccine exemption rates among young children.[36]

26. Zucker JR, Rosen JB, Iwamoto M, et al. Consequences of undervaccination—measles outbreak, New York City, 2018–2019. *N. Engl. J. Med.* 2020;382(11):1009–17. doi: 10.1056/NEJMoa1912514.

27. *Id.*

28. Health topics: Measles. New York City Health. https://web.archive.org/web/20200510145035/https://www1.nyc.gov/site/doh/health/health-topics/measles.page. Published May 10, 2020. Accessed June 13, 2022.

29. Id.

30. Zucker et al., *supra* note 26.

31. Patel, *supra* note 10.

32. Carlson A, Riethman M, Gastañaduy P, et al. Notes from the field: Community outbreaks of measles—Clark County, Washington, 2018–2019. *MMWR Morb. Mortal. Wkly. Rep.* 2019;68(19):446–47. doi: 10.15585/mmwr.mm6819a5.

33. *Id.*

34. *Id.*

35. Pike J, Melnick A, Gastañaduy P, et al. Societal costs of a measles outbreak. *Pediatrics*. 2021;147(4):e2020027037. doi: 10.1542/peds.2020-027037.

36. Sundaram ME, Guterman LB, Omer SB. The true cost of measles outbreaks during the postelimination era. *JAMA*. 2019; 321(12):1155–56. doi: 10.1001/jama.2019.1506.

Measles Outbreak Time Period	Number of Confirmed Cases	Percentage (%) of Infected Patients Confirmed to Be Either Unvaccinated or Only Partially Vaccinated for Measles	Economic Impact of Outbreak (does not include individual direct/indirect costs)	Key Characteristics of Measles Outbreak
October 2018 to November 2019 Rockland County, New York[37]	313[38]	91%[39]	—	Most patients lived in neighborhoods with low school vaccination rates. Documented measles vaccination coverage in schools in the outbreak area was only 77%, compared to 98% statewide in 2017–2018.[40]
April to August 2017, Hennepin County, Minnesota[41]	75[42]	94%[43]	**~$2.3M** on the response[44]	MMR vaccination coverage rates declined among communities in Minnesota before the outbreak. The decline in vaccination coverage in specific communities was reported to be in connection to the misunderstanding that autism was related to the MMR vaccine.[45]

37. New York State measles watch: Week ending 11/16/2019. New York State Health Connector. https://nyshc.health.ny.gov/web/nyapd/measles-watch. Accessed June 13, 2022.

38. *Id.*

39. Measles outbreak that sickened 312 in Rockland County, New York, declared over. CNN Health. https://www.cnn.com/2019/09/25/health/measles-outbreak-over-rockland-county-ny/index.html. Updated September 25, 2019. Accessed June 13, 2022.

40. McDonald R, Ruppert PS, Souto M, et al. Notes from the field: Measles outbreaks from imported cases in orthodox Jewish communities—New York and New Jersey, 2018–2019. *MMWR Morb. Mortal. Wkly. Rep.* 2019;68(19):444–45. doi: 10.15585/mmwr.mm6819a4.

41. Annual summary of communicable diseases, 2017: Measles, 2017. Minnesota Department of Health. https://www.health.state.mn.us/news/pressrel/2017/measles082517.html. Published 2018. Accessed June 13, 2022.

42. *Id.*

43. *Id.*

44. Banerjee E, Griffith J, Kenyon C, et al. Containing a measles outbreak in Minnesota, 2017: Methods and challenges. *Perspect. Public Health.* 2019;140(3):162–71. doi: 10.1177/1757913919871072.

45. Hall V, Banerjee E, Kenyon C, et al. Measles outbreak—Minnesota April–May 2017. *MMWR Morb. Mortal. Wkly. Rep.* 2017;66(27):713–17. doi: 10.15585/mmwr.mm6627a1.

Measles Outbreak Time Period	Number of Confirmed Cases	Percentage (%) of Infected Patients Confirmed to Be Either Unvaccinated or Only Partially Vaccinated for Measles	Economic Impact of Outbreak (does not include individual direct/indirect costs)	Key Characteristics of Measles Outbreak
May to June 2016, Pinal County, Arizona[46]	32[47]	Unknown	—	The outbreak occurred in a private detention facility. High MMR vaccination in the facility, along with containment measures, helped prevent the spread of the outbreak to the surrounding community.[48]
December 2014 to February 2015, Orange County, California[49]	125[50]	50%[51]	—	The outbreak was linked to attendance at Disney theme parks in California and highlighted how U.S. residents can be exposed to measles at venues with high volumes of international visitors. Of the patients, 88% were California residents, with cases linked to the outbreak also reported in seven other states, Canada, and Mexico. Among the vaccine-eligible patients, 67% of them were intentionally unvaccinated because of personal beliefs.[52]

46. Venkat H, Briggs G, Brady S, et al. Measles outbreak at a privately operated detention facility: Arizona, 2016. *Clin. Infect. Dis.* 2018;68(12):2018–25. doi: 10.1093/cid/ciy819.

47. *Id.*

48. *Id.*

49. *Id.*

50. Zipprich J, Winter K, Hacker J, et al. Measles outbreak—California, December 2014–February 2015. *MMWR Morb. Mortal. Wkly. Rep.* 2015;64(06):153–54.

51. *Id.*

52. *Id.*

Measles Outbreak Time Period	Number of Confirmed Cases	Percentage (%) of Infected Patients Confirmed to Be Either Unvaccinated or Only Partially Vaccinated for Measles	Economic Impact of Outbreak (does not include individual direct/indirect costs)	Key Characteristics of Measles Outbreak
May to July 2014, King County, Washington[53]	15[54]	93%[55]	—	After an unvaccinated child with measles symptoms returned to the United States following an international trip, an outbreak occurred in the community. Many children and adults in the community had no documentation of measles vaccination or knowledge of previous measles vaccination at the time of the outbreak.[56]
March to July, 2014 Holmes County, Ohio[57]	383[58]	89%[59]	—	In 2014, coverage with at least a single dose of MMR in the affected community was 14% before the outbreak, compared to the 91.9% two-dose MMR coverage among children in kindergarten within the general population in Ohio.[60]

53. Wendorf K. Notes from the field: Measles in a Micronesian community—King County, Washington, 2014. *MMWR Morb. Mortal. Wkly. Rep.* 2014;63(36):800.
54. *Id.*
55. *Id.*
56. *Id.*
57. Gastañaduy PA, Budd J, Fisher N, et al. A measles outbreak in an underimmunized Amish community in Ohio. *N. Engl. J. Med.* 2016;375(14):1343–54. doi: 10.1056/*NEJM*oa1602295.
58. *Id.*
59. *Id.*
60. *Id.*

Measles Outbreak Time Period	Number of Confirmed Cases	Percentage (%) of Infected Patients Confirmed to Be Either Unvaccinated or Only Partially Vaccinated for Measles	Economic Impact of Outbreak (does not include individual direct/indirect costs)	Key Characteristics of Measles Outbreak
April to May 2013, North Carolina[61]	23[62]	78%[63]	—	Most cases were concentrated among residents of a largely unvaccinated community in North Carolina.[64]
March to June 2013, Brooklyn, New York[65]	58[66]	100%[67]	**~$394,000** on the direct response[68]	All cases were linked to individuals with no documentation of measles vaccination at the time of exposure.[69]

61. Sullivan K, Moore ZS, Fleischauer AT. Notes from the field: Measles outbreak associated with a traveler returning from India—North Carolina, April–May 2013. *MMWR Morb. Mortal. Wkly. Rep.* 2013;62(36):753.

62. *Id.*

63. *Id.*

64. *Id.*

65. Arciuolo RJ, Brantley TR, Asfaw MM, et al. Notes from the field: Measles outbreak among members of a religious community—Brooklyn, New York, March–June 2013. *MMWR Morb. Mortal. Wkly. R*ep. 2013;62(36):752–53.

66. *Id.*

67. *Id.*

68. Rosen JB, Arciuolo RJ, Khawja AM, et al. Public health consequences of a 2013 measles outbreak in New York City. *JAMA Pediatr.* 2018;172(9):811–17. doi: 10.1001/jamapediatrics.2018.1024.

69. Arciuolo et al., *supra* note 65.

The Potential for Future Outbreaks

An increase in vaccine hesitancy has become a key barrier in maintaining high coverage rates across recommended routine vaccinations, including the MMR vaccine.[70] One driver of the rise in vaccine hesitancy across the country has been the spread of vaccine mis- and disinformation, especially on social media.[71] Mis- and disinformation have eroded public confidence in CDC-recommended vaccines. For example, the percentage of US adults who believe it is very important to have their children vaccinated has declined from 82 percent to 71 percent between 2008 and 2018.[72] More recently, research from Children's Hospital Los Angeles also noted a rise in recommended routine childhood vaccination hesitancy during the COVID-19 pandemic, largely due to parental concerns about vaccine side effects.[73] The volume of vaccine misinformation has only increased with the politicization of COVID-19 vaccines, which risks causing further resistance to vaccines and outbreaks as they become the subject of political debate.[74]

Disruptions to routine well-child visits because of the COVID-19 pandemic, and by extension fewer opportunities for providers to vaccinate children, have also put children and adolescents at risk of vaccine-preventable diseases.[75,76] During the early stages of the pandemic, stay-at-home orders and fear of contracting COVID-19 at healthcare facilities led to decreases in routine pediatric care.[77,78] Coinciding with

70. Olive et al., *supra* note 4.

71. Sharfstein JM, Callaghan T, Carpiano RM, et al. Uncoupling vaccination from politics: A call to action. *The Lancet*. 2021;398(10307):1211–12. doi: 10.1016/S0140-6736(21)02099-7.

72. Americans' views on vaccines and infectious disease outbreaks. Research! America and American Society for Microbiology. https://www.researchamerica.org/sites/default/files/MAY2018_VaccinePressRelease_final.pdf. Published May 2018. Accessed June 12, 2022.

73. He K, Mack WJ, Neely M, et al. Parental perspectives on immunizations: Impact of the COVID-19 pandemic on childhood vaccine hesitancy. *J Community Health*. 2022;47(1):39-52. doi: 10.1007/s10900-021-01017-9.

74. Sharfstein et al., *supra* note 71.

75. Centers for Disease Control and Prevention, *supra* note 1.

76. Murthy et al., *supra* note 5.

77. Murthy et al., *supra* note 5.

78. COVID-19 pandemic leads to major backsliding on childhood vaccinations, new WHO, UNICEF data shows. World Health Organization. https://www.who.int/news/item/15-07-2021-covid-19-pandemic-leads-to-major-backsliding-on-childhood-vaccinations-new-who-unicef-data-shows. Published July 15, 2021. Accessed June 12, 2022.

the decline in well-child visits, vaccine administration data from ten U.S. jurisdictions with high-performing vaccination information systems found substantially lower administered doses of routine childhood and adolescent vaccines at the beginning of the pandemic compared to the same period during 2018 and 2019. Vaccine administration rates increased after the initial phase of the pandemic, but the rebound was not enough to make up all the initial missed doses.[79]

Building and Maintaining Healthy and Resilient Communities by Ensuring High VCRs for Recommended Routine Vaccinations

Vaccination across the life course helps protect against preventable diseases. Even though the pandemic has introduced greater complexity into maintaining high VCRs for CDC-recommended vaccinations, it also has created opportunities to increase awareness and expand access to vaccinations.[80] Given the potential for future outbreaks of vaccine-preventable diseases, it is critical that the whole community, including healthcare professionals, public officials, and families, work together to ensure that everyone receives the recommended, routine, and catch-up vaccinations.

There are evidence-based policy and programmatic strategies that policy stakeholders can utilize to support recovery and improvement of CDC-recommended vaccination rates and build a resilient vaccination ecosystem:

- **Enable equitable access to vaccination services.**
  - Expand the pool of eligible vaccinators, in part through expanding scopes of practice (such as pharmacies), to create more points of care for patients to receive vaccinations from convenient and trusted sources.[81]
  - Eliminate out-of-pocket patient costs associated with vaccination services.[82]

---

79. Murthy, *supra* note 5.

80. U.S. House of Representatives. American Rescue Plan Act of 2021 (H.R. 1319). Washington: U.S. Government Printing Office, 2021;1–592.

81. Drozd E, Miller L, Johnsrud M. Impact of pharmacist immunization authority on seasonal influenza immunization rates across states. *Clin. Ther.* 2017;39(8):1563–80.e17. doi: 10.1016/j.clinthera.2017.07.004.

82. Bjork A, Morelli V. Immunization strategies for healthcare practices and providers. In: Hall E, Wodi AP, Hamborsky J, et al, eds. *Epidemiology and Prevention of Vaccine-Preventable Diseases.* 14th ed. Washington, D.C.: Centers for Disease

  - Create alternate vaccination sites, such as curbside and mobile vaccination clinics,[83,84] as well as offer walk-in and after-hours vaccination opportunities to increase convenience for parents and their children.[85]
  - Co-host vaccination clinics at schools. These can provide a convenient location for students, their family members, and people in the community to receive recommended, routine vaccinations.[86] Schools that are interested can reach out to their local public health departments. Additionally, schools can leverage colocated Federally Qualified Health Centers for providing immunizations (where established).
- **Enhance and fully leverage immunization information systems (IIS) to support vaccination across the life course.**[87]
  - Enable the safe and secure exchange of IIS data among states, providers, and public health agencies to improve data completeness and quality.
  - Leverage additional federal funding streams for data modernization to enhance IIS to efficiently and effectively manage vaccine ordering, inventory, and patient records.
  - Support the utilization of IIS reminder recall to encourage individuals to make appointments to get caught up on vaccinations. Combining a mix of reminder communication strategies (e.g., phone calls, emails, and mailings) can support parents in keeping their children up to date on their vaccinations.[88,89]

Control and Prevention; 2021:29–42. https://www.cdc.gov/vaccines/pubs/pinkbook/strat.html. Accessed June 12, 2022.

83. Interim guidance for routine and influenza immunization services during the COVID-19 pandemic. Centers for Disease Control and Prevention. https://www.cdc.gov/vaccines/pandemic-guidance/index.html. Updated April 6, 2021. Accessed June 12, 2022.

84. Bode SM, Gowda C, Mangini M, et al. COVID-19 and primary measles vaccination rates in a large primary care network. *Pediatrics*. 2021;147(1):e2020035576. doi: 10.1542/peds.2020-035576.

85. Frew PM, Lutz CS. Interventions to increase pediatric vaccine uptake: An overview of recent findings. *Hum. Vaccin. Immunother*. 2017;13(11):2503–11. doi: 10.1080/21645515.2017.1367069.

86. *Id.*

87. Suggestions to improve your immunization services. Immunization Action Coalition. https://www.immunize.org/catg.d/p2045.pdf. Published May 2017. Accessed June 12, 2022.

88. Frew et al., *supra* note 85.

89. Immunization Action Coalition, *supra* note 87.

- **Partner with and support diverse and varied voices within the community.**
    - Policy stakeholders and vaccination stakeholders should engage the education community, including the departments of education, to coordinate education and outreach activities that support getting back on track with routine vaccination.
    - Partnerships built during the pandemic to promote COVID-19 vaccination and improve vaccine confidence should be reinforced to support vaccination across all CDC-recommended vaccinations. This includes supporting community-based organizations and faith-based organizations.[90,91]
    - Support and implement digital and mainstream media campaigns from trusted messengers as part of outreach programs.[92]
    - Provide culturally and linguistically appropriate health education and outreach materials that tailor to the needs of diverse patient populations.[93,94]

Conclusion

The rise in vaccine hesitancy over the past several decades had already been linked with the resurgence of disease outbreaks in the United States, exemplified by recent experience with the measles virus.[95,96] When coupled with the disruptions to recommended routine vaccination brought on by the COVID-19 pandemic, the potential for further outbreaks looms

---

90. 12 COVID-19 vaccination strategies for your community. Centers for Disease Control and Prevention. https://www.cdc.gov/vaccines/covid-19/vaccinate-with-confidence/community.html. Reviewed November 3, 2021. Accessed July 14, 2022.

91. Thoumi A, Tewarson H, Johnson K. Prioritizing equity in COVID-19 vaccinations: Promising practices from states to reduce racial and ethnic disparities. Duke Margolis Center for Health Policy and National Governors Association. https://healthpolicy.duke.edu/sites/default/files/2021-03/Duke-NGA%20Equity-in-Covid-19-Vaccination.pdf. Published March 2021. Accessed July 14, 2022.

92. Bonnevie E, Rosenberg SD, Kummeth C, et al. Using social media influencers to increase knowledge and positive attitudes toward the flu vaccine. *PLoS One*. 2020;15(10):e0240828. doi:10.1371/journal.pone.0240828.

93. Thoumi et al., *supra* note 91.

94. COVID-19 vaccine equity toolkit. Kaiser Permanente. https://about.kaiserpermanente.org/content/dam/kp/mykp/documents/instructions/covid-19-vaccine-equity-toolkit-external.pdf. Published March 12, 2021. Accessed July 14, 2022.

95. World Health Organization, *supra* note 3.

96. Olive, *supra* note 4.

near.[97,98] Elevating information from trusted sources and strengthening systems to deliver essential health services are key steps communities can take to prepare for and respond to impending health threats.[99,100,101,102,103] The CDC's Call to Action on getting children caught up on recommended vaccines should serve as a warning to all communities that falling further behind on vaccination rates could have dire consequences.[104,105,106] Building confidence in vaccines and vaccination and bolstering recommended, routine vaccination are critical next steps in preventing disease outbreaks.

Funding

This research was funded by Merck Sharp & Dohme LLC, a subsidiary of Merck & Co., Inc., Rahway, NJ, USA. The funder contributed to the design of the study, collection, analysis, and interpretation of data as well as the writing and revision of the manuscript.

Acknowledgments

The authors would like to thank Drs. Stephanie Kujawski, Rachel Mitrovich, and Manjiri Pawaskar for their thoughtful review of the manuscript. The authors would further like to thank Mock5 for their support in manuscript formatting.

Author Contributions

All authors contributed to study conception and study design. All authors contributed to the writing of the manuscript. All authors reviewed and approved the final version of the manuscript.

97. Olive, *supra* note 4.
98. Murthy, *supra* note 5.
99. Drozd et al., *supra* note 81.
100. Centers for Disease Control and Prevention, *supra* note 83.
101. Frew, *supra* note 85.
102. Immunization Action Coalition, *supra* note 87.
103. Bonnevie et al., *supra* note 92.
104. Centers for Disease Control and Prevention, *supra* note 6.
105. Centers for Disease Control and Prevention, *supra* note 7.
106. U.S. Department of Health and Human Services, *supra* note 8.

Conflict of Interest Statement

L.C., A.B., and K.M. are current employees of Merck Sharp & Dohme LLC, a subsidiary of Merck & Co., Inc., Rahway, NJ, USA, and may hold equity interest in Merck & Co., Inc., Rahway, NJ, USA.

Contact Information

*Corresponding author
Alexandra Bhatti
351 North Sumneytown Pike, North Wales, PA 19454, USA
Email: Alexandra.Bhatti@merck.com
Merck & Co, Inc., Rahway, NJ, USA

Chapter 2

A Jewish Perspective on Vaccines, Acceptance, and Hesitancy

Roger Price

In the Beginning

Judaism has been described appropriately as the religious civilization of the Jewish people,[1] a people that can trace its origins back more than 3,000 years to the Ancient Near East.[2] Judaism's initial encounter with vaccines is much more recent, of course, but it does extend to the very beginnings of the modern development of vaccines in Europe just over 200 years ago.

At the end of the 18th century of the Common Era, smallpox in Europe was common, contagious, and often deadly.[3] In England, Dr. Edward Jenner realized that certain individuals who contracted cowpox seemed immune to smallpox. In 1796, he tested his idea by inoculating a young boy with matter scraped from a local dairymaid who contracted

1. *See* Mordecai M. Kaplan, *Judaism as a Civilization* (Jew. Pub. Soc., 2010), Ch. XIV–XV.

2. *See generally* Melvin Konner, *Unsettled: An Anthropology of the Jews* (Viking Compass, 2003); Israel Finkelstein & Neil Asher Silberman, *The Bible Unearthed* (Free Press, 2001).

3. *See* Stefan Riedel, "Edward Jenner and the history of smallpox and vaccination," *Proc.* (Bayl. Univ. Med. Cent., 2005) 18(1): 3/14, https://www.ncbi.nlm.nih.gov/pmc/articles/PMC1200696/#:~:text=In%201757%2C%20an%208%2Dyear,His%20name%20was%20Edward%20Jenner; *see also* Kendall Smith, "Edward Jenner and the Small Pox Vaccine," *Front. Immunol* (2011) 2:21: 1/9, https://www.ncbi.nlm.nih.gov/pmc/articles/PMC3342363/.

cowpox. Later, he injected the boy with smallpox material, but the lad never became infected.[4] After publication of his experience, news of Jenner's success spread rapidly.[5]

Those who know their English history know that there were few Jews in England in the late 18th century, Jews having been expelled from England in 1290 CE and generally not very welcomed even 500 years later.[6] There were, however, a good number of Jews in Eastern Europe at that time.

The Jews of the town of Breslov, located about 1,500 miles east of London in what is today central Ukraine, were led by a young Hassidic master, Rebbe Nachman (b. 1772). Rebbe Nachman heard of Jenner's success with smallpox and issued a mandate. He required that all infants over three months old be inoculated.

Why did Rebbe Nachman issue this mandate? Here are some clues:

- It was not because he had compelling data from the Breslov Institute of Health about the safety and efficacy of the procedure.
- It was not because the Breslov Drug Administration provided assurance about the integrity of the product used or manufacturing process involved.
- It was not because the scientific underpinnings of Jenner's procedure—even the substances and dosages involved—were well understood.

Given the state of the science, while Rebbe Nachman was no doubt influenced by anecdotal reports about Jenner's success, he was motivated primarily by Jewish values.

Selected Jewish Values Concerning Life and Safety

The Jewish values that informed Rebbe Nachman were the products of texts and experience. The foundational text of the Jewish people is the Torah, which means instruction. You may know it as the Five Books of Moses or the first part of the Hebrew Bible.

4. *See* Riedel, *supra* note 3, at 7–8/14; Smith, *supra* note 3, at 3–5/9.
5. *See* Riedel, *supra* note 3, at 10/14; Smith, *supra* note 3, at 6/9.
6. *See* Shira Schoenberg & Mitchell Bard, "United Kingdom Virtual Jewish History Tour," https://www.jewishvirtuallibrary.org/united-kingdom-virtual-jewish-history-tour.

The following passages from the Torah may be familiar to you:[7]

- Gen. 1:27 God created humankind *b'tzelem elohim*, in God's own image.
- Ex. 20:23 You shall not murder.
- Lev. 18:5 You shall keep these laws and rules . . . and live by them.
- Lev. 19:16 You shall not stand idly by the blood of your neighbor.
- Lev. 19:18 You shall love your neighbor as yourself.
- Deut. 30:19 Choose life.

These precepts may not be as familiar:

- Lev. 19:28 You shall not desecrate or harm your body.
- Deut. 4:9, 15 You shall take exceeding care of your selves.
- Deut. 22:8 You shall make a parapet around the roof of your house.

The Talmud is a collection of commentaries from the first millennium of the Common Era. Here, among many discussions concerning the value of life, are two often-cited concepts that reinforce one another:

- The overriding principle is that of *pekuach nefesh*. It holds that all of the commandments, laws, regulations, and rules of Judaism—with three exceptions (not relevant here)—can be disregarded to save a life.[8]
- In a bit of poetic hyperbole, we also find in the Talmud the understanding that if anyone were to take a life, it would be as if that person destroyed a whole world, but if anyone were to save a life, it would be as though that person saved a whole world.[9]

Subsequent rabbinic interpretations in the Middle Ages emphasized the importance of both guarding one's health and guarding against disease. For instance, the 12th-century Spanish-born physician and philosopher Moshe ben Maimon, also known as Maimonides or Rambam, wrote that Jews have a positive duty to use proactive measures to protect against a foreseeable harm.[10] Similarly, the 16th-century legal scholar and codifier Joseph Karo stated that Jews have a religious obligation to

7. Other translations of all non-English original sources may well vary. Citations to internet addresses were accessible and accessed in or about early April 2023.

8. BT Yoma 82a.9. The exceptions are, essentially, for idolatry, murder, and improper sexual conduct.

9. BT Sanhedrin 37a.13.

10. *See* Maimonides, *Mishneh Torah, Hilchot De'ot 4:1; Rotzei'ach 1:6, 14.*

take affirmative steps to prevent an anticipated danger to themselves or others.[11]

These texts and traditions can be boiled down to two fundamental responsibilities all Jews have. One is for self-care. The other is to sustain members of the community.[12]

So, we should not be surprised that, when faced with the foreseeable harm of infectious disease, Rebbe Nachman mandated vaccinations. We should not be surprised that he selected a then modern parapet of sorts, put to use then to guard against a potential danger. We should not be surprised that he wrote that "we must be careful about the health of children" because whoever "does not vaccinate every baby against smallpox, he is like one who sheds blood."[13]

From Smallpox to Measles and COVID-19

The values that motivated Rebbe Nachman just over two centuries ago motivate Jews of all denominations today, resulting in overwhelming, if not universal, support for government approved vaccines and immunization safety protocols, including mandates. After all, the Talmud also says *dina d'malkhuta dina*: the law of the land is the law.[14]

Writing for the Conservative movement about compulsory immunization in Jewish parochial, or day, schools, Rabbi Joseph Prouser surveyed the history of Jewish opinion on vaccinations, including Orthodox views, and concluded that there is in the Jewish tradition a "well established preference for preventive medicine as a religious mandate." And failure to immunize, he said, is a "serious, compound violation of Jewish law." He concluded, "there is *no basis* in Jewish law to support a request *for a religious exemption* from state-mandated immunization."[15]

Reform and Reconstructionist scholars have reached similar conclusions. Writing a response to question from a Reform congregation about the propriety of excluding from religious school children who had

11. *See* Joseph Karo, *Shulchan Aruch, Chosen Mishpat* 427.8.

12. *See* Rabbi Bradley Shevit Artson, "L'Chaim: Jewish Wisdom for a Time of Pandemic," *Jewish Journal* (Mar. 18, 2020), https://jewishjournal.com/commentary/opinion/312306/jewish-wisdom-for-a-time-of-pandemic/.

13. *See* David Prouser, "Compulsory Immunization in Jewish Day Schools," (Rabbinical Assembly, 2005), https://www.rabbinicalassembly.org/sites/default/files/public/halakhah/teshuvot/20052010/prouser_immunization.pdf, at 14/29.

14. *See, e.g.*, BT *Bava Batra* 54b, *Nedarim* 28a.4, *Gittin* 10b.13.

15. *See* Prouser, *supra* note 13, at 15–16, 29/29 (emphasis supplied).

not received standard immunizations, Rabbi Mark Washofsky noted that "(t)here are no valid Jewish religious grounds to support refusal to immunize as a general principle."[16] Likewise, from a Reconstructionist perspective, Rabbi David Teutsch observed that "since the duty to heal is communal," a decision to avoid vaccinating a child is ethical only when "parents believe that no one should be vaccinated or when the vaccine poses a grave health risk to a particular child."[17]

Again, given the duration and extent of adoption of the relevant Jewish health ethics value system, we should not be surprised that among America's many faith communities, Jews generally scored highest on vaccine acceptance during the 2020–22 COVID-19 pandemic. More specifically, Jewish Americans were "by far" the most likely religious group to be the COVID-19 vaccine accepters, with an 85 percent acceptance rate.[18] While "majorities of Americans of all major religious groups report(ed) at least moderate concerns about COVID-19 vaccines," only 47 percent of Jewish Americans did and their level of major concerns was 14 percent, the lowest such description among the surveyed population.[19]

Herd Immunity and the Challenge of Religious Exemptions to Vaccine Mandates

When enough people within a community become immune to a disease, either though vaccination or through overcoming natural infection, the bacteria or virus that causes the disease has relatively limited opportunities to infect further and that community achieves what is called herd immunity. The required portion necessary to achieve herd immunity varies from disease to disease, but reaching the appropriate level is important to provide indirect protection to individuals whose own immune systems cannot protect them.[20]

16. Mark Washofsky, ed., *Reform Responsa for the Twenty-First Century* (CCAR, 2010), v. 1, at 113–15.

17. David Teutsch, *A Guide to Jewish Practice* (RRC Press, 2011), v. 1, at 505.

18. *See* Pub. Rel. Res. Inst. and Inter. Youth Corp. "Religious Identities and the Race Against the Virus" (2021), https://www.prri.org/wp-content/uploads/2021/04/PRRI-IFYC-Apr-2021-Vaccine-D.pdf, at 11, 23/41.

19. *Id.* at 20–21/41.

20. *See* Mayo Clinic Staff, "Herd immunity and COVID-1: What you need to know," https://www.mayoclinic.org/diseases-conditions/coronavirus/in-depth/herd-immunity-and-coronavirus/art-20486808; Christine Yu, WebMD, "What Is Herd Immunity?," https://www.webmd.com/covid/what-is-herd-immunity.

As the novel, highly contagious pathogen that causes COVID-19 began to spread in early 2020, no protective vaccines were available and the level of natural immunity needed to achieve herd immunity was unclear. Since then, COVID-19 and its variants have caused considerable death and damage, but because the virus has changed so much, there is still a question as to whether herd immunity can be achieved solely or predominantly by vaccination or at all.[21] Nevertheless, because the vaccines available in the United States have proven "to be effective in reducing the risk of severe disease, hospitalization, and even death," they remain a critical part of any public health program.[22]

One challenge to containing the virus, and maximizing our chance to achieve herd immunity, arises from claims of religious exemptions to public and private mandates for vaccinations. In the United States, interference by a governmental body with the free exercise of one's religion is generally prohibited by the First Amendment to the U.S. Constitution.[23] Moreover, Title VII of the Civil Rights Act of 1964 forbids religious discrimination, with religion being defined broadly to include not only a belief in a Supreme Being as understood in well-established religions but also "moral or ethical beliefs as to what is right and wrong" as long as they are "sincerely held with the strength of traditional religious views."[24] Additionally, as of May, 2022, over 40 states and the District of Columbia have enacted similar protections.[25]

Yet, while there are anecdotal reports of individuals who claim that getting a COVID vaccine violates their religious or moral beliefs, due

---

21. *See* Health Hive, "What Herd Immunity for COVID-19 Means In 2023," https://hive.rochesterregional.org/2023/02/herd-immunity-covid#:~:text=Herd%20immunity%20happens%20when%20enough,the%20disease%20to%20spread%20further; Jun She, et al., "Challenges of vaccination and herd immunity in COVID-19 and management strategies," *Clin. Respir J.* (Nov. 2022), 16(11): 708–16, https://www.ncbi.nlm.nih.gov/pmc/articles/PMC9539035/.

22. *See* Jun She, et al., *supra* note 21.

23. For a history of religious exemptions, *see* Brian Dean Abramson, et al., "Vaccine Exemptions," Ch. 8 in *Vaccine, Vaccination, and Immunization Law* (Amer. Health Law. Assn., Bloomberg Law, 2d ed., 2022); Coll. of Phys. Phila., "History of Vaccines—Vaccine Exemptions" (2023), https://historyofvaccines.org/getting-vaccinated/vaccine-faq/vaccination-exemptions.

24. *See* 29 C.F.R. Sec. 1605.1; *see also* EEOC, "*Section 12: Religious Discrimination*" (Jan. 15, 2021).

25. *See* Nat. Conf. of State Legis., "States With Religious and Philosophical Exemptions From School Immunization Requirements" (May 25, 2022), https://www.ncsl.org/health/states-with-religious-and-philosophical-exemptions-from-school-immunization-requirements.

to privacy, data collection, and other issues, it is not at all clear how many Americans have made or would make such a claim or to which religious group, if any, they belong. The reality is that most established denominations (and the religions that most people observe or practice) do not have theologically based objections to vaccinations in general.[26] And even among the faith-healing traditions, such as Christian Science or Dutch Reformed churches, allowance is made for those who would get vaccinated.[27] So, while, according to a 2021 survey, about 30 percent of Americans unvaccinated against COVID-19 expressed an interest in securing an exemption because of religious values, only 10 percent claimed that the teachings of their religion precluded vaccinations. And there is some indication that their objections are less doctrinally based and more personal or political.[28]

At the same time, while the extent and identity of exemption claimers are clouded, three things are clear. First, applying for an exemption in order to decline vaccination is not onerous, there are interest groups ready and willing to help, and in at least some instances there is considerable activity.[29] Second, the legal landscape concerning religious objections to vaccine mandates appears to be changing and that change has generated challenges.[30] Third, and critically, even if just 10 percent of the population rejects vaccination, protecting them and the other 90 percent

26. *See* Vanderbilt Faculty & Staff Health and Wellness, "Immunizations and Religion" (2013), https://www.vumc.org/health-wellness/news-resource-articles/immunizations-and-religion.

27. *See* Diane Juffras, "An In-Depth Look at Religious Exemptions from COVID-19 Vaccine Mandates," UNC Sch. of Gov't. (Oct. 8, 2021), https://www.vumc.org/health-wellness/news-resource-articles/immunizations-and-religion.

28. *See* PRRI-IFYC Staff, "Religious Identities and the Race Against the Virus" (Dec. 9, 2021), https://www.prri.org/research/religious-identities-and-the-race-against-the-virus-american-attitudes-on-vaccination-mandates-and-religious-exemptions/; Russell P. Johnson, U. Chi. Div. Sch., "Are Vaccine Exemptions Actually Religious?" (Feb. 4, 2022), https://divinity.uchicago.edu/sightings/articles/are-vaccine-exemptions-actually-religious.

29. *See* Rachael Levy & Megan Messerly, "Health workers' vaccine mandate undone by religious exemptions," *Politico* (Feb. 28, 2022), https://www.politico.com/news/2022/02/28/covid-vaccine-exemption-hospital-00011951; *see also* Liberty Counsel Action, "Covid Vaccine," https://lcaction.org/vaccine.

30. *See* Richard Hughes IV, "The Supreme Court And The Future Of State Vaccine Requirements," *Health Affairs* (July 7, 2022), https://www.healthaffairs.org/do/10.1377/forefront.20220705.879853; Zalman Rothchild, "Individualized Exemptions, Vaccine Mandates, and the New Free Exercise Clause," *Yale L. J.* (Apr. 29, 2022), https://www.yalelawjournal.org/forum/individualized-exemptions-vaccine-mandates-and-the-new-free-exercise-clause.

of the population from an infectious disease becomes that much harder and more costly.

Vaccine Hesitancy and Resistance in the Jewish Community

Although highly vaccine receptive, the Jewish American community is not homogeneous. Within that community there are considerable differences in theological beliefs and degrees of religious and cultural practices. And there are different gradations of assimilation into the larger national culture as well, often marked by different levels of educational achievement and economic well-being.[31]

Consequently, despite the broad and deep consensus regarding vaccines and vaccination mandates, there has been some hesitancy and some resistance to them in certain subsections of the larger Jewish community. Part of this distinctly minority attitude may be based on a particular feature of Jewish law and is relatively easy to address. Part of this attitude, however, is grounded in matters more complex.

Let us consider the challenge on principle first. From time to time, some Jews have raised particular concerns about the ingredients in vaccines. The usual basis for such concern derives from the Torah's classification of some animals as kosher, that is, fit for consumption, and others as not fit. For example, cows are fit, but pigs are not; chickens are fit, but pheasants are not; salmon are fit, but shrimp are not.[32]

You can find the ingredients for government-approved vaccines on the website of the Centers for Disease Control and Prevention (CDC).[33] There you will see that some vaccines contain cells from animals deemed unfit, including monkey cells, human cells, and even pig cells. Why pork? Because gelatin from pork is sometimes used as a stabilizer in flu and

31. *See* Pew Research Center, "Jewish Americans in 2020" (May 11, 2021), at 56–92/248, https://www.pewresearch.org/religion/2021/05/11/jewish-americans-in-2020/.

32. *See* Lev. 11: 2–45. Pigs are identified as impure in Lev. 11:7. Muslims also classify some products as permissible to be consumed (i.e., as *Halal*) and others as not (i.e., *Haram*) under Islamic law, or *Sharia*, the primary sources for which are *Al-Quran* and *Al-Hadith*. The flesh of swine is specifically prohibited. *See* Mardian, et al., "Sharia (Islamic Law) Perspectives of Covid-19 Vaccines," *Front. Trop. Dis.*, 20 (2021), https://doi.org/10.3389/fitd.2021.788188.

33. *See* CDC, "What's in Vaccines?," https://www.cdc.gov/vaccines/vac-gen/additives.htm and "Vaccine Excipient Summary," https://www.cdc.gov/vaccines/pubs/pinkbook/downloads/appendices/b/excipient-table-2.pdf.

other vaccines.[34] In the case of vaccines approved in the United States for COVID-19, none contain any animal material, much less pork cells, so this particular issue is moot as to those vaccines.[35]

Moreover, according to authorities on *kashrut*, that is, the laws and practices of all things kosher, even where pork or other impure substances are present in a formulation, the perceived problem largely goes away because *kashrut* prohibitions apply only to ingredients that are consumed.[36] They do not, therefore, apply to substances that are administered by injection, by a nasal spray, or in the form of creams, ointments, or suppositories. In short, any objection to administration of a non-oral vaccine on *kashrut* grounds would be unwarranted.

Consequently, the only possible legitimate objection based on *kashrut* could be to oral vaccines, and even there, especially in the absence of an alternative treatment, the number of offending cells is generally considered to be *de minimis*, they cannot be seen with the naked eye (a formal, if scientifically archaic, test for impurity), and, in any event, the primary directive of *pikuach nefesh* should override any concerns.

The more difficult challenge of vaccine hesitancy is a communal one. It is an attitude based not on any single commandment or text, but one that arises in certain Orthodox communities, especially in the close-knit and self-protective Hasidic and Litvish groups of Jews known as the *Haredim*, a word that literally means those who tremble, suggesting the intensity of their commitment to act in accordance with the word of God as they understand it.

These are Jews who are religiously engaged, whose lifestyle is typified by large families who live in densely populated areas, and who sometimes distinguish themselves from other groups by language and dress. Formal secular education is limited, and poverty is common.[37] Crucially, they engage in numerous and significant communal activities, including group prayer three times daily and Sabbath meals for extended families.

34. *See* Joan Cavaco Silva, "What are flu vaccines made of and why?" (2020), https://www.medicalnewstoday.com/articles/321207.

35. *See* CDC, "Overview of COVID-19 Vaccines," https://www.cdc.gov/coronavirus/2019-ncov/vaccines/different-vaccines/overview-COVID-19-vaccines.html.

36. *See* David Samson, "Are vaccines kosher?," https://www.yeshiva.co/ask/10.

37. *See* Tehilla Berger Lipsky & Ezra Gabbay, "Sociocultural and Religious Perspectives Toward the COVID-19 Pandemic in the Haredi Jewish Community," *J. Relig. Health* (2022), 5/18, https://www.ncbi.nlm.nih.gov/pmc/articles/PMC9483331/. By contrast, the majority of Jewish Americans live in households earning $100,000 or more and almost 30 percent hold post-graduate degrees. *See* Pew, *supra* note 31, at 193, 201/248.

Their insular communities are also places where measles outbreaks occurred in 2018–19 and places that were disproportionately affected by COVID-19 in 2020.[38]

Most recently, in July 2022, in Rockland County, New York, a county with a large concentration of *Haredim*, a young Orthodox man was diagnosed with the first case of polio in a decade in the United States. At that time, the early childhood vaccination rate in Rockland was the lowest in New York at 42 percent, and the polio vaccination rate in one zip code in that county was only 37 percent, also the lowest in the state of New York.[39] Similarly, Williamsburg, a neighborhood in Brooklyn with a large Orthodox Jewish population, has had New York City's lowest rate of polio vaccination with only 56 percent of children under five years old vaccinated, compared to 86 percent in all of New York City.[40]

COVID-19 has now prompted several studies that demonstrate both the challenges of communicable diseases, especially among tight-knit religious communities, and the role that Jewish values and practices have played and can play in mitigating the danger of transmission in such communities.

One study, known as the MITZVA cohort study, looked at over 9,500 Orthodox Jews in various communities in 12 states and how they were impacted in March 2020, during which time Jews around the world were celebrating Purim, a holiday that commemorates a Biblical tale about the planned destruction of Persian Jews by a high-ranking political official. Typically, during Purim Jews gather together in synagogues to hear the story recited and interact socially outside of the synagogue to provide gifts and food to members of the community. This particular time period was also early in our understanding of the COVID-19 pandemic, well before ideas about physical distancing and mask wearing were promoted.[41]

---

38. *See* Hurubie Meko, "First Polio Case in Nearly a Decade is Detected in New York State," *New York Times* (July 21, 2022), https://www.nytimes.com/2022/07/21/nyregion/polio-case-new-york.html; *see also* Jacob Henry, "First US case of polio in nearly a decade is an Orthodox Jewish man," *NY Jewish Week* (July 21, 2022), https://www.jta.org/2022/07/21/ny/first-us-case-of-polio-in-nearly-a-decade-is-an-orthodox-jewish-man.

39. *See* Henry, *supra* note 38; *see also* Dana Smith, "A mutated virus, anti-vaxxers and a vulnerable population: how polio returned to the US," *The Guardian* (Aug. 29, 2022), https://www.theguardian.com/us-news/2022/aug/29/polio-us-vaccines-new-york-rockland-county.

40. *See* Jacob Henry, "Polio in NYC Wastewater," *Intermountain Jewish News* (Aug. 19, 2022), https://www.ijn.com/polio-nyc-wastewater/.

41. *See* Israel Zyskind, et al., "SARS-CoV-2 Seroprevalence and Symptom Onset in Culturally Linked Orthodox Jewish Communities Across Multiple Regions in the

Another, much smaller study, which may be called the NYU study, sought to understand communal knowledge and attitudes about COVID-19 and vaccines in New York's *Haredi* communities. Information for this survey was gathered later than that in the MITZVA study, specifically in December 2020 and January 2021.[42]

The results of both surveys were consistent with the fact that infections were higher in these socially and culturally bonded communities than in other neighboring areas.

The NYU study added a historical and sociological perspective. It noted that prior to the recent measles outbreak, the percentage of those vaccinated in the surveyed communities was less than 15 percent (15 percent!), and that the efforts of New York officials to increase vaccinations were viewed as "curtailing individual liberties and threatening the integrity" of the community. Whether that view was accurate is debatable, but there is no doubt that the tension felt in the *Haredi* community about perceived political motivations and overt actions of vaccine advocates in 2020 was palpable.[43]

How to Handle a Vaccine Objector

Both the MITZVA and NYU studies indicate a lack of health equity in an identifiable socially and culturally bonded community and, also, provide us with information concerning methodologies to mitigate vaccine hesitancy in such a community to the direct benefit of that and of neighboring communities.

Those who object to vaccine mandates do so largely for one of three reasons:

United States," *JAMA Network Open* (Mar. 10, 2021), 4(3): e212816, https://jamanetwork.com/journals/jamanetworkopen/fullarticle/2777318. In this instance, MITZVA is a partial acronym for Multi-institutional Study Analyzing Anti-CoV-2 Antibodies, which also evokes the Hebrew word *mitzvah*, often meaning good deed.

42. *See* Ellie R. Carmody, et al., "Knowledge and Attitudes Toward Covid-19 and Vaccines Among a New York Haredi-Orthodox Jewish Community," *J. Community Health* (May 17, 2021) 46(6): 1161–69, https://www.ncbi.nlm.nih.gov/pmc/articles/PMC8127857/#. It is identified here as the NYU study because the protocol for this study was approved by the New York University Langone Health Institutional Review Board and because it was funded, in part, by a fellowship at the NYU Grossman School of Medicine.

43. *See* Lipsky & Gabbay, *supra* note 37, at 4/18.

- They may have received misinformation and reject the science behind the vaccine.
- They may claim that their objection is based on some religious principle.
- They may be acting consistent with what they perceive is the norm of their cohort. That is, not vaccinating may be a marker of group identity. As discussed in his book *The Righteous Mind*, NYU professor of ethical leadership Jonathan Haidt points out that religion can bind, and it also can blind.[44]

Fortunately, both the MITZVA and NYU studies also contain helpful observations about how certain insular Jewish neighborhoods function and may be approached.

The MITZVA cohort study stated, albeit without any citations, that before government and private restrictions on mass gatherings were put in place in the spring of 2020, Orthodox rabbis and leadership organizations were already developing "culturally sensitive policies" relating to religious services and gatherings. To learn more, I spoke with one of the authors of the study, Dr. Avi Rosenberg, an award-winning assistant professor of pathology at the Johns Hopkins University School of Medicine. Dr. Rosenberg told me of creative ways during a pandemic that prayer quorums were achieved, how religious teachings were home delivered, and, perhaps most remarkably, that eight-week overnight (sleepaway) summer camps for over 25,000 kids were operated while secular camps were closed.

The NYU study asked specifically who the survey participants trusted the most and the least for medical information. State and local health departments and major secular news and social media outlets ranked at the bottom of the list. The most trusted sources were a personal physician, an Orthodox physician network, and a rabbi or other religious authority.

This study contended that in order to achieve effective intervention, it is critical that messaging on COVID-19 and vaccines be (1) tailored to the self-protective socio-religious group and (2) conveyed by a known and trusted authority. To achieve that goal in the *Haredi* community, however, any intervenor would have to understand that the *Haredim* are not uniform in their approach to vaccines and vaccinations. For instance, vaccination hesitancy and vaccinations rates are quite different in different

44. Jonathan Haidt, *The Righteous Mind* (Vintage Books, 2012): 222, Ch. 11.

segments of the community, such as the Satmars, Bobovers, and Chabad/Lubavitch.[45]

Consistent with the imperative of understanding the community, reporting following the 2022 polio scare identified two points of interest. One was that some communal organizations in the at-risk neighborhoods were quick to urge their people to get vaccinated. The other was that while economic and political decisions in Orthodox communities were made by men, health decisions were made by women. And they were, reportedly, knowledgeable and proactive.[46] Engaging these female health deciders may provide another avenue for secular personnel who want to expand health care to an underserved population.

Our Obligations Continue

When Judaism meets science today on the field of epidemiology, it is both amazing and gratifying to see how Jews across almost the entire spectrum of contemporary Jewish life apply traditional commitments to personal and communal health and readily and extensively embrace the protections that government-approved vaccines offer. But if we do not reach all members of our community, we will have failed in our obligation to protect one another and, worse, we will have failed to save the lives, and worlds, that could have been saved.

Insular *Haredi* Jews present a set of challenges to those who want to protect against the spread of infectious diseases within their community and beyond it. They are not, however, the only socially and culturally bonded community that presents such challenges. For instance, and while their religious orientation is quite different and they tend to be more rural based than *Haredi* populations in the United States, Amish communities share with the *Haredim* strong faith in a Supreme Deity, intense commitment to family and community, a lack of knowledge about and regard for science, and a distrust of government officials. They also share a disproportionately low level of vaccination and a disproportionately high

45. *See* Mark Trencher, "2021 COVID-19 Attitudes and Vaccine Sentiment in the U.S. Orthodox Jewish Community" (Apr. 2021), https://www.jewishdatabank.org/databank/search-results?search=nishma.

46. *See* Jeneen Interlandi, "How to Fight Polio with Cultural Sensitivity" (Aug. 17, 2022), https://www.nytimes.com/2022/08/17/opinion/polio-vaccine-orthodox-jewish-religion.html.

incidence of contracting diseases such as measles and COVID-19.[47] Drilling down further, it is also true that vaccine hesitancy is not even limited to tight, predominantly religious groups. It can be found throughout the nation among many diverse individuals, including, for instance, both libertarians and progressives.[48]

More important than whether the *Haredi* situation is unique or not, there is, within the broader Jewish community, an ancient understanding that all Jews are, to a degree, responsible each for the other, and that concern prompts our discussion here.[49] Fortunately, the obligation to reach out and reach in to the hard to reach is consistent with the aspirational goal of the CDC to provide greater access to vaccines for minority groups who by virtue of one or more factors such as limited education, reduced language fluency, lower income, and lack of trust are adversely affected to a greater than average extent during an outbreak of viral disease.[50]

Now, some may argue that the predicament in which the *Haredim* find themselves is a result more of internal choice than external discrimination, but even if that were true, the adverse health consequences in their community would still deserve attention. A virus neither knows nor cares that any human being is susceptible to infection because of invidious discrimination or religious practice or personal or communal hesitancy. The sad fact is that a virus such as measles morbillivirus, SARS-CoV-2, or poliovirus anywhere creates risk everywhere. And the broader community cannot be safe as long a component of it can harbor and transmit that virus. Faced with this reality, we must be true to our time-tested values and help where we can. As our ancestors taught, "You are not obligated to complete the work, but neither are you free to desist from it."[51]

That help begins with an understanding, based on studies such as the ones discussed above, that insular communities that object to vaccines are not necessarily doing so as a result of critical thinking, but may be

47. *See* Anna Huntsman, "COVID-19 Has Hit the Amish Community Hard. Still, Vaccines are a Tough Sell," NPR (Apr. 28, 2021), https://www.npr.org/sections/health-shots/2021/04/28/990986056/covid-19-has-hit-the-amish-community-hard-still-vaccines-are-a-hard-sell.

48. *See* David Myers, "Vaccine hesitancy is not a uniquely Haredi problem," *Forward* (July 25, 2022), https://forward.com/opinion/511863/vaccine-hesitancy-haredi-jews-orthodox-hasidic-polio/.

49. *See* My Jewish Learning, "All of Israel are Responsible for One Another," https://www.myjewishlearning.com/article/all-of-israel-are-responsible-for-one-another/.

50. *See* CDC, "COVID-19 Vaccine Equity for Racial and Ethnic Minority Groups," https://www.cdc.gov/coronavirus/2019-ncov/community/health-equity/vaccine-equity.html.

51. *Pirke Avot* [Sayings of the Fathers] 2:21.

engaged in a kind of motivated reasoning, wanting to act in a manner consistent with the customs of their group.

Consequently, attempting to persuade people that their opinions are not well based in fact or even in the tenets of their faith is not likely to be successful, especially if the would-be persuader does not share their religious outlook and affiliation.

If there is to be a chance at successful persuasion, it will more likely come from an understanding about what concerns the objector has and a tailored message from a trusted source about values that the objector shares with the public health community. Those values may be one or a combination of several of the values discussed earlier. For example, vaccines, and masks, too, can be seen as modern parapets that help protect us directly and, through the creation of herd immunity, also guard the elderly and immunocompromised among us with protection they would not otherwise have.[52]

The values first approach may lead a religiously observant Jewish objector to understand that accepting a vaccination is an important way to fulfill the objector's twin responsibilities of self-care and sustaining one another. Hopefully, the objector may also come to realize how many worlds can be saved by getting a values-infused, life-affirming shot in the arm.

52. For more models of engagement, *see* Lipsky and Gabbay, *supra* note 37, at 12–13/18.

Chapter 3

Does God Want You to Be Vaccinated? The Legal Status of Religious Exemptions

Matthew Brown and Richard Hughes IV

Introduction

For over a century, states and their subdivisions have used vaccine requirements to curb the spread of infectious disease. Since the Supreme Court of the United States' seminal *Jacobson v. Massachusetts* decision in 1905, states have relied on settled law to implement these requirements both to stem the tide of virulent outbreaks and to build herd immunity to prevent deadly outbreaks from occurring.[1]

States have furthermore relied on established law allowing them to exempt certain individuals from vaccination requirements. These exemptions universally include medical exemptions for those for whom vaccination is contraindicated; most states also exempt those with religious and, in some cases, philosophical objections to vaccination.[2] Crucially, however, courts—although not the Supreme Court—made it clear in the decades preceding the COVID-19 pandemic that religious exemptions to

1. "Based on the Supreme Court's recognition [in *Jacobson*] of [states' authority to mandate vaccination under the police power], states and localities have enacted vaccination mandates for certain populations and circumstances." Wen W. Shen, *State and Federal Authority to Mandate COVID-19 Vaccination*, CONG. RSCH. SERV. (May 17, 2022) at 5, https://crsreports.congress.gov/product/pdf/R/R46745.

2. *Vaccination Exemptions*, HISTORY OF VACCINES, https://historyofvaccines.org/getting-vaccinated/vaccine-faq/vaccination-exemptions (last visited May 1, 2023).

state vaccination requirements are not legally obligatory.[3] Thus, while many states opted to include religious exemptions in their vaccination requirements, some opted not to allow for religious exemptions, and those states' policy choices were upheld by courts against constitutional challenges.[4]

The COVID-19 pandemic generated a renewed scrutiny of vaccine law. States and state subdivisions that implemented vaccination requirements without religious exemptions faced court challenges.[5] Those challenges were almost entirely unsuccessful; courts either upheld states' prerogative to choose not to offer religious exemptions[6] or, as in the two most notable cases before the Supreme Court, *Does v. Mills* and *Dr. A. v. Hochul*, declined to enjoin state mandates without religious exemptions.[7] Justice Neil Gorsuch, however, drew on COVID-19-era precedent to highlight a push to undermine what was once settled law. In *Mills* and *Hochul*, he dissented from the Court's denial of an injunction and argued that, contrary to precedent, religious exemptions should be obligatory under the Free Exercise Clause of the First Amendment.[8] And prospective plaintiffs paid attention: the Court recently rejected a First Amendment challenge to a state vaccination requirement, a challenge that echoed Justice Gorsuch's arguments in *Mills* and *Hochul*.[9]

This chapter traces the line of notable cases establishing the state prerogative to implement public health measures without religious exemptions. It then examines the current state of the law and the emerging

3. *E.g.*, Phillips v. City of New York, 775 F.3d 538 (2d Cir. 2015); Workman v. Mingo Cty. Bd. of Ed., 419 F. App'x 348 (4th Cir. 2011); McCarthy v. Boozman, 212 F. Supp. 2d 945 (W.D. Ark. 2002).

4. Dorit R. Reiss, *Litigating Alternative Facts: School Vaccination requirements in the Courts*, 21 U. Pa. J. Const. L. 207, 229 (2018) ("No court, state or federal, has ever struck down an immunization mandate, and many have upheld them.").

5. *E.g.*, We the Patriots USA, Inc. v. Hochul, 17 F.4th 266 (2d Cir. 2021) (New York healthcare worker requirement); Doe v. Mills, 16 F.4th 20 (2021) (Maine healthcare worker requirement); Dr. T. v. Alexander-Scott, 579 F. Supp. 3d 271 (2022) (Rhode Island healthcare worker requirement); Doe v. San Diego Unified Sch. Dist., 19 F.4th 1173 (9th Cir. 2021) (*SDUSD*) (California student vaccination requirement).

6. *See, e.g.*, *SDUSD*, 19 F.4th 1173.

7. Does v. Mills, 142 S. Ct. 17 (2021); Dr. A. v. Hochul, 142 S. Ct. 552 (2021).

8. *Mills*, 142 S. Ct. at 18 (Gorsuch, J., dissenting); *Hochul*, 142 S. Ct. at 552 (Gorsuch, J., dissenting).

9. Matt Naham, *Justice Sotomayor Rejects Emergency Application of NYC Firefighters, Cops, and Teachers Raising Religious Objections to COVID-19 Vaccine Mandate*, Law & Crime (Nov. 10, 2022, 11:46 a.m.), https://lawandcrime.com/supreme-court/justice-sotomayor-rejects-emergency-application-of-nyc-firefighters-cops-and-teachers-raising-religious-objections-to-covid-19-vaccines/.

tension between religious belief claims and public health measures, including a review of the requirements of Title VII of the Civil Rights Act of 1964 to understand the difficulty of scrutinizing religious exemption claims. It focuses in particular on Justice Gorsuch's dissents in *Mills* and *Hochul* and the possible circuit split those dissents portend. Finally, it previews arguments likely to come before the Supreme Court and how the Court can and should address them, considering established precedent, the legitimacy of sincere religious claims, and health equity.

Vaccine Requirements and Religious Exemptions: Established Precedent

A notable line of cases established states' power to mandate vaccination without religious exemptions. In 1905, the Supreme Court decided *Jacobson v. Massachusetts*,[10] the case of a Swedish immigrant pastor who refused to comply with the smallpox vaccination requirement of the city of Cambridge, Massachusetts.[11] Henning Jacobson was convicted of flouting the mandate and was fined $5.[12] He argued that the state, through its subdivision, had deprived him of liberty without due process of law under the 14th Amendment; although he was a minister, he did not claim that his religious belief allowed him to opt out of the mandate (the First Amendment had not been incorporated against the states at that time).[13] Rather, he claimed that past vaccinations had harmed him and his sons, and so he was afraid that the smallpox vaccine posed a danger to his health.[14]

Writing for a 7–2 Court, Justice John Marshall Harlan rejected Jacobson's constitutional claim.[15] He wrote that allowing Jacobson to exempt himself from the enforcement of the Cambridge vaccination requirement would render such a mandate unenforceable, "even at the command of the legislature, however widespread the epidemic of

10. Jacobson v. Massachusetts, 197 U.S. 11 (1905).

11. Leslie Landrigan, *Henning Jacobson Loses His Fight with the Board of Public Health over Vaccination*, New Eng. Hist. Soc'y, https://newenglandhistoricalsociety.com/henning-jacobson-loses-his-freedom-to-the-board-of-public-health/ (last visited Dec. 19, 2022).

12. *Id.*

13. *Jacobson*, 197 U.S. at 17–18 (cataloguing Jacobson's arguments, which do not include any appeal to the First Amendment); *see* Cantwell v. Connecticut, 310 U.S. 296, 303 (1940) (incorporating the First Amendment against the states).

14. Landrigan, *supra* note 11.

15. *Jacobson*, 197 U.S. at 37.

smallpox, and however deep and universal was the belief of the community and of its medical advisers, that a system of general vaccination was vital to the safety of all."[16] The Court thus upheld the vaccination requirement, which was not "arbitrary and oppressive," as a valid exercise of the state's police power.[17] In a now-famous passage, Justice Harlan wrote that "the liberty secured by the Constitution of the United States to every person within its jurisdiction [i.e., the liberty Jacobson claimed the mandate violated] does not import an absolute right in each person to be, at all times and in all circumstances, wholly freed from restraint. There are manifold restraints to which every person is subject for the common good."[18]

While *Jacobson* predated modern levels of judicial scrutiny,[19] it is read to have established "rational basis" scrutiny as the level of constitutional scrutiny to be applied to public health measures.[20] Under rational basis scrutiny, government action need only be "rationally related to a legitimate state interest."[21] In this context, courts have essentially held explicitly what *Jacobson* implied, that the state has a legitimate interest in preventing the spread of disease and that compulsory vaccination is rationally related to that interest.[22]

Although the Cambridge smallpox vaccination requirement did not contain any explicit exemptions,[23] the *Jacobson* Court took pains to distinguish between claims like Henning Jacobson's—those not supported by medical science[24]—and the claims of those who could demonstrate

---

16. *Id.*

17. *Id.* at 38.

18. *Id.* at 28.

19. *Cf.* United States v. Carolene Products Co., 304 U.S. 144, 152 n.4 (1938) (suggesting that, while the constitutionality of commercial legislation should be determined on "the assumption that it rests upon some rational basis," laws showing a prejudice toward "discrete and insular minorities . . . may call for a correspondingly more searching judicial inquiry").

20. Roman Cath. Diocese of Brooklyn v. Cuomo, 592 U.S. ____, ____, 141 S. Ct. 63, 70 (2020) (Gorsuch, J., concurring) ("[T]his Court essentially applied rational basis review to Henning Jacobson's challenge to [Cambridge's vaccine mandate].").

21. Klaassen v. Trustees of Ind. Univ., 549 F. Supp. 3d 836, 861 (N.D. Ind. 2021), citing City of Cleburne v. Cleburne Living Ctr., 473 U.S. 432, 440 (1985).

22. *See, e.g., Klaassen*, 549 F. Supp. 3d at 869–70 (cataloguing cases scrutinizing vaccination requirements under rational basis review); *see also* Workman v. Mingo County Bd. of Ed., 419 Fed. Appx. 348, 353–55 (4th Cir. 2011).

23. The mandate did explicitly exempt children with a doctor's certification. *Jacobson*, 197 U.S. at 30.

24. Jacobson seemed to the Court to be a fit subject for vaccination and not to have adduced any evidence that his fear of vaccines was well-founded. *Id.* at 39.

that being vaccinated would harm them, or those who, in today's medical parlance, have a contraindication to vaccination. The Court opined that requiring a person with a "particular condition of his health or body" making him unfit to be vaccinated (i.e., a contraindication) to submit to vaccination anyway would be "cruel and inhuman."[25] In such a case, a court could step in to protect the person's constitutional right to an exemption from the vaccination requirement.[26] Thus, the *Jacobson* Court implicitly recognized a substantive due process right not to be vaccinated if one has a medical contraindication.[27] The Court was quick to point out, however, that such cases are "extreme"—that is, they are exceptions, not the rule.[28] Medical science has come a long way since *Jacobson*, but it has only confirmed that the universe of *perceived* contraindications, even among healthcare providers, is greater than the universe of *actual* contraindications.[29] True medical contraindications are rare[30] and temporary.[31]

Two subsequent Supreme Court cases solidified *Jacobson*'s precedential strength and further delineated the scope of police powers. In 1922, the Supreme Court dismissed the appeal of Rosalyn Zucht, a

25. *Id.* at 38–39.

26. *Id.* at 39.

27. *Id.* at 38–39.

28. *Id.* at 38. It is unclear from the opinion how rarely the Court thought a genuine medical exemption should be granted; the opinion does not cite authority to support its conclusion that what would today be considered contraindications are "extreme."

29. *General Best Practice Guidelines for Immunization: Contraindications and Precautions*, Advis. Comm. on Immuniz. Practices (Mar. 15, 2022) at 53, https://www.cdc.gov/vaccines/hcp/acip-recs/general-recs/contraindications.pdf ("Clinicians or other health-care providers might misperceive certain conditions or circumstances as valid contraindications or precautions to vaccination when they actually do not preclude vaccination . . . . These misperceptions result in missed opportunities to administer recommended vaccines." (cleaned up)).

30. R. Opri et al., *True and False Contraindications to Vaccines*, 46 Allergologia et Immunopathologia 99, 103 (2018) (characterizing "true contraindications to vaccination" as "rare"); Megan Cerullo, *Want a medical exemption for the COVID-19 vaccine? Good luck with that.*, CBS News (Sept. 23, 2021, 6:00 a.m.), https://www.cbsnews.com/news/covid-vaccine-mandate-medical-exemption (quoting a physician stating that the "severe allergic reactions" that would constitute contraindications for mRNA COVID-19 vaccines are "very, very rare—like one in a million"). Indeed, hospitalization is not a contraindication for vaccination; on the contrary, the CDC recommends that healthcare providers view hospitalization as an *opportunity* for vaccination. *General Best Practice Guidelines*, *supra* note 29, at 52–53.

31. Those who cannot be vaccinated now may be able to be vaccinated when the contraindication abates or disappears. *General Best Practice Guidelines*, *supra* note 29, at 51.

child excluded from San Antonio's public school for failure to be vaccinated.[32] Zucht argued that, because "there was then no occasion for requiring vaccination," the San Antonio ordinance requiring vaccination of schoolchildren deprived her of her liberty without due process of law.[33] While raising a substantive due process argument as Henning Jacobson had, Zucht sought to differentiate the circumstances of the Cambridge smallpox threat from that of San Antonio's attempts to prevent the spread of disease in the absence of an imminent threat. The *Zucht* Court held that *Jacobson* had settled the question that states can mandate vaccination and that the state's "broad discretion required for the protection of the public health" encompassed the power to mandate vaccination even absent an outbreak or emergency.[34] All states would enact compulsory vaccination policies for schoolchildren in the decades following *Zucht* to prevent outbreaks.[35] These compulsory policies have been widely credited for the reduction of vaccine preventable disease in the 20th century.[36]

In 1944, the Supreme Court relied on *Jacobson* to uphold the conviction of Sarah Prince for violating Massachusetts's child labor law for forcing her niece to distribute religious pamphlets.[37] In contrast to *Jacobson* and *Zucht*, Prince argued that the Massachusetts statute violated her right to freedom of religious practice and her right as her niece's guardian to direct the child's behavior.[38] In upholding the constitutionality of Massachusetts's child labor law, the Court nevertheless cited *Jacobson* for the proposition that the state can interfere with parental rights and religious practice as *parens patriae*, whether in the context of vaccination or in the context of child labor laws.[39] The *Jacobson-Zucht-Prince* line

32. Zucht v. King, 260 U.S. 174, 177 (1922).

33. *Id.* at 175.

34. *Id.* at 176–77.

35. *History of vaccine requirements and vaccine research highlights*, Mayo Clinic, https://www.mayoclinic.org/coronavirus-covid-19/history-disease-outbreaks-vaccine-timeline/requirements-research (last visited May 1, 2023) ("In the U.S. [by 1980], all states have vaccine-related laws that pertain to children before they go to school.").

36. *See, e.g.*, Walter A. Orenstein & Rafi Ahmed, *Simply Put: Vaccination Saves Lives*, 114 Proc. Nat'l Acad. Scis. 4031, 4031 (2017) (cataloguing the reduction in 2016 in cases of nine vaccine-preventable diseases from the 20th-century average and attributing the reduction to childhood vaccination).

37. Prince v. Massachusetts, 321 U.S. 158, 159, 171 (1944).

38. *Id.* at 164.

39. *Id.* at 166–67 ("[N]either rights of religion nor rights of parenthood are beyond limitation. . . . [The parent] cannot claim freedom from compulsory vaccination for

of cases established a firm precedent in favor of states' power to mandate vaccination, notably without affording any exemptions except for those necessary to accommodate a legitimate medical contraindication.

Although after *Zucht* the Supreme Court would not consider another constitutional challenge to state vaccination policies until the COVID-19 pandemic and, until the pandemic, had never heard an explicit religious challenge to a vaccine requirement, other federal and state courts did hear such challenges and consistently considered the law settled.[40] For example, as recently as 2015 in *Phillips v. City of New York*, the Second Circuit Court of Appeals upheld the temporary exclusion from school of unvaccinated children during a chickenpox outbreak against a free exercise challenge.[41] The court upheld the state's vaccination requirement on substantive due process grounds, following *Jacobson*, and on free exercise grounds, following *Jacobson* and *Prince*.[42] Synopsizing the consensus of courts on whether religious exemptions are constitutionally required, the court declared, "New York could constitutionally require that all children [i.e., without exemption] be vaccinated in order to attend public school. New York law *goes beyond what the Constitution requires* by allowing an exemption for parents with genuine and sincere religious beliefs."[43]

---

the child more than for himself on religious grounds. The right to practice religion freely does not include liberty to expose the community or the child to communicable disease or the latter to ill health or death."); the doctrine of *parens patriae* (Latin for "parent of the nation") refers here to the state's power to provide special protection of children and persons deemed incompetent.

40. *E.g.*, Phillips v. City of New York, 775 F.3d 538 (2d Cir. 2015); Workman v. Mingo Cty. Bd. of Ed., 419 F. App'x 348 (4th Cir. 2011); McCarthy v. Boozman, 212 F. Supp. 2d 945 (W.D. Ark. 2002); Whitlow v. Cal. Dept. of Ed., 203 F. Supp. 3d 1079 (S.D. Cal. 2016); Davis v. State, 451 A.2d 107 (Md. 1982); Wright v. DeWitt Sch. Dist., 385 S.W.2d 644 (Ark. 1965); Brown v. Smith, 24 Cal. App. 5th 1135 (2018). *See also* Marie Killmond, *Why Is Vaccination Different? A Comparative Analysis of Religious Exemptions*, 117 Colum. L. Rev. 913, 915 (2017) ("While vaccination is a hot political topic, it is largely settled as a matter of law.").

41. *Phillips*, 775 F.3d at 540.

42. *Id.* at 542–43.

43. *Id.* at 543 (emphasis added).

The Tension between Public Health and Religious Claims in the COVID-19 Era

Since *Zucht*, states have chosen to require schoolchildren to be vaccinated against a range of pathogens as a condition of public school admission.[44] By contrast, states have generally not required vaccination of their adult populations. Instead, pressure on adults to be vaccinated has generally stemmed from employment relationships: some private companies in certain industries[45]—healthcare, notably[46]—or state entities[47] require their workers to be vaccinated or else be reassigned, placed on leave, or fired. When a state entity issues a vaccination requirement pursuant to its police power, religious objectors rely on the Free Exercise Clause; when a private employer requires its employees to be vaccinated, religious-objector employees rely on the protections of Title VII of the Civil Rights Act of 1964, which prohibits employer discrimination on the basis of religious belief and requires employers to offer employees reasonable accommodation for their religious beliefs unless such accommodation would work an

---

44. *History of vaccine requirements and vaccine research highlights*, *supra* note 35.

45. Several private companies required their employees to receive a COVID-19 vaccination. *E.g.*, *Over 96% of Tyson Foods' Active Workforce is Vaccinated*, TYSON (Oct. 26, 2021), https://www.tysonfoods.com/news/news-releases/2021/10/over-96-tyson-foods-active-workforce-vaccinated; David K. Li, *United CEO says vaccine mandate appears to have ended weekly deaths of employees from Covid*, NBC NEWS (Jan. 11, 2022, 10:01 a.m.), https://www.nbcnews.com/news/us-news/united-ceo-says-vaccine-mandate-appears-ended-weekly-deaths-employees-rcna11760; Haley Messenger, *From Amex to Walmart, here are the companies mandating the Covid vaccines for employees*, NBC NEWS (Jan. 25, 2022, 9:44 p.m.), https://www.nbcnews.com/business/business-news/amex-walmart-are-companies-mandating-covid-vaccine-employees-rcna11049 (listing private companies requiring employees to be vaccinated).

46. *See, e.g.*, Chris Costa, *Mills announces COVID-19 vaccine requirement for Maine health care workers*, NEWS CENTER MAINE (Aug. 12, 2021, 11:05 p.m.), https://www.newscentermaine.com/article/news/health/coronavirus/vaccine/governor-janet-mills-announces-covid-19-vaccine-requirement-for-maine-health-care-workers/97-ca8bfbcc-c06e-4065-be06-47ad531c3010 ("[Maine's vaccine requirement for health-care workers] follow[ed] announcements by Maine's two largest hospital systems, MaineHealth and Northern Light Health, announcing they would both require health-care workers to get the vaccine.").

47. *E.g.*, Ore. Exec. Order No. 21-29 (2021) at 4, *available at* https://www.oregon.gov/gov/eo/eo-21-29.pdf (requiring that employees and contractors of the Oregon executive branch be fully vaccinated by October 18, 2021, or within six weeks of FDA approval of a COVID-19 vaccine, whichever is later).

undue hardship on the employer.[48] Importantly, a "reasonable accommodation" for an employee's objection to vaccination need not be an exemption from the requirement.[49] The two legal paradigms may also overlap: during the COVID-19 pandemic, some states required their healthcare workers to submit to COVID-19 vaccination or be placed on leave or fired. Legal challenges to those requirements in some cases alleged that the state both violated the Free Exercise Clause and compelled, or acted in concert with, a private employer to violate Title VII.[50]

All states, consonant with *Jacobson*, allow exemptions for medical contraindications; 44 states also allow exemptions for sincerely held religious belief, while 6 do not.[51] States and their subdivisions impose their own qualifications for and administration of religious[52] and medical[53] exemptions. The claiming of an exemption generally requires filling out and presenting to the appropriate agency a standard form reflecting the state's exemption requirements.[54]

---

48. 42 U.S.C. § 2000e(j) (prohibiting employer discrimination against employees on the basis of religion; excluding from the definition of "religion" practices an employer cannot "reasonably accommodate . . . without undue hardship on the conduct of the employer's business"); Trans World Airlines, Inc. v. Hardison, 432 U.S. 63, 84 (1977) (holding that an "undue hardship" on employers is more than a "de minimis cost" of religious accommodation).

49. We the Patriots USA, Inc. v. Hochul, 17 F.4th 266, 292 (2d Cir. 2021) (employees may be granted a religious accommodation that is not an exemption from the mandate).

50. *E.g.*, *We the Patriots*, 17 F.4th at 273 (holding that New York's requirement that healthcare workers be vaccinated against COVID-19 without offering religious exemption from the mandate did not force employers to violate Title VII); Doe v. Mills, 16 F.4th 20, 35 (2021) (rejecting claim that hospitals, "in concert with the state appellees," violated Title VII).

51. *States with Religious and Philosophical Exemptions from School Immunization Requirements*, NAT'L CONF. OF STATE LEGISLATURES (May 25, 2022), https://www.ncsl.org/research/health/school-immunization-exemption-state-laws.aspx (listing California, Connecticut, Maine, Mississippi, New York, and West Virginia as offering no religious exemptions and reporting that Connecticut, Maine, and New York eliminated religious exemptions in the last three years).

52. Robert Bednarczyk et al., *Current landscape of nonmedical vaccination exemptions in the United States: impact of policy changes*, 18 EXPERT REV. VACCINES 175, 175 (2019).

53. Stephanie Stadlin et al., *Medical Exemptions to School Immunization Requirements in the United States—Association of State Policies With Medical Exemption Rates* (2004–2011), 206 J. INFEC. DISEASE 989, 989 (2012).

54. Cf. *Medical Exemption Form*, ARIZ. DEPT. HEALTH SVCS., https://www.azdhs.gov/documents/preparedness/epidemiology-disease-control/immunization/school-childcare/medical-exemption-form.pdf (last visited Dec. 22, 2022) (requiring signature

Although there has long been tension between religious belief claims and state enforcement of vaccination requirements, the COVID-19 pandemic brought that tension into much starker light. Faced with state and private-sector mandates to accept one of the newly developed COVID-19 vaccines or lose their job, a large number of adults claimed religious exemptions to the mandates. These claimants often professed a religious belief in opposition to vaccines derived from cells harvested from aborted fetuses.[55] Other objections include beliefs that vaccines alter a person's DNA,[56] that they are unnecessary because God will protect the body from sickness, and that the body is a sacred vessel that should not be polluted with unnatural substances.[57] Such claims often stand in contrast to the teachings of organized religion: most organized religions are at least neutral to vaccination, and some spiritual leaders—Pope Francis, notably—openly favor vaccination.[58] According to Vanderbilt

---

of licensed physician or nurse practitioner, written description of vaccine subject to exemption and reason for exemption, whether exemption is temporary or permanent, and attestation of parent or guardian); *Certificate of Immunization*, GA. DEPT. PUB. HEALTH, https://www.gadoe.org/wholechild/Documents/SchoolNurse/Revised-3231-2014.pdf (last visited Dec. 22, 2022) (including medical exemption documentation on child immunization form; allowing licensed physician, physician assistant, advanced practice registered nurse, or qualified health department employee to fill out and sign form; requiring no explanation of reason for medical exemption or parental attestation).

55. *See, e.g.*, Meredith Wadman, *Abortion opponents protest COVID-19 vaccines' use of fetal cells*, SCIENCE (June 5, 2020), https://www.science.org/content/article/abortion-opponents-protest-covid-19-vaccines-use-fetal-cells (quoting Catholic and other faith leaders urging governmental agencies to eschew use of aborted fetal cell lines in vaccine development, framing objection as matter of individual conscience); *see also* Priyanka Runwal, *Here are the facts about fetal cell lines and COVID-19 vaccines*, NAT'L GEOGRAPHIC (Nov. 19, 2021), https://www.nationalgeographic.com/science/article/here-are-the-facts-about-fetal-cell-lines-and-covid-19-vaccines ("[O]ne common reason people give for religious exemptions is the link between vaccines and human fetal cells").

56. *See, e.g.*, Austin Stevenson, *"My body is a temple": Vaccine hesitancy, religious exemptions, and the integrity of Christian witness*, ABC RELIGION & ETHICS (Oct. 11, 2021), https://www.abc.net.au/religion/vaccines-religious-exemptions-and-christian-witness/13580026 (presenting fear of DNA alteration as example of religious objection to COVID-19 vaccination).

57. *Id.*; *Cultural Perspectives on Vaccination*, HISTORY OF VACCINES, https://historyofvaccines.org/vaccines-101/ethical-issues-and-vaccines/cultural-perspectives-vaccination (last visited Dec. 20, 2022).

58. Mark E. Wojcik, *Sincerely Held or Suddenly Held Religious Exemptions to Vaccination?*, AM. BAR ASS'N (July 5, 2022), https://www.americanbar.org/groups/crsj/publications/human_rights_magazine_home/intersection-of-lgbtq-rights-and

University Medical Center, the major Christian denominations in the United States (Roman Catholic, Orthodox, Baptist, Lutheran, Methodist, Presbyterian, Episcopalian, Mormon) do not oppose vaccination, nor do other major religions (Hinduism, Islam, Judaism); even the Church of Scientology holds no theological opposition to vaccination.[59] Only a few Christian sects (Dutch Reformed Congregations and various faith-healing sects) theologically oppose vaccination.[60]

Nevertheless, the law protects only sincere religious belief;[61] whether a religious objector claims an exemption from a state's vaccination requirement or a private employer's, the sincerity of the claimant's belief, however idiosyncratic or unorthodox, determines the validity of the exemption claim. Although government, including courts, may not judge the validity of religious beliefs, "the threshold question of sincerity . . . must be resolved in every case."[62]

But the sincerity of religious claims is difficult to judge. The COVID-19 pandemic, and the vaccine requirements arising in response to it, gave rise to an online cottage industry instructing nonreligious objectors in claiming religious exemptions by couching their objections in religious terms.[63] Many objectors relied on the protections of Title VII

-religious-freedom/sincerely-held-or-suddenly-held/#:~:text=Vaccination%20is%20widely%20accepted%20in,to%20protect%20life%20and%20health (noting that Pope Francis supports vaccination and that other denominations do not officially oppose it; citing research finding theological opposition to vaccination in only a few Christian sects).

59. *Immunizations and Religion*, VAND. U. MED. CTR., https://www.vumc.org/health-wellness/news-resource-articles/immunizations-and-religion (last visited Dec. 20, 2022).

60. *Id.*

61. *See* Employment Div., Dep't of Human Res. v. Smith, 494 U.S. 872, 893 (1990) (O'Connor, J., concurring) (emphasizing sincerity as condition of First Amendment protection); *see also* Bushouse v. Local Union 2209, UAW, 164 F. Supp. 2d 1066, 1075 (N.D. Ind. 2001) (holding that only sincere beliefs must be accommodated under Title VII and that "an inquiry into the sincerity and religious nature of an employee['s] . . . purported beliefs [may be conducted] before the duty to accommodate [under Title VII] arises.").

62. United States v. Seeger, 380 U.S. 163, 185 (1965).

63. Dorit Reiss, *People lie about their 'religious' objections to vaccines. Proving it is hard.*, WASH. POST (Oct. 15, 2021, 11:55 a.m.), https://www.washingtonpost.com/outlook/religious-exemptions-law-vaccines-dishonesty/2021/10/15/df405c38-2d0d-11ec-8ef6-3ca8fe943a92_story.html ("It's easy to find people online, for example, coaching others on how to pretend that freedom of worship is the real issue.").

of the Civil Rights Act of 1964; such claims relied on courts' customary deference to individuals' claimed beliefs.[64]

COVID-19-era cases illustrate the difficulty of scrutinizing religious beliefs. For example, in *Together Employees v. Mass. General Brigham, Inc.*,[65] the District Court for the District of Massachusetts refused to enjoin MGB's (the company that owns and operates Mass General Hospital in Boston) vaccination requirement for employees.[66] The court held that allowing the plaintiffs to remain unvaccinated would result in undue hardship—that is, unvaccinated workers would be more than a *de minimis* harm to MGB's business.[67] In so holding, however, the court was at considerable pains to countenance the plaintiffs' right to express and practice their religion. The court was "mindful" of Title VII's "capacious definition of religion"[68] and was hesitant to scrutinize the plaintiffs' sincerity of belief, noting that other courts have tended to avoid unseemly skepticism of deeply held beliefs by assuming that such beliefs are sincere and instead deciding Title VII discrimination cases on other grounds.[69] The court was particularly hesitant in light of the plaintiffs' apparently unorthodox beliefs—it was concerned about resorting to the tenets of organized religions to judge the sincerity of idiosyncratic beliefs that nevertheless may be sincere and religious in nature.[70] The court openly admitted its difficulty: it made the same assumption as to the plaintiffs' sincerity, "with some misgivings."[71] The court went on to decide the religious discrimination claim on its determination that, for MGB, a healthcare provider corporation of considerable stature, allowing employees to remain unvaccinated would be an undue hardship, thus avoiding any inquiry into the sincerity of the plaintiffs' beliefs.[72]

---

64. *See, e.g.*, Sambrano v. United Airlines, Inc., 2022 U.S. App. LEXIS 4347, at *4 n.2 (5th Cir. Feb. 17, 2022) ("United's bizarre inquisition into the sincerity of its employees' beliefs is somewhat at odds with our usual approach of taking parties at their word regarding their own religious convictions.").

65. 573 F. Supp. 2d 412 (D. Mass. 2021).

66. *Id.* at 424.

67. *Id.* at 435.

68. *Id.* at 441.

69. *Id.*

70. *Id.* at 440 ("[C]ourts should also be wary of the real danger, in evaluating both the nature of a belief and its sincerity, that they may tend to favor well-established or widely practiced religions [at] the expense of new or disfavored ones.").

71. *Id.* at 441.

72. *Id.* at 431, 437 (acknowledging that MGB is a "major hospital and healthcare network"; finding undue hardship).

In certain cases, however, courts have been able to scrutinize religious claims and determine them not to be sincere.[73] For example, in *Aukamp-Corcoran v. Lancaster General Hospital*,[74] a nurse sued her former employer for firing her instead of offering her a religious accommodation when she refused to submit to the employer's mandatory influenza vaccination.[75] The District Court for the Eastern District of Pennsylvania granted the defendant employer's summary judgment motion, holding that the plaintiff's claimed religious objection to the vaccine was not sincere—and that, even if it were sincere, allowing the plaintiff to remain unvaccinated would undermine the hospital's safety efforts.[76] Unique facts allowed the court to determine that the plaintiff's claim was insincere: she had submitted to the same influenza vaccination in prior years before objecting to it; she had tried to obtain a medical exemption before claiming a religious objection and was unsuccessful; and she had posted to a secular Facebook group coaching members to claim religious exemptions even if their objections were not religious in nature.[77]

Just as COVID-19-era cases in lower courts illustrated the difficulty of scrutinizing individual religious claims, COVID-19-era Supreme Court cases represented the expansion of constitutional protections for religious claimants. Prior to COVID-19, the Court judged the claims of plaintiffs alleging governmental interference with their religious practice according to the rubric established by *Employment Division v. Smith*[78] and *Church of the Lukumi Babalu Aye v. City of Hialeah*.[79] In *Smith*, the Court held that Oregon's criminal statute outlawing the possession of peyote did not run afoul of the Free Exercise Clause, even though it incidentally burdened Native American religious practice involving the use of peyote, because the law was neutral toward religion (i.e., did not target religious practice) and generally applicable to the entire populace.[80] In *Lukumi*, the Court held that the City of Hialeah's prohibition of animal sacrifice must be judged under strict scrutiny,

73. *E.g.*, Phillips v. City of New York, 775 F.3d 538, 541 (2015) (reporting magistrate's finding, based on plaintiff's testimony, that plaintiff's objection was "health-related and did not constitute a genuine and sincere religious belief").

74. 2022 U.S. Dist. LEXIS 29355 (E.D. Penn. Feb. 17, 2022).

75. *Id.* at 3–8.

76. *Id.* at 18, 24.

77. *Id.* at 4–7.

78. Employment Div., Dep't of Human Res. v. Smith, 494 U.S. 872 (1990).

79. Church of the Lukumi Babalu Aye, Inc. v. City of Hialeah, 508 U.S. 520 (1993).

80. *Smith*, 494 U.S. at 878.

because, in contrast to the law at issue in *Smith*, the prohibition targeted Santeria religious practices involving animal sacrifice.[81]

Thus, under those cases, the constitutionality of laws impacting religious exercise is judged using the rational basis test—the test Justice Neil Gorsuch said the *Jacobson* Court applied[82]—if the laws are "generally applicable and neutral toward religion."[83] If the law in question is not neutral (that is, it discriminates against religion on its face or it targets religious practice) and generally applicable (that is, it "prohibits religious conduct while permitting secular conduct that undermines the government's asserted interest in a similar way" or it allows for a system of "individualized exemptions"), its constitutionality is judged according to strict scrutiny,[84] requiring a showing that the law in question "serves a compelling state interest and employs the least restrictive means available for doing so."[85]

The Supreme Court handed down a series of decisions during the COVID-19 era that built upon the *Smith-Lukumi* framework and showed increased solicitude for religious claims. In *Fulton v. City of Philadelphia*, the Court elaborated on the concept of general applicability.[86] There, the City of Philadelphia stopped referring foster children to a Catholic foster family referral agency, because the agency refused to place children with same-sex couples for religious reasons.[87] The City's foster care contract forbade the refusal to place children based upon prospective parents' sexual orientation, except in the "sole discretion" of a city officer.[88] The Court took issue with this "formal system of entirely discretionary exemptions"[89] and held that "the creation of a formal mechanism for granting exceptions renders a policy not generally applicable, . . . because it 'invite[s]' the government to decide which reasons for not complying with the policy are worthy of solicitude."[90]

81. *Lukumi*, 508 U.S. at 533–34.

82. Roman Cath. Diocese of Brooklyn v. Cuomo, 592 U.S. ___, ___, 141 S. Ct. 63, 70 (2020) (Gorsuch, J., concurring).

83. *Mills*, 142 S. Ct. at 18 (Gorsuch, J., dissenting).

84. Kennedy v. Bremerton Sch. Dist., 142 S. Ct. 2407, 2422 (2022).

85. *Mills*, 142 S. Ct. at 18 (Gorsuch, J., dissenting) (citing *Lukumi*, 508 U.S. at 531–32 and *Smith*, 494 U.S. at 879).

86. Fulton v. City of Philadelphia, 141 S. Ct. 1868 (2021).

87. *Id.* at 1874.

88. *Id.* at 1878.

89. *Id.*

90. *Id.* at 1879.

In response to state-level restrictions on religious gatherings in the early days of the COVID-19 pandemic, the Court held in *Tandon v. Newsom* that such restrictions violate the Free Exercise Clause when they treat "*any* comparable secular activity more favorably than religious exercise."[91] In particularly notable language, Justice Neil Gorsuch wrote in concurrence in *Roman Catholic Diocese of Brooklyn v. Cuomo* that, "[e]ven if the Constitution has taken a holiday [in allowing for restrictions on religious observance for public health reasons] during this pandemic, it cannot become a sabbatical."[92] Justice Gorsuch's language evinces a view that, contrary to *Jacobson*, *Zucht*, and *Prince*, religious considerations must trump public health considerations in policymaking, whether such policy is in response to an outbreak of disease or in anticipation of one; in his view, failing to prioritize religious claims over public health is tantamount to refusing to apply the Free Exercise Clause at all.[93] Indeed, Justice Gorsuch took pains to note that Chief Justice Roberts' concurrence in *South Bay United Pentecostal Church v. Newsom* "reached back 100 years in the U.S. Reports to grab hold of . . . *Jacobson*," a case Gorsuch considered entirely inapposite to the current tension between religious claims, which are explicitly protected in the Constitution, and public health policy.[94] Justice Gorsuch's focus on the primacy of religion in constitutional law[95] demonstrates a willingness to allow individuals to use religious claims to make themselves, in Justice Harlan's words, "laws unto themselves."[96] This solicitude for religious claims became even clearer in dissents he wrote in the first two cases ever to reach the Supreme Court challenging vaccination requirements on religious grounds: *Does v. Mills* and *Dr. A. v. Hochul*.[97]

The Supreme Court's highest-profile COVID-19 vaccine requirement decisions dealt with the Biden administration's unprecedented

91. Tandon v. Newsom, 141 S. Ct. 1294, 1296 (2021).

92. Roman Catholic Diocese of Brooklyn v. Cuomo, 141 S. Ct. 63, 70 (2020).

93. Justice Gorsuch considered the Court's earlier decision in *South Bay United Pentecostal Church v. Newsom*, 140 S. Ct. 1613 (2020), allowing a California ban on large religious gatherings in the early days of the pandemic to stand, "mistaken" and opined that courts "must resume applying the Free Exercise Clause." *Id.*

94. *Id.* at 71.

95. *See* Peter Manus, *Justice Gorsuch's Crusade: The Inviolable Power of Religion*, 28 B.U. Pub. Int. L.J. 195, 221 (2019) ("To Judge Gorsuch, faith-based behavior, once established as genuine, is virtually immune from judicial scrutiny.").

96. Jacobson v. Massachusetts, 197 U.S. 11, 26 (1905).

97. Does v. Mills, 142 S. Ct. 17 (2021); Dr. A. v. Hochul, 142 S. Ct. 552 (2021).

attempts to mandate vaccination at the federal level,[98] but the first COVID-19-vaccine-related cases to reach the Court were challenges to state-level vaccination requirements without religious exemptions.[99] In *Does v. Mills* and *Dr. A. v. Hochul*, the Court declined to enjoin state vaccination requirements for healthcare workers in Maine and New York, respectively.[100] Maine and New York had, in 2019, repealed their religious exemptions from mandatory vaccination for schoolchildren.[101] Then, in 2021, those states mandated that healthcare workers be vaccinated against COVID-19, on penalty of losing their jobs, and, consistent with their 2019 actions, provided no exemption for sincerely held religious beliefs.[102] The circumstances surrounding the announcements of the Maine and New York vaccination requirements differed in one important respect, however: whereas Maine governor Janet Mills announced the vaccine requirement without commentary on religious matters,[103] New York governor Kathy Hochul, in conjunction with the rollout of her state's requirement, publicly stated her views on the religious obligation of New Yorkers to be vaccinated and the invalidity of religious views contrary to vaccination.[104]

98. Biden v. Missouri, 595 U.S. ___, 142 S. Ct. 647 (2022) (upholding Centers for Medicare and Medicaid Services' vaccination requirement for healthcare workers at facilities participating in Medicare or Medicaid); Nat'l Fed'n Indep. Bus. v. Dept. Labor, Occupational Safety & Health Admin., 595 U.S. ___, 142 S. Ct. 661 (2022) (striking down Occupational Safety and Health Administration's vaccination requirement for employees of businesses with 100 or more employees).

99. *Mills*, 142 S. Ct. at 18 (Gorsuch, J., dissenting); *Hochul*, 142 S. Ct. at 552 (Gorsuch, J., dissenting).

100. *Mills*, 142 S. Ct. at 18; *Hochul*, 142 S. Ct. at 552.

101. *States With Religious and Philosophical Exemptions From School Immunization Requirements*, NAT'L CONF. STATE LEGISLATURES (Jan. 10, 2022), https://www.ncsl.org/research/health/school-immunization-exemption-state-laws.aspx.

102. Doe v. Mills, 16 F.4th 20, 28 (2021); We the Patriots USA, Inc. v. Hochul, 17 F.4th 266, 272 (2021).

103. Costa, *supra* note 46; *see* David Marino, *Religious group sues Gov. Mills over vaccine mandate for health care workers*, WGME (Aug. 26, 2021), https://wgme.com/news/coronavirus/religious-group-sues-gov-mills-over-vaccine-mandate-for-health-care-workers (reporting on lawsuit challenging Maine vaccine requirement; not mentioning any religious statements made by Maine government officials).

104. Brendan Lyons, *New challenge to vaccine mandate cites Hochul's statements on God*, TIMES UNION (Oct. 5, 2021, 7:47 p.m.), https://www.timesunion.com/state/article/New-challenge-of-vaccine-mandate-cites-Hochul-s-16509151.php ("[Governor Hochul] said, 'I need you to be my apostles. I need you to go out and talk about it and say, we owe this to each other. We love each other. Jesus taught us to love one another and how do you show that love but to care about each other enough to say, please get the vaccine . . . .' The lawsuit contends additional remarks

Anonymous healthcare-worker plaintiffs filed suit in federal district court, alleging First Amendment infringement;[105] after unfavorable decisions, they appealed to the First and Second Circuits, respectively.[106] Both circuit courts again ruled in favor of the states' broad authority to enact public health measures and held that the First Amendment did not require the states to provide religious exemptions from their vaccination requirements.[107]

The Supreme Court declined to enjoin the state mandates. Justice Gorsuch, however, dissented from the denial of an injunction in both cases and showed the same solicitude for religious claims in the vaccination context as he did in the public gathering context.[108]

Justice Gorsuch's dissent in *Mills*, joined by Justices Thomas and Alito, argues, in essence, that the Supreme Court's landmark COVID-19 free exercise jurisprudence in the public gathering context should result in the application of strict scrutiny to vaccination requirements.[109] He starts from the well-established framework of *Smith* and *Lukumi*, accepting the premise that laws that are not neutral and generally applicable should receive strict scrutiny. He first argues, citing *Lukumi* and *Fulton*, that Maine's law is not generally applicable because it offers "individualized exemptions . . . , but only if they invoke certain preferred (nonreligious) justifications."[110] He then turns to the Court's COVID-19-era decisions to support his argument that Maine's lack of a religious exemption violates the Free Exercise Clause, relying in particular on *Tandon v. Newsom*'s "most favored nation" approach to free exercise cases (strictly scrutinizing laws that treat "*any* comparable

---

by Hochul indicate anyone whose religious beliefs conflict with her own on vaccines are 'invalid,' and that she said Pope Francis agrees with her position. The governor has also publicly stated that God is responsible for the creation of the COVID-19 vaccines, the complaint states.").

105. Doe v. Mills, 2021 U.S. Dist. LEXIS 197251, at *1 (D. Maine Oct. 13, 2021); Dr. A. v. Hochul, 2021 U.S. Dist. LEXIS 199419, at *9, 15 (Oct. 12, 2021).

106. *Mills*, 16 F.4th at 28; *Hochul*, 17 F.4th at 272.

107. *Mills*, 16 F.4th at 31–35 ("Providing a medical exemption does not undermine any of Maine's three goals, let alone in a manner similar to the way an exemption for religious objectors would."); *Hochul*, 17 F.4th at 281.

108. *Mills*, 142 S. Ct. at 18 (Gorsuch, J., dissenting); *Hochul*, 142 S. Ct. at 552 (Gorsuch, J., dissenting).

109. *Mills*, 142 S. Ct. at 19 (Gorsuch, J., dissenting) (finding that Maine's mandate treats a "comparable secular activity more favorably than religious exercise," citing Tandon v. Newsom, 593 U.S. ___, 141 S. Ct. 1294 and Fulton v. City of Philadelphia, 593 U.S. ___, ___, 141 S. Ct. 1868 (2021)).

110. *Id.*

secular activity more favorably than religious exercise").[111] Predictably, Justice Gorsuch proceeds to portray medical exemptions as comparable to religious exemptions, such that any differentiation in their treatment would trigger strict scrutiny.[112] In particular, he asserts that there is no basis to assume that "those invoking medical reasons to avoid the vaccination requirement" would present any less risk for being willing to wear personal protective equipment and undergo testing than "those invoking religious reasons" would.[113] He goes on to assert that "unvaccinated medical objectors" and "unvaccinated religious objectors" pose the same risk to healthcare infrastructure; thus, he argues, "medical exemptions and religious exemptions are on comparable footing when it comes to the State's asserted interests."[114]

Justice Gorsuch, joined by Justice Alito, likewise dissented from the Court's denial of an injunction in *Hochul*.[115] As he did in *Mills*, he argued that, under *Smith* and *Church of Lukumi*, New York's vaccination requirement should be subject to strict scrutiny as not neutral or generally applicable.[116] In *Hochul*, however, he added the argument that the circumstances surrounding the enactment of the mandate suggested an animus toward religion by the state.[117]

In the crux of his dissent, Justice Gorsuch dismissed the difference between religious exemptions and medical exemptions. He brushed off as "speculation" the state's argument that greater numbers of religious exemptions make religious exemption a greater risk to the state's asserted interest than medical exemption poses—general applicability is not a "numbers game," he argued.[118] Then, in particularly revealing language, he posited that the state's mandate could survive strict scrutiny if it "restricted vaccine exemptions to a particular number divided in a nondiscriminatory manner between medical and religious objectors."[119]

---

111. *Tandon*, 141 S. Ct. at 1296.

112. *Mills*, 142 S. Ct. at 19–20 (Gorsuch, J., dissenting).

113. *Id.* at 19–20.

114. *Id.* at 20.

115. Dr. A. v. Hochul, 595 U.S. ___, ___, 142 S. Ct. 552, 552 (2021).

116. *Id.* at 556.

117. Former governor Andrew Cuomo announced the vaccination requirement but promised that it would contain a religious exemption; when Governor Cuomo resigned, his successor, Governor Kathy Hochul, announced the imposition of a vaccination requirement with no religious exemption and made public statements questioning the religious sincerity of vaccine objectors. *Id.* at 553–54. *See also* Lyons, *supra* note 104 and accompanying text.

118. *Hochul*, 595 U.S. at 556.

119. *Id.* at 556–57.

A Coming Circuit Split?

Justice Gorsuch's repeated attacks on the *Jacobson-Zucht-Prince* precedent are not merely one jurist's lone effort; they are one aspect of a growing movement to undermine *Jacobson*'s basic principle that individuals may not, simply by claiming a conflicting belief, opt out of a reasonable and nonoppressive public health measure. The Supreme Court as a whole may be primed to place individual religious claims above the state's police power:[120] Justices Thomas and Alito have shown their agreement with Justice Gorsuch's views,[121] and Justices Kavanaugh and Barrett may yet agree with Gorsuch, too.[122] Furthermore, at least one prominent legal scholar has begun to characterize the consensus understanding of *Jacobson*'s basic principle as a "myth,"[123] and lower courts have issued decisions citing Justice Gorsuch's dissents with approval.[124]

The lower court decisions following *Mills* and *Hochul* reveal the potential for a circuit split to arise, giving the Court the occasion to undermine *Jacobson* and the constitutional consensus regarding religious exemptions articulated in *Phillips*. One circuit court has already weighed in on the side of the established consensus: in *Doe v. San Diego Unified School District* (*SDUSD*), the Ninth Circuit upheld a school district's COVID-19 vaccination requirement with medical exemptions but

---

120. Regarding religious objections to vaccine mandates, Prof. Reiss believes "the Supreme Court has begun to change its mind about what the Constitution requires." Reiss, *supra* note 63.

121. Justices Gorsuch and Thomas joined Justice Alito's concurrence in *Fulton* arguing for overruling *Smith*, which Justice Alito says does little to protect religious belief against laws with "devastating effect[s] on religious freedom." Fulton v. City of Philadelphia, 141 S. Ct. 1868, 1883 (Alito, J., concurring). Justice Gorsuch penned his own concurrence in *Fulton*, joined by Justices Thomas and Alito, emphasizing his agreement with Justice Alito that *Smith* should be overruled. 141 S. Ct. at 1926.

122. Justices Barrett and Kavanaugh concurred in *Mills* to stress that their decision was based on the novelty of the case and the lack of full briefing, not on the underlying merits. Does v. Mills, 142 S. Ct. 17, 18 (2021); Allie Reed, *Covid Vaccination Mandate Religious Exemptions Give Hospitals Leeway*, Bloomberg Law (Feb. 25, 2022, 4:35 a.m.), https://news.bloomberglaw.com/health-law-and-business/covid-vaccine-mandate-religious-exemptions-give-hospitals-leeway ("'One of the touchstones of the Supreme Court ideologically is religion,' and 'there's a determined five-member majority of the court' that might 'preference religion over public health,' [Prof. Lawrence] Gostin said.").

123. Josh Blackman, *The Irrepressible Myth of* Jacobson v. Massachusetts, 70 Buff. L. Rev. 131 (2022).

124. *See, e.g.*, Air Force Officer v. Austin, 2022 U.S. Dist. LEXIS 26660, at *3–10 (M.D. Ga. Feb. 15, 2022).

without religious exemptions.[125] The court grappled with the relevant Supreme Court precedent, from *Smith* and *Lukumi* to *Fulton* and *Tandon* to *Mills* and *Hochul*, and it concluded that the district's mandate was facially neutral (i.e., that it did not mention religion at all), that it did not aim to suppress religious belief, and that it was generally applicable.[126]

The *SDUSD* court's discussion of general applicability is particularly important. The court noted that, under the *Fulton* standard for general applicability, the medical exemption did not "undermine the government's asserted interest in a similar way" that a religious exemption would: because medical exemptions are objectively limited to Centers for Disease Control and Prevention (CDC)-recognized contraindications and precautions and require a physician's certification, they advance health and safety; religious exemptions, which are not matters of objectively verifiable fact and can be claimed by anyone, do not advance health and safety.[127] Moreover, the relative number and duration of medical and religious exemptions make them not comparable in the free exercise analysis: whereas medical exemptions are temporary and rare, religious exemptions would be permanent and possibly quite common. Thus, as the court said, "although 'it may be feasible for [SDUSD] to manage the COVID-19 risks posed by a small set of objectively defined and largely time-limited medical exemptions,' 'it could pose a significant barrier to effective disease prevention to permit a much greater number of permanent religious exemptions.'"[128]

This focus on the number and extent of medical and religious exemptions is a crucial factor and harkens back to *Jacobson*. *Jacobson*, although not a free exercise case, grounded its rationale on the collective good that vaccination does and the harm that would be done by allowing individuals to opt out without medical necessity.[129] The same consideration is apparent in *SDUSD*, and it is consonant with the purpose of vaccination and vaccination requirements: in order to protect public health—including the health of the most vulnerable—vaccination must be widespread,[130] and allowing a large number of opt outs that do not

125. Doe v. San Diego Unified Sch. Dist., 19 F.4th 1173, 1176 (9th Cir. 2021).

126. *Id.* at 1177–78.

127. *Id.*

128. *Id.* at 1178, quoting We the Patriots USA, Inc. v. Hochul, 17 F.4th 266, 286 (2d Cir. 2021).

129. *See* Vaccine Requirements and Religious Exemptions: Established Precedent, *supra*.

130. The greater the percentage of a population is vaccinated against a particular pathogen, the slower that pathogen spreads because it rarely encounters a susceptible

themselves advance a health-related goal undermines public health by increasing the risk of outbreaks.[131]

The *SDUSD* court also addressed the issue of individualized exemptions. The school district's medical exemption policy was "limited," allowing exemptions only for contraindications or precautions recognized by the CDC and requiring the certification of a physician.[132] Because the medical exemption mechanism was "rigid" and did not vest authority in a government official to make "discretionary exceptions," the court held that it was generally applicable.[133]

Conversely, in *Air Force Officer v. Austin*, the U.S. District Court for the Middle District of Georgia enjoined the Department of Defense's COVID-19 vaccination requirement as applied to one reservist.[134] The court sided with Justice Gorsuch in *Hochul* and against the Ninth Circuit in *SDUSD*, holding that, under *Fulton*, whether a servicemember remains unvaccinated for religious or nonreligious reasons, he or she poses a "similar hazard" to the military's goal of preventing the spread of COVID-19 within its ranks.[135] The court pointedly followed Justice Gorsuch's language in *Hochul*, declaring that its mind would not be changed by the possibility of an influx of religious accommodation requests as a result of an injunction; "the general applicability test doesn't turn on [a] numbers game."[136] Although decisions like the district court's in *Austin* are the exception and not the rule, the issue remains live before the courts: in November 2022, Justice Sotomayor, the justice assigned to hear emergency requests arising out of the Second Circuit, rejected an emergency request to enjoin New York City's COVID-19 vaccination

---

individual. Paul Fine et al., *"Herd Immunity": A Rough Guide*, 52 Clinical Infec. Diseases 911, 912 (2011). When a certain percentage of a population is immunized, the population achieves what is known as "herd immunity" or "community protection," whereby the pathogen's "chain of human-to-human transmission [is] interrupted," even though not all of the population is immunized. Orenstein & Ahmed, *supra* note 36, at 4031.

131. Saad B. Omer, *Why small groups of vaccine refusers can make large groups of people sick*, Wash. Post (Nov. 29, 2018), https://www.washingtonpost.com/outlook/2018/11/29/why-small-groups-vaccine-refusers-can-make-large-groups-people-sick/ (increased vaccine refusal rates and clustering of refusers lead to "more and larger outbreaks").

132. *SDUSD*, 19 F.4th at 1178.

133. *Id.* at 1180.

134. Air Force Officer v. Austin, 2022 U.S. Dist. LEXIS 26660, at *3 (M.D. Ga. Feb. 15, 2022).

135. *Id.*

136. *Id.* at *30–31.

requirement for public sector workers.[137] The plaintiffs in the case, New Yorkers for Religious Liberty, argued that New York City's mandate is not neutral toward religion and not generally applicable—an argument that tracks Justice Gorsuch's dissents in *Mills* and *Hochul*.[138]

Although the Supreme Court denied certiorari in *Does v. Mills* on the question of whether states that offer medical exemptions to their vaccination requirements must also offer religious exemptions,[139] the growing movement to undermine *Jacobson* will likely result in the Court tackling that very question soon. When it does, it should find the Ninth Circuit's reasoning in *SDUSD* persuasive. After all, vaccination is indeed a "numbers game"—its effectiveness as a public health measure comes through large percentages of the population being vaccinated.[140] Furthermore, religious exemptions, whose validity depends on the credibility of the claimant, are not "comparable" to medical exemptions, whose validity depends on the independent, objective judgment of a physician or (in some cases) other medical professional. In the end, the Supreme Court should reinforce the longstanding precedent of *Jacobson*, *Zucht*, *Prince*, and cases like *Phillips*, holding that states may enact vaccination requirements that do not allow individuals, merely by invoking religion, to become "a law unto [themselves]."[141] Although states may choose to make religious exemptions to their vaccination requirements available based on political considerations,[142] they should know that the Constitution does not tie their hands.

---

137. Naham, *supra* note 9.

138. Emergency Application for an Injunction Pending Appellate Review at 15-25, New Yorkers for Religious Liberty v. City of New York, No. 22A389 (U.S. Nov. 2, 2022).

139. Doe v. Mills, 595 U.S. ___, 142 S. Ct. 1112, 2022 U.S. LEXIS 949 (Feb. 22, 2022).

140. *See* Fine et al., *supra* note 130, at 912; *see also* Orenstein & Ahmed, *supra* note 36, at 4031.

141. Jacobson v. Massachusetts, 197 U.S. 11, 26 (1905).

142. According to polling, the American public is closely divided on whether religious exemptions from mandatory vaccination should be available. *Religious Identities and the Race Against the Virus: American Attitudes on Vaccination Mandates and Religious Exemptions*, Pub. Religion Rsch. Inst. (Nov. 28, 2021) at 17, https://www.prri.org/research/religious-identities-and-the-race-against-the-virus-american-attitudes-on-vaccination-mandates-and-religious-exemptions/ (58 percent of Americans in favor of allowing religious exemptions from required vaccination, and 41 percent opposed). Views on whether religious exemptions should be available vary by political and religious affiliation, *id.* at 17–18, suggesting that political pressures may vary by state based on the political and religious makeup of each state's populace.

Prescriptions

Courts, state legislatures, and public health regulators can take additional steps to shore up legal protections for vaccination requirements without religious exemptions. First, they should consider the public health impact of permitting large numbers of individuals to opt out of vaccination. In *Brown v. Stone*, the Mississippi Supreme Court struck down a religious exemption from school-age vaccination as violative of the Equal Protection Clause of the 14th Amendment, "in that it would require the great body of school children to be vaccinated and at the same time expose them to the hazard of associating in school with children exempted under the religious exemption who had not been immunized."[143] Although *Brown v. Stone* is unique, it illustrates that the vaccinated, and the public at large, bear a substantial burden when a portion of the populace can rely on their unique religious beliefs to avoid vaccination.[144] The COVID-19 pandemic has shone a brighter light on that burden, as the SARS-CoV-2 virus has mutated into more vaccine-resistant strains. Indeed, there is evidence to show that the populations of states that allow religious exemptions are at greater risk of vaccine-preventable disease than those of states that have ended religious exemptions.[145]

Second, courts and public health regulators should be more willing to scrutinize religious claims for their sincerity, looking to cases like *Aukamp-Corcoran v. Lancaster General Hospital* for inspiration. As the Supreme Court has acknowledged, the threshold question of sincerity is

143. Brown v. Stone, 378 So. 2d 218, 223 (Miss. 1979).

144. *See* Gordana Pelčić et al., *Religious exception for vaccination or religious excuses for avoiding vaccination*, 57 Croat. Med. J. 516, 516 (2016) (noting link between religious opt-outs from vaccination and disease outbreaks); *see also* Sarah Pulliam Bailey, *Some anti-vaccination parents cite religious exemptions. Measles outbreaks could change that*, Wash. Post (Feb. 21, 2019, 3:25 p.m.), https://www.washingtonpost.com/religion/2019/02/21/some-anti-vaccination-parents-cite-religious-exemptions-measles-outbreaks-could-change-that/ (noting link between clusters of vaccine opt outs and dip in herd immunity; noting Maryland exception to availability of opt out "during an emergency or epidemic of disease").

145. *See* Bednarczyk et al., *supra* note 52, at 11 ("Non-medical exemptions have epidemiological implications of increasing individual disease risk and population risk for disease outbreaks."); *see also* Sindiso Nyathi et al., *The 2016 California policy to eliminate nonmedical vaccine exemptions and changes in vaccine coverage: An empirical policy analysis*, PLOS Medicine (Dec. 23, 2019), https://www.ncbi.nlm.nih.gov/pmc/articles/PMC6927583/pdf/pmed.1002994.pdf.

one that must be answered in every case;[146] to take every claim as sincere without question invites rampant abuse and risks making a mockery of sincere religious claims. Given the rapid growth of social media and the many online sources coaching individuals to claim religious objections to vaccination,[147] courts will increasingly find that the records of the cases they hear will allow them to judge the sincerity of religious claims more accurately than they could in years past. Rather than defaulting to the position that individuals' religious claims are sincere, courts should be unafraid to judge some claims insincere when the evidence warrants.

Third, public health authorities should pay closer attention to lagging standards in granting medical exemptions.[148] True medical contraindications are rare, yet some clusters of workers have successfully claimed medical exemptions in statistically improbable numbers.[149] Such abuse of the medical exemption system tends to justify Justice Gorsuch's cynical equivalence of those who seek exemptions for religious and medical reasons, thereby undermining the legal foundation for allowing for vaccination requirements without religious exemptions. It also brings states closer to losing the "numbers game" of achieving high vaccination rates for public health.[150] States can tighten medical exemption standards by following the American Medical Association's advice to allow licensed physicians only—not other health professionals—to validate medical exemption requests.[151] They can also require, as West Virginia does, that

---

146. United States v. Seeger, 380 U.S. 163, 185 (1965).

147. *See* Dorit Reiss, *Religious Exemptions to Vaccines and the Anti-Vax Movement*, Bill of Health (July 16, 2021), https://blog.petrieflom.law.harvard.edu/2021/07/16/religious-exemptions-to-vaccines-and-the-anti-vax-movement/ (cataloguing Facebook activity coaching viewers to "[game] the system" in seeking religious exemptions).

148. *See, e.g.*, Ross Silverman & Gabriel Bosslet, *Preventing Misuse of COVID-19 Vaccine Medical Exemptions*, Bill of Health (Aug. 23, 2021), https://blog.petrieflom.law.harvard.edu/2021/08/23/covid-vaccine-medical-exemptions/ (flagging problem of medical exemption abuse and describing California physicians' violation of practice standards in writing unwarranted medical exemptions).

149. Emily Hopkins & Andrea Suozzo, *Vaccine Medical Exemptions Are Rare. Thousands of Nursing Home Workers Have Them*, ProPublica (Apr. 21, 2022, 5:00 a.m.), https://www.propublica.org/article/vaccination-rates-nursing-home-workers.

150. *See* Jodie McVernon, *Vaccination: A Numbers Game that Adds Up*, Pursuit (Nov. 18, 2016), https://pursuit.unimelb.edu.au/articles/vaccination-a-numbers-game-that-adds-up (characterizing vaccination to protect public health as a "numbers game" and arguing for higher vaccination rates to maximize public health).

151. *AMA PolicyFinder, Nonmedical Exemptions from Immunizations H-440.970*, AMA, https://policysearch.ama-assn.org/policyfinder/detail/vaccine%20exemption?uri=%2FAMADoc%2FHOD.xml-0-3985.xml (last visited Mar. 19, 2022) ("[The

any provider validating a medical exemption must have personally examined the claimant and must specifically state the basis for the exemption, and they can designate a knowledgeable officer to review medical exemption requests to weed out spurious claims.[152] They can require, as New York does, that medical exemptions from vaccination must be based on the guidance of the Advisory Committee on Immunization Practices (ACIP) or other objective standard of care-based criteria, not merely on individual physicians' conceptions of medical risk.[153] Also, just as courts can scrutinize the sincerity of religious belief, states can use their professional licensing authority to police the behavior of physicians who sign off on medical exemption requests in extraordinary numbers.

Vaccination, Exemptions, and Health Equity

Achieving high rates of vaccination advances health equity.[154] As COVID-19 showed, infectious disease can disproportionately impact disadvantaged communities.[155] Therefore, equity requires that state health policy include measures to prevent vaccine-preventable diseases, and eliminating religious exemptions leads to higher vaccination rates. Public health policy should attempt to eliminate inequities in disease outcomes by broadening vaccines' protection against disease as widely as possible, and vaccination requirements without religious exemptions can relieve the outsized burden of disease on disadvantaged populations.

AMA] believes that nonmedical (religious, philosophic, or personal belief) exemptions from immunizations endanger the health of the unvaccinated individual and the health of those in his or her group and the community at large"; the AMA "supports legislation eliminating nonmedical exemptions from immunization" and supports limiting "medical vaccine exemption authority to only licensed physicians.").

152. Silverman & Bosslet, *supra* note 148.

153. N.Y. Comp. Codes R. & Regs. tit. 10, § 66-1.1(l) (2019); Goe v. Zucker, 43 F.4th 19 (2d Cir. 2022), *cert. denied*, Goe v. McDonald, 598 U.S. ___ (2023).

154. *Emphasizing Equity in COVID-19 Vaccine Requirements*, Made to Save (Sept. 1, 2021), https://madetosave.org/2021/09/01/requirements/.

155. Vaughn Barry et al., *Patterns in COVID-19 Vaccination Coverage, by Social Vulnerability and Urbanicity—United States, December 14, 2020–May 1, 2021*, 70 Morbidity & Mortality Wkly. Rep. 818, 819 (2021) ("Counties with higher levels of social vulnerability have been disproportionately affected by COVID-19.").

Chapter 4

Free Exercise Challenges to Vaccine Mandates: The Destabilization of the Law and Its Implications

*Wendy E. Parmet and Faith Khalik**

For more than two centuries, states have employed vaccine mandates to prevent the spread of communicable diseases.[1] For almost all of that time, such laws were not viewed as incompatible with the First Amendment's protections for religious liberty. Indeed, states only began to offer religious exemptions to vaccine mandates in the 1960s.[2] By 2020, most state laws requiring that children be vaccinated to attend school allowed for religious or personal belief exemptions.[3] Nevertheless, courts consistently held that the absence of a religious exemption did not violate the Free Exercise Clause of the First Amendment.[4] That is no longer the case. Since the start of the COVID-19 pandemic, the Supreme Court and lower

*This work was supported by ChangeLab Solutions as part of the Act for Public Health Partnership. The views expressed here are solely those of the authors and are not necessarily those of ChangeLab Solutions or other members of the Act for Public Health Partnership. The authors wish to thank Linda Tvrdy for her assistance.

1. Lawrence O. Gostin & Lindsay Wiley, Public Health Law: Power, Duty, Restraint 348 (3d ed. 2016).

2. Dorit Rubinstein Reiss, *Thou Shalt Not Take the Name of the Lord Thy God in Vain: Use and Abuse of Religious Exemptions from School Immunization Requirements*, 65 J. Hastings L. J. 1551, 1559 (2014).

3. *States with Religious and Philosophical Exemptions from School Immunization Requirements*, National Conference of State Legislatures, https://www.ncsl.org/research/health/school-immunization-exemption-state-laws.aspx (May 25, 2022).

4. *See infra* text accompanying notes 22–30.

federal courts have issued a series of decisions that have upended free exercise doctrine, raising new questions as to the constitutionality and feasibility of vaccine mandates.

This chapter explores that doctrinal shift and its implication for vaccine mandates. It begins by reviewing the pre-pandemic legal consensus. Next, it describes the Supreme Court decisions that have destabilized free exercise law and opened the door to constitutional challenges to both COVID-19 and traditional childhood vaccine mandates. After reviewing these cases, the chapter discusses their implications for vaccine mandates, public health, and health equity moving forward.

Pre-COVID-19 Foundations

Although the Supreme Court has never held that the Free Exercise Clause does not compel religious exemptions to vaccine mandates, numerous Supreme Court decisions offer strong support for that conclusion. The earliest was *Jacobson v. Massachusetts*, which rejected the Reverend Henning Jacobson's challenge to a Cambridge, Massachusetts, law requiring that all residents be vaccinated against smallpox during an outbreak.[5] *Jacobson* was decided in 1905, before the Court "incorporated" the First Amendment's Free Exercise Clause into the 14th Amendment. Hence, it was not, strictly speaking, a free exercise case, even though Jacobson had religious objections to vaccination.[6] Nevertheless, in rejecting Jacobson's argument that the mandate violated the 14th Amendment, the Court explained that "in every well-ordered society charged with the duty of conserving the safety of its members the rights of the individual in respect of his liberty may at times, under the pressure of great dangers, be subjected to such restraint, to be enforced by reasonable regulations, as the safety of the general public may demand."[7] The Court added that an individual "may be compelled, by force if need be, against his will and without regard to his personal wishes or his pecuniary interests, or even his *religious or political convictions*, to take his place in the ranks of the army of his country, and risk the chance of being shot down in its defense."[8]

Nearly 20 years later, in *Zucht v. King*, the Court reaffirmed and expanded on *Jacobson* by rejecting a 14th Amendment challenge to a

---

5. 197 U.S. 11 (1905).

6. Wendy E. Parmet, *Rediscovering* Jacobson *in the Era of COVID-19*, 100 B.U. L. Rev. Online 117, 121 (2020).

7. 197 U.S. at 29.

8. *Id.* (emphasis added).

law that required students to be vaccinated to attend school, even in the absence of an outbreak.[9] *Zucht* was also decided before the Court had held that the Free Exercise Clause applied to the states and did not consider a religious liberty claim. Nevertheless, the Court was adamant that the constitutionality of vaccine mandates had been "settled," "long before this suit was instituted."[10]

The Court continued to adhere to that view even after it held in 1940 that the Free Exercise Clause applied to the states.[11] Most notably, in rejecting a free exercise claim to Massachusetts' child labor laws, the Court in *Prince v. Massachusetts* cited *Jacobson*, stating that a parent "cannot claim freedom from compulsory vaccination for the child more than for himself on religious grounds. The right to practice religion freely does not include liberty to expose the community or the child to communicable disease or the latter to ill health or death."[12]

Later, in *Sherbert v. Verner*, the Supreme Court once again cited *Jacobson* while discussing a free exercise claim.[13] In concluding that the state had violated the First Amendment by denying unemployment compensation to a women who refused to work on her Sabbath, the Court offered *Jacobson* as an example of a situation in which the Free Exercise Clause did not limit a state's regulation, because "[t]he conduct or actions so regulated . . . posed some substantial threat to public safety, peace or order."[14]

In 1990, the Court in *Employment Division v. Smith*[15] retreated from *Sherbert*, holding that the Free Exercise Clause "does not relieve an individual of the obligation to comply with a 'valid and neutral law of general applicability on the ground that the law proscribes (or prescribes) conduct that his religion prescribes (or proscribes).'"[16] Thus, under *Smith*, neutral laws of general applicability that could easily characterize most vaccine mandates are generally subject only to rational basis review and must be upheld if they are rationally related to a legitimate state interest.[17]

---

9. 260 U.S. 174 (1922).
10. Zucht v. King, 260 U.S. 174, 176 (1922).
11. Cantwell v. Connecticut, 310 U.S. 296 (1940).
12. Prince v. Massachusetts, 321 U.S. 158, 166–67 (1944) (citing *Jacobson*, 197 U.S. 11 and People v. Pierson, 176 N.Y. 201 (1903)).
13. 374 U.S 398 (1963).
14. *Id.* at 403.
15. 494 U.S. 872 (1990).
16. *Id.* at 879 (quoting United States v. Lee, 455 U.S. 252, 263 n.3 (1982) (Stevens, J., concurring)).
17. *Id.* at 884–89.

Smith, which was widely read as lessening protections for religious liberty, was controversial. Reacting to the ruling, Congress quickly passed the Religious Freedom Restoration Act (RFRA),[18] which requires courts to apply strict scrutiny whenever plaintiffs establish that a law substantially burdens their exercise of religion. In *City of Boerne v. Flores*, the Court ruled that Congress lacked the power to command courts to apply strict scrutiny when analyzing free exercise claims against the states, as opposed to the federal government.[19] That meant that *Smith*'s holding that strict scrutiny did not apply to free exercise challenges to neutral state rules of general applicability remained in effect.

To be sure, *Smith* did suggest that cases raising so-called hybrid claims, where religious liberty was coupled with another claim, might receive more rigorous scrutiny.[20] Moreover, only three years after *Smith*, in *Church of Lukumi Babalu Aye v. City of Hialeah*, the Court made clear that "[a]t a minimum, the protections of the Free Exercise Clause pertain if the law at issue discriminates against some or all religious beliefs or regulates or prohibits conduct because it is undertaken for religious reasons."[21] Thus, laws that target religion, even if they are neutral on their face regarding religion, are subject to strict scrutiny. So, for example, a law that fined schools with low vaccination rates might be subject to strict scrutiny if there was evidence showing that it was enacted to target religious schools.

Even with these caveats, pre-COVID-19, *Jacobson*, *Zucht*, *Prince*, and *Smith* were widely taken as teaching that the Free Exercise Clause did not require state vaccine mandates to have or grant religious exemptions.[22] For example, in 2011, the Fourth Circuit in *Workman v. Mingo County Board of Education* rejected a free exercise challenge to West Virginia's childhood vaccine law (which did not have a religious exemption) by citing the above-noted Supreme Court decisions, as well as several lower court cases that had rejected such claims over the course of

18. 107 Stat. 1488, 42 U.S.C. 2000bb.

19. 521 U.S. 507, 534–36 (1997).

20. 494 U.S. at 881.

21. 508 U.S. 520, 532 (1993).

22. In *Brown v. Stone*, the Mississippi Supreme Court stated that granting religious exemptions "would discriminate against the great majority of children whose parents have no such religious convictions" in violation of the Equal Protection Clause of the 14th Amendment. 378 So. 2d 218, 223 (Miss. 1979).

decades.[23] Later, in *Phillips v. City of New York*,[24] the Second Circuit cited *Workman* and *Jacobson* in denying a First Amendment challenge to a New York law that authorized the Commissioner of Public Health to bar unvaccinated children (including those who had received a religious exemption) from attending school after a fellow student was diagnosed with chicken pox.

The same year that *Phillips* was decided, California responded to a measles outbreak associated with Disneyland by enacting Senate Bill 277 (SB277), which repealed the state's personal belief exemption (which could encompass religious objections) for childhood vaccines.[25] Free exercise litigation quickly followed. In *Brown v. Smith*, the California Court of Appeals rejected the plaintiffs' free exercise claims, citing *Prince* and *Workman* and noting that the plaintiffs had failed to point to any "pertinent authority to the contrary."[26] A federal district court reached a similar conclusion in *Whitlow v. California*.[27] That court also rejected the plaintiffs' argument that SB277 violated the Free Exercise Clause because it granted some secular but no religious exemptions, stating "nowhere in [*Smith*] does the Supreme Court state that if the government provides a secular exemption to a law or regulation that it must also provide a religious exemption."[28]

In 2019, in response to another measles outbreak, New York repealed the religious exemption to its own childhood vaccine law. Once again, the repeal was challenged on free exercise grounds. In a lengthy opinion that examined whether the repeal targeted religion under *Church of Lukumi Babalu Aye*, a state court concluded that the repeal would pass muster even if strict scrutiny was applied.[29] The court explained, "[p]rotecting public health, and children's health in particular, through attainment of threshold inoculation levels for community immunity

23. 419 Fed. Appx. 348 (4th Cir. 2011).

24. 775 F.3d 538 (2d Cir. 2015). *See also* Caviezel v. Great Neck Pub. Schs., 500 Fed. Appx. 16 (Table) (2d Cir. 2012).

25. Dorit Rubinstein Reiss, *Litigating Alternative Facts: School Vaccine Mandates in the Courts*, 21 U. Pa. J. Const L. 207, 215–18 (2018).

26. Brown v. Smith, 235 Cal. Rptr. 3d 218, 225 (Ct. App. 2018). *See also* Love v. State Dep't of Educ., 240 Cal. Rptr. 3d 861, 873 (Ct. App. 2018) (agreeing with *Brown*, 235 Cal. Rptr. at 218).

27. 203 F. Supp. 3d 1079 (S.D. Cal. 2016).

28. *Id.* at 1086.

29. *See* F.F. v. State, 114 N.Y.S. 3d 852, 858–59 (N.Y. Misc. 2019) *aff'd*, F.F. v. State, 194 A.D.3d 80 (App. Div. 3d Dept. 2021).

from vaccine-preventable, highly contagious diseases that pose the risk of severe health consequences . . . is unquestionably a compelling state interest."[30]

The Evolution of Free Exercise Law during the Pandemic

In early 2020, to stem the spread of COVID-19, states throughout the country issued a wide range of social distancing laws that shuttered businesses and other activities, including in-person worship.[31] In response, litigants brought myriad lawsuits against federal, state, and local governments based on a wide range of legal theories, leading to over 1,000 judicial decisions.[32] Many of these lawsuits claimed that public health orders violated the Free Exercise Clause of the First Amendment.[33]

Initially, most courts read *Jacobson* as requiring them to grant substantial deference to officials during a health emergency and *Smith* as teaching that neutral laws of general applicability are subject only to rational basis review.[34] In May 2020, the Supreme Court appeared to agree. In *South Bay United Pentecostal Church v. Newsom*, the Court by a 5–4 vote refused to issue an emergency injunction blocking California's 25 percent capacity cap on in-person worship.[35] As is typical with a case from the Court's emergency (or "shadow") docket, the majority did not publish an opinion. But in a concurring opinion, Chief Justice Roberts noted that the challenged order appeared to treat worship similarly to other "secular gatherings . . . where large groups of people gather in close proximity for extended periods of time."[36] He also cited *Jacobson* for the point that the Constitution "principally entrusts" health and safety to "politically accountable officials."[37]

---

30. *Id.* at 867.

31. Wendy E. Parmet, *From the Shadows: The Public Health Implications of the Supreme Court's COVID-Free Exercise Cases*, 49 J. L. Med. & Ethics 564, 565 (2021).

32. Wendy E. Parmet & Faith Khalik, *Judicial Review of Public Health Powers Since the Start of the COVID-19 Pandemic: Trends and Implications*, 113 Am. J. Pub. Health 280, 280 (2023).

33. *Id.* at 282.

34. Wendy E. Parmet, *The COVID Cases: A Preliminary Assessment of Judicial Review of Public Health Powers During a Partisan and Polarized Pandemic*, 57 S. Diego L. Rev. 999, 1026 (2020).

35. 140 S. Ct. 1613 (2020).

36. *Id.* at 1613 (Roberts, C.J., concurring).

37. *Id.*

Given the pre-pandemic state of the law, neither the majority's decision nor Roberts' opinion was surprising. What was surprising was Justice Kavanaugh's dissent, which Justices Thomas and Gorsuch joined.[38] In it, Kavanaugh argued that by placing looser restrictions on some secular spaces, including retail stores and pharmacies, California had treated worship less favorably than comparable secular activities.[39] To Kavanaugh, this meant that strict scrutiny was required, which he believed the order failed precisely because the state acted as if comparable activities did not have to be strictly restricted in order to protect health.[40]

Two months later in *Calvary Chapel Dayton Valley v. Sisolak*, the Supreme Court refused to block another state restriction on religious worship.[41] Once again there was no majority opinion. But in three different dissents, Justices Alito, Kavanaugh, and Gorsuch argued that the state's order was unconstitutional because it treated worship less favorably than (in their view) comparable secular activities.[42] In his own dissent, Alito added that *Jacobson* was irrelevant because it was not a First Amendment case.[43]

In October 2020, Justice Amy Coney Barrett replaced Justice Ruth Bader Ginsburg on the Supreme Court,[44] cementing a strong conservative majority. Almost immediately, that majority adopted what had been the dissenters' views about free exercise challenges to COVID-19 restrictions. In November 2020, in *Roman Catholic Diocese v. Cuomo*, the Court by a 5–4 vote enjoined a New York law that set capacity caps on worship in COVID-19 "hot zones."[45] What was noteworthy about the case was not the outcome—the Court might well have reached the same decision under *Lukumi*—but the majority's approach. According to the Court, strict scrutiny was required because the state had treated some secular activities, including retail shops and acupuncture facilities, more favorably than religious activities.[46] Critically, in reaching that conclusion, the Court failed to grant health officials any deference in determining

38. *Id.* at 1614 (Kavanaugh, J., dissenting).

39. *Id.* at 1615.

40. *Id.*

41. 140 S. Ct. 2603 (2020).

42. *Id.*

43. *Id.* at 2608 (Alito, J., dissenting).

44. *Oath Ceremony: The Honorable Amy Coney Barrett*, Supreme Court of the United States, https://www.supremecourt.gov/publicinfo/press/oath/oath_barrett.aspx.

45. 141 S. Ct. 63 (2020).

46. *Id.* at 66–67.

which secular activities were comparable to religious worship in terms of spreading COVID-19.[47]

After ruling that strict scrutiny was required, the Court held that the state's order failed that rigorous test. In so doing, the Court accepted that the state had a compelling interest in preventing the spread of COVID-19 but found that "there is no evidence that the applicants have contributed to the spread of COVID-19 [and] there are many other less restrictive rules that could be adopted to minimize the risk to those attending religious services."[48]

The Court's treatment of *Jacobson* was even more ominous. Although *Jacobson* was widely considered the Court's most important public health law case, the majority in *Roman Catholic Diocese* never discussed it. Further, in his concurring opinion, Justice Gorsuch castigated the Chief Justice for even citing *Jacobson* in *South Bay.*[49] Gorsuch also repeated Justice Alito's argument from *Calvary Chapel*[50] that *Jacobson* was irrelevant to First Amendment claims.[51]

Following *Roman Catholic Diocese*, the Supreme Court issued several additional decisions from its emergency docket blocking COVID-19 restrictions on free exercise grounds.[52] Some of the decisions, like *Roman Catholic Diocese*, concerned orders that specifically regulated worship. However, in February 2021, the Court blocked a restriction on indoor gatherings that neither mentioned nor targeted worship.[53] Then on April 9, 2021, in *Tandon v. Newsom*, the Court enjoined a California order limiting the number of people who could gather in private residences that was challenged by plaintiffs who wished to hold a bible study group in a private home.[54] Although the order did not single out or even mention worship, the Court held that strict scrutiny was required because the state "treats some comparable secular activities more favorably than at-home religious exercise, [by] permitting hair salons, retail stores, personal care services, movie theaters, private suites at sporting events and concerts, and indoor restaurants to bring together more than three households at a time."[55] Critically, in reaching that conclusion, the Court cited

47. Parmet, *supra* note 31, at 569.
48. 141 S. Ct. at 67.
49. *Id.* at 70 (Gorsuch, J., concurring).
50. 140 S. Ct. 2603, 2608 (2020) (Alito, J., dissenting).
51. 141 S. Ct. 63 at 70 (Gorsuch, J., concurring).
52. Parmet, *supra* note 31, at 570–71.
53. Gateway Church v. Newsom, 141 S. Ct. 1460 (2021).
54. 141 S. Ct. 1294 (2021).
55. *Id.* at 1297.

Justice Gorsuch's concurrence in *Roman Catholic Diocese*, explaining that "[c]omparability is concerned with the risks varies activities pose, not the reasons why people gather."[56] Thus, the state had to treat shopping as comparable to at-home gatherings so long as the Court, without relying on any evidence, thought that they posed similar risks. This effectively granted religious activity "most favored nation status."[57] No religious activity could be regulated more strictly than *any* comparable secular activity, even if most secular activities were similarly (or even more strictly) regulated.

The Court was not finished altering free exercise law. In June 2021, in *Fulton v. City of Philadelphia*, the Court held that Philadelphia's Department of Human Services violated the Free Exercise Clause by not contracting with a Catholic charity that refused to place children with same-sex couples.[58] In granting review, the Court had raised the question of whether *Smith* should be overruled. Ultimately, in a unanimous decision, the Court chose not to do that.[59] Instead, it ruled that the city's policy was subject to strict scrutiny under *Smith* because the city agency had discretion to grant the charity an exemption from its nondiscrimination policy.[60] In effect, the very possibility of an exemption triggered strict scrutiny if it was not granted. Taken together with *Tandon*, *Fulton* raised the possibility that courts might find vaccine mandates unconstitutional either for not having a religious exemption or, when they have one, for not granting it to a particular plaintiff.

The COVID-19 Vaccine Cases

In December 2020, the FDA granted emergency use authorization to Pfizer-BioNTech's COVID-19 vaccine.[61] The FDA authorized Moderna's

56. *Id.* at 1296 (citing 141 S. Ct. at 70 (Gorsuch, J., concurring)).

57. Zalman Rothschild, *Individualized Exemptions, Vaccine Mandates, and the New Free Exercise Clause*, 131 YALE. L. J. 1106 (2022).

58. 141 S. Ct. 1868 (2021).

59. *Id.* at 1881. Three justices, however, would have overruled *Smith.* 141 S. Ct. at 1883 (Alito, J., dissenting); 141 S. Ct. at 1926 (Gorsuch, J., dissenting).

60. *Id.* at 1878.

61. News Release, FDA, *FDA Approves First COVID-19 Vaccine* (Aug. 23, 2021), https://www.fda.gov/news-events/press-announcements/fda-approves-first-covid-19-vaccine.

vaccine shortly thereafter, and by the end of the 2020, around 2.8 million people in the United States had received a COVID-19 vaccine.[62]

By March 2021, more than half of older Americans had already been vaccinated against COVID-19.[63] Yet, by summer 2021, as the Delta variant surged, health officials expressed concern about low vaccination uptake. In July, a group of epidemiology and infectious disease professional organizations urged COVID-19 vaccine requirements for healthcare workers.[64] In the weeks that followed, some state and local governments imposed mandates for healthcare workers or certain public employees.[65] The Department of Veterans Affairs mandated vaccination for "the most patient-facing" healthcare workers,[66] and President Biden announced a vaccine-or-test requirement for federal employees and contractors.[67]

Following full FDA approval of the Pfizer vaccine in August 2021, the Pentagon announced a mandate for all military personnel; some states, school systems, and private companies followed suit.[68] In November 2021, the White House announced two more vaccine-or-test mandates: one by the Occupational Health and Safety Administration (OSHA) for employers with at least 100 employees and one by the Centers for Medicare and Medicaid Services for healthcare workers at

---

62. Derek Hawkins & Meryl Kornfield, *Trump administration falls far short of vaccination goals as new virus variant looms*, WASH. POST (Dec. 31, 2020), https://www.washingtonpost.com/nation/2020/12/31/coronavirus-covid-updates/.

63. Liz Hamel, Grace Sparks & Mollyann Brodie, *KFF COVID-19 Vaccine Monitor: Experiences with Vaccine Access and Information Needs* (Mar. 9, 2021), https://www.kff.org/coronavirus-covid-19/poll-finding/kff-covid-19-vaccine-monitor-experiences-vaccine-access-information-needs/.

64. David J. Weber et al., *Multisociety Statement on Coronavirus Disease 2019 (COVID-19) Vaccination as a Condition of Employment for Healthcare Personnel*, 43 INFECTION CONTROL & HOSPITAL EPIDEMIOLOGY 3 (2022).

65. Mirna Alsharif et al., *New York City to Require its Health Care Workers to get Vaccinated or Submit to Weekly Tests*, CNN (July 21, 2021), https://www.cnn.com/2021/07/21/us/new-york-city-vaccine-healthcare-requirement/index.html.

66. Jennifer Steinhauer, *V.A. Issues Vaccine Mandate for Health Care Workers, a First for a Federal Agency*, N.Y. TIMES (July 26, 2021), https://www.nytimes.com/2021/07/26/us/politics/veterans-affairs-coronavirus-covid-19.html.

67. Annie Linskey et al., *Biden to federal workers: Get vaccinated or face restrictions*, WASH. POST (July 29, 2021), https://www.washingtonpost.com/politics/biden-coronavirus-vaccines-federal-workers/2021/07/29/333ae9ac-f069-11eb-a452-4da5fe48582d_story.html.

68. *COVID-19 Updates: F.D.A.'s Vaccine Approval Leads Pentagon and Others to Add Requirements*, N.Y. TIMES (Aug. 23, 2021; updated Oct. 27, 2021), https://www.nytimes.com/live/2021/08/23/world/covid-delta-variant-vaccine.

Medicare- and Medicaid-participating facilities.[69] By February 2022, half of all states had vaccine mandates in place for at least some state employees.[70] Some, but not all, of these mandates included religious exemptions.[71]

Most organized religions supported the vaccines.[72] Nevertheless, in part due to the fact that "cell lines stemming from abortions" were used during the vaccines' testing or production, some individuals opposed the vaccines on religious grounds.[73] Others opposed them because they thought they were unsafe, unnecessary, or part of a government plot to curtail liberty.[74]

Initially, some racial and ethnic minority groups were hesitant to get vaccinated, likely due in part to the long history of injustices within the public health and healthcare systems.[75] Historically vaccine mandates as well as compulsory vaccination (in which individuals are given no option to reject vaccination) have targeted minority and other vulnerable populations. For example, in 1900, the San Francisco Board of Health issued a vaccine mandate for people of Chinese descent, claiming they were more likely to contract and spread bubonic plague.[76] A short time later, during the same smallpox outbreak that led to *Jacobson*, health officials in Boston, Massachusetts, accompanied by guards, forcibly vaccinated

---

69. Press Release, White House, *Fact Sheet: Biden Administration Announces Details of Two Major Vaccination Policies* (Nov. 4, 2021), https://www.whitehouse.gov/briefing-room/statements-releases/2021/11/04/fact-sheet-biden-administration-announces-details-of-two-major-vaccination-policies/.

70. Dee Pekruhn & Eram Abbasi, *Vaccine Mandates by State: Who is, Who isn't, and How?*, Leading Age (Feb. 9, 2022), https://leadingage.org/workforce-vaccine-mandates-state-who-who-isnt-and-how/.

71. *Id.*

72. Natalie Dascoulias, *COVID-19 vaccine religious exemptions: Where do different religions stand on COVID-19 vaccinations?*, Local SYR (Sept. 21, 2021), https://www.localsyr.com/health/coronavirus/covid-19-vaccine-religious-exemptions-where-do-different-religions-stand-on-covid-19-vaccinations/.

73. D. Gareth Jones, *Religious Concerns About COVID-19 Vaccines: From Abortion to Religious Freedom*, 61(3) J. Religion & Health 2233 (2022).

74. Tara C. Smith & Dorit Rubinstein Reiss, *Digging the rabbit hole, COVID-19 edition: anti-vaccine themes and the discourse around COVID-19*, 22(10) Microbes & Infection 608 (2020).

75. *See* Michel Martin, *Race and The Roots of Vaccine Skepticism*, NPR (Dec. 20, 2020), https://www.npr.org/2020/12/20/948614857/race-and-the-roots-of-vaccine-skepticism; Long H. Nguyen et al., *Self-reported COVID-19 vaccine hesitancy and uptake among participants from different racial and ethnic groups in the United States and United Kingdom*, 13:636 Nature Communications 1 (2022).

76. Wong Wai v. Williamson, 103 F. 1 (1900).

Italian, African American, and other railroad workers.[77] The risk of such discriminatory approaches to vaccination remains salient. In 2020, two French doctors suggested that the use of tuberculosis vaccines for COVID-19 should first be tested on people in Africa, "where there are no masks, no treatments, no resuscitation."[78] Somewhat paradoxically, the willingness to compel vaccination in an inequitable manner can coexist with structural barriers that reduce vulnerable populations' access to vaccines.[79]

Whatever the mix of motivations that fuel vaccine hesitancy, some individuals who objected to the COVID-19 vaccines raised religious objections. As Dorit Reiss explained, even before COVID-19, individuals often couched secular objections to vaccines as religious objections in order to take advantage of religious exemptions.[80] Because the Constitution does not limit its protection for religious liberty to individuals whose views align with the tenets of any particular religion, or even of any organized religion,[81] and courts grant significant deference to individuals who claim that a law burdens their sincerely held (even if idiosyncratic) religious beliefs,[82] individuals can prevail on free exercise claims even if their objections to vaccines rely largely or solely on secular reasons.

The imposition of COVID-19 vaccine mandates quickly prompted litigation. Opponents brought a range of claims. Most were rejected.[83] However, claims brought under the Free Exercise Clause and/or RFRA fared better than other individual rights challenges to COVID-19-related laws.[84] Importantly, challenges were brought both against mandates that

---

77. Wendy E. Parmet, Richard A. Goodman & Amy Farber, *Individual Rights versus the Public's Health 100 Years after* Jacobson v. Massachusetts, 352 N. Eng. J. Med. 652, 653 (2005).

78. *Coronavirus: France Racism Row over Doctors' Africa Testing Comments*, BBC (Apr. 3, 2020), https://www.bbc.com/news/world-europe-52151722.

79. Rebecca F. Wilson et al., *Call Out Racism and Inequity in Reports on Vaccine Intentions*, 7 Nat. Hum. Behav. 300 (2023).

80. Reiss, *supra* note 2, at 1570–73. One New Mexico study found that 54.9 percent of those seeking exemptions for school vaccinations were doing so for "philosophical or personal reasons." Angela Tang et al., *Vaccine Exemption of Children in New Mexico*, 2014(4) New Mexico Epidemiology, https://www.nmhealth.org/data/view/report/161/.

81. *E.g.*, Boone v. Boozeman, 202 A.2d 889, *modified* 214 A. 2d 408 (N.J. 1965); Dalli v. Bd. of Educ., 358 Mass. 753 (1971)(vaccine mandate limited to members of a recognized religion violates the First Amendment).

82. *See, e.g.*, Thomas v. Rev. Bd. of Ind. Employment Security Div., 450 U.S. 707, 714 (1981).

83. Parmet & Khalik, *supra* note 32, at 283.

84. *Id.*

lacked exemptions and from denials of exemptions to mandates that included them. The discussion below reviews how courts have analyzed both types of claims.

Cases Challenging Lack of Religious Exemptions

The most critical issue in religious challenges to COVID-19 mandates that lacked religious exemptions was the standard of review. As noted above, pre-COVID-19, courts generally held that such mandates were neutral rules of general applicability and, under *Smith*, subject only to rational basis review.[85] Since the evolution of the court's free exercise jurisprudence, that conclusion has become less certain.

In several cases, plaintiffs argued that a mandate that has a medical exemption as mandates generally do[86] but not a religious exemption is not a neutral law of general applicability because it fails *Tandon*'s comparability test. Some district courts agreed. For example, in *Dr. A. v. Hochul*, a federal district court in New York relied on *Tandon* to hold that the inclusion of a medical but not religious exemption meant that the mandate had not treated religious activity as favorably as a comparable secular activity.[87] As a result, strict scrutiny was required. The court then went on to find that the mandate failed that test precisely because the state had not shown why it could achieve its goals while offering a medical, but not religious, exemption.[88]

The Second and Ninth Circuits have rejected that analysis as applied to COVID-19 vaccine mandates, ruling that medical exemptions are not comparable to religious exemptions. In reviewing both the *Dr. A.* case and another lower court ruling that granted a preliminary injunction, the Second Circuit held that New York's mandate was a neutral law of general applicability subject only to rational basis review.[89] In *Doe v. San Diego Unified School District*, the Ninth Circuit rejected a challenge to a COVID-19 vaccination mandate for students, stating "[l]imitation of the medical exemption [to contraindications recognized by the Centers for Disease Control and Prevention] in this way serves the primary interest for imposing the mandate protecting student 'health and safety' and so does not undermine the District's interests as a religious exemption would."[90]

85. *See supra* text accompanying notes 22–30.
86. *See* National Conference of State Legislatures, *supra* note 3.
87. 567 F. Supp. 3d 363, 375 (N.D.N.Y. 2021) *rev'd*, 17 F.4th 266 (2d Cir. 2021).
88. *Id.* at 376.
89. We the Patriots USA, Inc. v. Hochul, 17 F.4th 266 (2d Cir. 2021).
90. Doe v. San Diego Unified School Dist., 19 F.4th 1173, 1178 (9th Cir. 2021).

Initially, the First Circuit reached a similar conclusion. In *Does 1-6 v. Mills*, it upheld a lower court's refusal to preliminarily enjoin Maine's vaccine mandate for healthcare workers, reasoning that medical exemptions further the state's goal of protecting health, whereas religious exemptions undermine it.[91] The court also found that even if strict scrutiny applied, the mandate would likely pass muster because there were no less restrictive means for achieving the state's goal of protecting patients from COVID-19.[92] However, when the case came back to that court in 2023 on review of the district court's dismissal of the complaint, the appeals court reversed.[93] In so doing, the First Circuit looked to *Tandon* and determined that the plaintiffs' contention that religious exemptions were comparable to medical exemptions raised issues of fact that precluded dismissing the case on the pleadings.

On October 29, 2021, the Supreme Court rejected the *Does 1-6* plaintiffs' request for emergency relief from Maine's mandate.[94] However, not all the justices agreed. In a dissent joined by Justices Thomas and Alito, Justice Gorsuch argued that because the state permitted medical exemptions, the absence of a religious mandate should be subject to strict scrutiny.[95] He added that although he accepted "[f]or purposes of resolving this application" that "'[s]temming the spread of COVID-19' qualifies as 'a compelling interest,'" it could not do so "forever."[96] He then concluded that the mandate could not survive strict scrutiny because the state had not shown that a mandate without a religious exemption was the least restrictive means available to achieving the state's public health goal.[97]

A few months later, the Court refused to issue emergency relief in the *Dr. A.* case.[98] Once again, Justices Thomas, Alito, and Gorsuch dissented. In a dissent that only Alito joined, Gorsuch argued that statements by Governor Hochul "that religious objections to COVID-19 vaccines are theologically flawed" evinced animosity to religion.[99] He also rejected the argument that religious exemptions were not comparable to medical exemptions, stating, "this Court's general applicability test doesn't

91. 16 F.4th 20, 31 (1 Cir. 2021).

92. *Id.* at 33.

93. Lowe v. Mills, 68 F.4th 706 (1st 2023).

94. Does 1-3 v. Mills, 142 S. Ct. 17 (2021).

95. *Id.* at 18 (Gorsuch, J., dissenting).

96. *Id.* at 20–21 (Gorsuch, J., dissenting) (quoting Roman Catholic Diocese of Brooklyn v. Cuomo, 141 S. Ct. 63, 68-69 (2020) (per curiam).

97. *Id.* at 22.

98. 142 S. Ct. 552 (2021).

99. *Id.* at 554–55 (Gorsuch, J., dissenting).

turn on that kind of numbers game. At this point in the proceedings, the only question is whether the challenged law contains an exemption for a secular objector that 'undermines the government's asserted interests in a similar way' an exemption for a religious objector might."[100] He then pointed to the fact that other states have found that they could "satisfy [their] COVID-19 public health goals without coercing religious objectors to accept a vaccine" as showing that the mandate was not narrowly tailored to achieve a compelling state interest.[101]

Despite these dissents, the Court has continued to resist the invitation to review a free exercise challenge of a COVID-19 vaccine mandate that lacks a religious exemption, leaving the constitutionality of such mandates uncertain.

Cases Challenging Denial of Requested Exemptions

As noted above, the possibility of a religious exemption may not save a mandate from constitutional invalidation.[102] In several notable cases, plaintiffs have alleged that the state's refusal to grant them an exemption that existed, at least on paper, violated the Free Exercise Clause and/or RFRA.

In one of the earliest such cases, *Dahl v. Board of Trustees of Western Michigan University*, plaintiffs were university athletes who sought and were denied religious exemptions from the university's policy barring unvaccinated athletes from participating in inter-collegiate sports.[103] In a decision that the Sixth Circuit later affirmed, the district court ruled for plaintiffs and quoted *Fulton*, stating, "[a] law is not generally applicable if it 'invite[s]' the government to consider the particular reasons for a person's conduct by providing a 'mechanism for individualized exemption.'"[104] In contrast, in *Lukaszczyk v. Cook County*, the Seventh Circuit emphasized the lack of a factual record in rejecting employees' free exercise challenge to the county's decision to deny religious exemptions to someone who had previously accepted a flu vaccine.[105]

100. *Id.* at 556 (quoting Fulton v. City of Philadelphia, 141 S. Ct. 1868, 1877 (2021)).

101. *Id.* at 557.

102. *See supra* text accompanying notes 58–60.

103. 558 F. Supp. 3d 561 (W.D. Mich. 2021), *aff'd*, 15 F.4th 728 (6th Cir. 2021).

104. *Id.* at 564 (quoting *Fulton*, 141 S. Ct. 1686, 1877).

105. Lukaszczyk v. Cook County, 47 F.4th 587 (7th Cir. 2022).

Several, but not all,[106] federal courts have also found for plaintiffs challenging the denial of religious exemptions from the federal vaccine mandates.[107] Because these mandates were subject to RFRA, strict scrutiny was clearly applicable.[108] Nevertheless, rulings by the Fifth and Sixth Circuits holding that the mandates could not survive strict scrutiny are notable.[109] In *US Navy Seals v. Austin*, for example, the Fifth Circuit pointed to the Navy's lack of an explanation for the denial of plaintiffs' request for an exemption and that the sailors "engage in life-threatening actions that may create risks of equal or greater magnitude than the virus."[110]

The Supreme Court has not weighed in on the merits of these cases. However, in *Austin v. U.S. Navy Seals 1-26*, it granted the government's request to limit the scope of a lower court's injunction "insofar as it precludes the Navy from considering respondents' vaccination status in making deployment, assignment, and other operational decisions."[111] In dissent, Justices Alito and Gorsuch argued that the Court should have rejected the government's request because the Navy forced plaintiffs "to choose between violating their religious beliefs and the punishment that the Navy threatened" in violation of both RFRA and the Free Exercise Clause.[112]

Childhood Vaccine Cases

The controversy and contestation surrounding the COVID-19 vaccines has spilled over to other vaccines. According to a December 2022 report by the Kaiser Family Foundation, the percentage of adults who say that healthy children should receive the measles-mumps-rubella (MMR) vaccine in order to attend school dropped from 82 percent in 2019 to only 71 percent in 2022.[113] Further, in 2022, 28 percent of adults (up from

106. For example, a federal district court denied the plaintiff's claim in *Short v. Berger*, 593 F. 3d 3944 (C.D. Ca. 2022), *appeal dismissed mem.*, 2022 WL 2421096 (9th Cir. May 17, 2022).

107. *See infra* text accompanying notes 108–111. *See also* Colonel Financial Management Officer v. Austin, 2022 WL 3643512 (M.D. Fla. 2022).

108. *See supra* text accompanying notes 18–19.

109. US Navy Seals 1-26 v. Biden, 27 F.4th 336 (5th Cir. 2022); Doster v. Kendall, 54 F.4th 398 (6th Cir. 2022), *vacated as moot*, Kendall v. Doster, No. 23-154, 2023 WL 8531840 (S.Ct. 2023).

110. 27 F.4th at 351.

111. Austin v. U.S. Navy Seals 1-26, 142 S. Ct. 1301 (2022).

112. *Id.* at 1304 (Alito, J., dissenting).

113. Lunna Lopes et al., *KFF COVID-19 Vaccine Monitor: December 2022*, KFF (Dec. 16, 2022), https://www.kff.org/coronavirus-covid-19/poll-finding/kff-covid-19-vaccine-monitor-december-2022/.

16 percent in 2019) said that parents should be able to reject vaccination for their children even if doing so created a risk to others.[114] In this climate, the courts' new, though still uncertain, approach to free exercise claims offers a tempting invitation to challenge vaccine mandates. Such litigation is only beginning.

In the first year of the pandemic, before *Fulton* and *Tandon* were decided, courts continued to reject free exercise challenges to mandates regarding non-COVID-19 vaccines. For example, in *C.F. v. New York City Dep't of Health & Mental Hygiene*, a state court denied a free exercise challenge to a health department order requiring all residents over the age of six months who lived or worked in affected areas of Brooklyn to be vaccinated or pay a fine, unless they had a medical exemption.[115] After relying on *Jacobson*, the Court distinguished its holding from Justice Gorsuch's rejection of that case in *Roman Catholic Diocese*, noting that Gorsuch's views "did not command a majority and, even these views do not foretell an abandonment of the *Jacobson* [rational basis] standard."[116]

In another case decided shortly before *Tandon* and *Fulton* were decided, a New York court in *F.F. v. State* held that the state's repeal of its religious exemption for school vaccination requirements was neutral and generally applicable and thus subject only to rational basis scrutiny.[117] The court distinguished the case before it from *Roman Catholic Diocese*, saying that there, "the regulation created a favored class of businesses and it thus needed to justify why houses of worship were excluded from that favored class," while in *F.F.*, "the religious exemption previously created a benefit to the covered class, and now the elimination of the exemption subjects those in the previously covered class to vaccine rules that are generally applicable to the public."[118]

Even after the Supreme Court issued its rulings in *Fulton* and *Tandon*, a federal court in Connecticut held that the state's vaccine law, which allows for medical but not religious exemptions, was subject to rational

114. *Id.*

115. 191 A.D. 3d 52 (N.Y. App. Div. 2020).

116. *Id.* at 72. *See also* W.D. v. Rockland Cty, 521 F. Supp. 3d 358, 399–400 (2021), *rev'd in part*, M.A. v. Rockland Cty. Dep't of Health, 53 F.4th 29 (2d Cir. 2022) (rejecting free exercise challenge to law barring unvaccinated students from attending school during an outbreak).

117. F.F. v. State, 194 A.D.3d 80 (N.Y. App. Div. 2021).

118. *Id.* at 87–88.

basis scrutiny.[119] In reaching that conclusion, the court relied heavily on *Phillips*, which it took as binding precedent in the Second Circuit.[120]

Following that ruling, the Second Circuit issued two decisions with potentially inconsistent reasoning. In *M.A. v. Rockland Country,* which concerned a challenge of a public health order barring unvaccinated children from attending school during a measles outbreak, the Second Circuit ruled that summary judgement was inappropriate because more factfinding was necessary to determine how the state treated different groups of children and whether officials had acted with animus.[121] The court also questioned why those who had received medical exemptions were treated differently and viewed statements by officials calling "anti-vaxxers" "ignorant" as possible evidence of anti-religious animus.[122]

More recently, in *We the Patriots USA, Inc. v. Connecticut Office of Early Childhood Development,123* a different panel from the Second Circuit rejected another challenge to Connecticut's childhood vaccine law. In that case, the court distinguished *Rockland*, noting that the *Rockland* court had not reached a final decision on the constitutional question.[124] The *We the Patriots* court also ruled that Connecticut's repeal of its religious mandate was not motivated by animus against religion and that the religious exemption was not comparable to the medical exemption because only the latter serves the state's interest in protecting health.[125]

Not all lower courts have agreed with the Second Circuit's analysis in *We the Patriots USA*. Most notably, in *Borsage v. Edney,* a federal court ruled that Mississippi violated the Free Exercise clause by offering a medical but not religious exemption to its childhood vaccine mandate.[126] And following the First Circuit's ruling in *Lowe*, a federal district judge in Maine refused to dismiss a Free Exercise challenge to that state's repeal of its religious exemption.[127] As of January 1, 2024, the Supreme Court has not ruled on a post-pandemic challenge to a state's vaccine law,

---

119. We the Patriots USA v. CT Office of Early Child Development, 579 F. Supp. 3d 290 (D. Conn. 2022), *aff'd in relevant part*,76 F.4th 130 (2d Cir. 2023).

120. *Id.*

121. 53 F.4th 29, 36 (2d Cir. 2022).

122. *Id.* at 38.

123. We the Patriots USA, Inc., v. Conn. Off. of Early Childhood Development, 76 F.4th 130 (2d Cir. 2023).

124. *Id.* at 147.

125. *Id.* at 151-153.

126. Borsage v. Edney, No. 1:22cv233-HSO-BWR, 2023 WL 299484 (S.D. Miss. 2023).

127. Fox v. Makin, No. 2:22-cv-00251-GZS, 2023 WL 5279518 (D. Me. Aug. 16, 2023).

but given the conflicting rulings from lower courts, it seems quite possible that the high court will do so in the not-so-distant future.

The Future of Vaccine Mandates and Religious Liberty Claims

The new instability in vaccine law combined with decreasing support by the public for mandates raises serious questions as to the continued viability of state-imposed vaccine mandates. Today, any refusal to grant a religious exemption faces constitutional risk as courts have enjoined mandates with and without religious exemptions as violating religious liberty.

From a public health perspective, this is troubling. Pre-pandemic research showed that mandates helped to improve vaccination rates among children.[128] Further, as Mello and colleagues report, "states that have eliminated personal-belief or religious exemptions (while maintaining medical exemptions) have lower exemption rates and higher vaccination rates."[129] Early evidence also suggests that mandates helped to boost COVID-19 vaccination rates, at least in some settings.[130]

In addition, despite their problematic use in the past, mandates can reduce health inequities. Citing fluoridation of drinking water and smoking bans as universal measures that reduced health inequities, Lakshmi Ganapathi and Ramnath Subbaraman explain: "[m]andates rely on the simple public health principle that universal application of an intervention can be a powerful tool for reducing disparities.[131] "In contrast," they write, "public education alone often worsens health inequities," as individuals with more income and greater levels of education have more access to health information and services than those with lower incomes or lower levels of education.[132] Relatedly, the very existence of a mandate may obligate, ethically and politically if not legally, governments and

128. Kevin M. Malone & Alan R. Hinman, Vaccination Mandates: The Public Health Imperative and Individual Rights, *available at* http://www.cdc.gov/vaccines/imz-managers/guides-pubs/downloads/vacc_mandates_chptr13.pdf.

129. Michelle M. Mello et al., *Effectiveness of Vaccination Mandates in Improving Uptake of COVID-19 Vaccines in the USA*, 400 The Lancet 535 (2022).

130. *Id.*

131. Lakshmi Ganapathi & Ramnath Subbaraman, *The equity-enhancing power of mandates*, Boston Globe (Dec. 29, 2021), https://www.bostonglobe.com/2021/12/29/opinion/equity-enhancing-power-mandates/.

132. *Id.*

employers to ensure access to the vaccine that is required. If, on the other hand, vaccination is left purely to individual choice, governments and employers may feel less of a need to facilitate access to those who are uninsured or lack a regular source of healthcare. This failure to ensure accessibility can exacerbate inequities with respect to vaccine-preventable diseases.

These public health and equity benefits of mandates are imperiled, but not doomed, by the Court's new free exercise jurisprudence. Critically, despite the varied rulings from lower courts and the dissenting opinions of three Supreme Court justices, the Supreme Court has not chosen to overturn a state's vaccine mandate.[133]

Somewhat paradoxically, vaccine mandates with religious exemptions may face greater jeopardy than those without such exemptions. Indeed, the willingness of some courts to block the military's mandate is especially noteworthy, given the courts' traditional deference to the armed forces. However, the appellate decisions blocking the military's mandate, though not the lower court decisions, were decided under RFRA; therefore, they did not hold that strict scrutiny would have been applicable under the First Amendment.[134]

The decisions relating to the denial of exemptions also demonstrate the fact-dependent nature of such cases. The Supreme Court in *Fulton* emphasized that the defendant had "sole discretion" over the granting of exemptions.[135] And in cases such as *Dahl* and *Austin*, the courts stressed that the defendants had granted few exemptions and did not appear to take the exemption process seriously. [136] Likewise, a decision by a district court in Ohio finding that a mandate by Cleveland's Municipal Court violated the plaintiffs' First Amendment rights focused on the lack of a compelling explanation for the defendant's decision to deny a requested religious exemption.[137] In another case, the Seventh Circuit dismissed a

133. Does 1-3 v. Mills, 142 S. Ct. 17 (2021); Dr. A. v. Hochul, 142 S. Ct. 552 (2021) *vacated as moot*, Kendall v. Doster, No. 23-154, 2023 WL 8531840 (S.Ct. 2023).

134. Doster v. Kendall, 54 F.4th 398 (6th Cir. 2022); U.S. Navy Seals 1-26 v. Biden, 27 F.4th 336 (5th Cir. 2022).

135. 2022 WL 17261374, 141 S. Ct. 1868, 1878 (2021).

136. Dahl v. Board of Trustees of West- ern Michigan University 558 F. Supp. 3d 561 (W.D. Mich. 2021), *aff'd*, 15 F.4th 728 (6th Cir. 2021); Austin v. U.S. Navy Seals 1-26, 142 S. Ct. 1301 (2022).

137. Grantonz v. Earley, 2021 WL 5866978 (N.D. Oh. 2021). *See also* Harris v. Univ. of Massachusetts, Lowell, 557 F. Supp. 3d 304, 315 (D. Ma. 2021) (denying plaintiffs' free exercise claim, noting that there was no evidence that the defendants administered their exemption in a way that "burdens some religions but not others").

challenge to mandates with exemptions because plaintiffs failed to compile a sufficient record.[138]

These cases illustrate that the constitutionality of the denial of requested exemptions may depend on the specific facts in the record. In particular, these cases suggest that mandates may escape strict scrutiny (or even survive it) if they cabin officials' discretion within well-designed procedures and the state can demonstrate that officials followed those procedures, granted a significant number of requests, and offered strong reasons for denials.[139] In doing so, however, officials will need to avoid rejecting requests on the grounds that the objectors' views do not adhere to those of an established religion.[140] Officials will also likely have to be very deferential to individuals' claims that their religious objections are sincerely held.[141]

Yet, even if vaccine mandates can survive the inevitable free exercise challenges, the deeper question is whether mandates can continue to serve as effective public health tools. Although well-crafted mandates can improve vaccination rates and potentially reduce health inequities,[142] they can also serve as a rallying cry for anti-vaccination activism and partisan warfare.[143] Litigation's role in fomenting that contestation is not wholly clear, but high-profile court cases and judicial opinions (especially by Supreme Court justices) that emphasize the burdens that vaccine mandates place on religion can shine attention on and provide legitimacy for anti-vaccination sentiment. Thus, by unsettling a once well-settled area of the law, and inviting new legal challenges to mandates, the new free exercise jurisprudence may undermine a longstanding public health tool.

---

138. Lukaszczyk v. Cook Cty., 47 F.4th at 587 (7th Cir. 2022).

139. In an interesting case decided before *Tandon* and *Fulton*, the Eighth Circuit rejected a free exercise challenge to Missouri's requirement that individuals file a form in order to request a religious exemption. B.W.C. v. Williams, 990 F.3d 614 (8th Cir. 2021). After *Tandon* and *Fulton*, a Missouri court rejected a claim under the state's RFRA. Baker v. Crossroads Academy-Central St., 648 S.W. 3d 790 (Mo. Ct. App. 2022).

140. *See* Thomas v. Rev. Bd. of Ind. Employment Security Div., 450 U.S. 707, 714 (1981).

141. Rothschild, *supra* note 57, at 1121–32.

142. *See supra* text accompanying notes 126–27.

143. Kevin Bardosh et al., *The unintended consequences of COVID-19 vaccine policy: why mandates, passports and restrictions may cause more harm than good*, 7(5) BMJ GLOBAL HEALTH 1 (2022).

Chapter 5

Regulatory and Patent Drivers for Vaccines and Other Treatments for Infectious Diseases and Considerations for Balancing Innovation and Collaboration for Future Public Health Emergencies

Brian Malkin and Katherine Pappas

Introduction

Considering the legal response to infectious diseases such as COVID-19 and the heavy toll such diseases extract from society, much attention is due to the question of what drives innovation and how our regulatory frameworks do—or do not—incentivize the dedication of resources to improve society's ability to overcome infectious diseases. This chapter addresses the intersection of regulatory and intellectual property, which concerns both small-molecule drugs and large-molecule biological and their respective lower-cost versions, generics and biosimilars. In the process, we discuss the U.S. Food and Drug Administration's (FDA's) evolving role in policy issues relating to pharmaceutical intellectual property (IP) including how the FDA and the U.S. Patent and Trademark Office (USPTO) may collaborate more on patent prosecution and post grant proceedings, best practices in IP law for vaccines, and IP waivers and pledges not to enforce patent rights and how these were impacted during the COVID-19 pandemic. As our conclusion, we propose that regulators and legislators consider developing specific guidelines, regulations, or statutory provisions to better address the balance between innovation and collaboration during a public health emergency situation and how to transition that balance from an emergency to nonemergency situation to advance world health objectives.

The FDA's Role in Policy Issues Relating to Pharmaceutical IP

The U.S. FDA has its own complex IP framework, including as defined through the Hatch-Waxman Act and the Biologics Price Competition and Innovation Act (BPCIA). These provisions aim to increase generic pharmaceuticals and biosimilars (respectively) with the goal to lower pharmaceutical and biologics pricing, while providing mechanisms for early determination of patent coverage for the aspiring follow-on. However, when it comes to patent rights, the FDA's role has been purely "ministerial." In practice, this means the FDA asks brand companies for patent information but does not perform any analysis of patent coverage or validity. With respect to drugs falling under the Hatch-Waxman Act, an innovator or "brand" applicant must submit to the FDA for listing in the "Orange Book"[1] all patents that claim the reference-listed drug (RLD) or a method of using it; this Orange Book listing then triggers potential litigation if another company submits an application to make a generic version of the RLD and certifies that the proposed generic will not infringe any of the Orange Book-listed patents or it believes the listed patents to be invalid or unenforceable (known as a "Paragraph IV" or "PIV" certification or "patent challenge").[2] But because the FDA merely lists

1. The Orange Book is the common name for an FDA publication, *Approved Drug Products with Therapeutic Equivalence Evaluations*, available at https://www.fda.gov/drugs/drug-approvals-and-databases/approved-drug-products-therapeutic-equivalence-evaluations-orange-book.

2. The BPCIA does not use the same Orange Book scheme as the Hatch-Waxman Act, but it also has a pre-launch patent dispute mechanism, which is known colloquially as the "patent dance," because rather than prospective patent infringement based on a patent listing in the Orange Book, it involves a voluntary exchange of patent information and mutual decision of which patents to litigate at filing and pre-launch stages.

the identified patents in the Orange Book without performing any patent coverage or validity analysis, there is an inherent hazard that invalid, not infringed, or unenforceable patents may be wielded by brand companies to prevent earlier generic competition without even a cursory review by the FDA. This risk has increased over recent years as patent law precedent has developed more exacting standards for disclosure of inventions. Surprisingly, the FDA has recently taken a more active role, penning a letter to the USPTO expressing concerns and offering to collaborate.

Executive Order 14036, Directing FDA and USPTO Collaboration

In July of 2021, President Biden issued Executive Order 14036, which expressed concern that "too often, patent and other laws have been misused to inhibit or delay—for years and even decades—competition from generic drugs and biosimilars, denying Americans access to lower-cost drugs."[3] In the Executive Order, the President directed the Secretary of Health and Human Services to "help ensure that the patent system, while incentivizing innovation, does not also unjustifiably delay generic drug and biosimilar competition beyond that reasonably contemplated by applicable law," and directed a letter exchange between the FDA and USPTO to discuss relevant concerns of the FDA.[4]

FDA Letter to USPTO

In light of the Executive Order, the FDA penned a letter to the USPTO in September 2021, seeking to further develop the FDA's engagement with the USPTO.[5] In that letter, the FDA expressed its commitment "to incentivizing innovation and fostering competition by approving high-quality, affordable, safe, and effective therapies including generic drugs and biosimilar and interchangeable biological products."[6] But it also noted its commitment "to identifying abuses of the system that can impede competition," going on to delineate a few such concerns as well as suggestions and questions for the USPTO.

First, the FDA expressed concern that too many patents are being granted for the same types of technology, allowing brand companies to create "patent thickets" that keep generics off the market by increasing

3. Executive Order 14036, available at https://www.whitehouse.gov/briefing-room/presidential-actions/2021/07/09/executive-order-on-promoting-competition-in-the-american-economy/.

4. *Id.* at § 5(p)(vi).

5. September 10, 2021, FDA Letter to USPTO, available at https://www.fda.gov/media/152086/download.

6. *Id.* at 1.

litigation burdens.[7] Next, it expressed concern about patent "evergreening," a practice of obtaining patents for post-approval or secondary changes to previously approved drugs—for example, for different formulations of the same drug, new delivery systems, or new methods of use. As the FDA explained, brand sponsors often will seek approvals for these modifications just as the earlier patents are expiring, effectively extending protection against would-be competitors.[8] And third, the FDA expressed concern that brand sponsors engage in "product-hopping," a practice of submitting a new application for a slightly modified drug product and switching the market to the new product right before generic or biosimilar competition on the previously approved product is set to commence. When paired with new patent protection of the related modification, this can effectively forestall competition, despite the fact that the prior product (and related generic or interchangeable biosimilar) remains safe and effective.[9]

The FDA then launched into a series of suggestions and questions directed at the USPTO. First, it offered to support USPTO examiners' work by "offering training on FDA's public information and databases that may help the USPTO locate pertinent references and determine whether particular documents constitute prior art to a claimed invention" and offering to collaborate in determining appropriate patent term extensions.[10] Next, it asked for the USPTO's perspective on what it identified as possible misuses of the patent system, particularly the creation of patent thickets, product hopping, and evergreening.[11] It went on to solicit the USPTO's views on whether additional resources or time for examiners would "help ensure the right balance of rewarding innovation and facilitating competition" for complex subject matter such as pharmaceutical patents.[12] Finally, it noted that the Patent Trial and Appeals Board (PTAB) is "a relatively new body that offers a mechanism for reviewing the patentability of claims," namely through the post grant review (PGR) and inter partes review (IPR) processes—the FDA asked for any available data on how these PTAB proceedings may effect Orange Book–listed patents and/or patents covering biological products, and offered to

7. *Id.* at 3.
8. *Id.*
9. *Id.* at 3–4.
10. *Id.* at 4.
11. *Id.* at 4–5.
12. *Id.* at 5.

discuss "how the PTAB framework might be optimized to support timely availability of generic drugs."[13]

USPTO's Responsive Letter to FDA

The USPTO responded to the FDA's letter in July 2022.[14] In its response, the USPTO listed a series of prioritized initiatives to strengthen the patent system for all technologies. The USPTO's recitation of these initiatives shines a light on how the USPTO views the current patent system's strengths and weaknesses, even highlighting areas where we may expect to see changes in coming years. And, on the other side of the coin, it also indicates areas where the USPTO's views are not necessarily aligned with those expressed by the FDA.

The first initiative listed by the USPTO is to create a formal mechanism to collaborate with the FDA, including to create joint public engagement opportunities, provide USPTO examiners training and resources in collaboration with the FDA, explore consistency in representations made to the two agencies, and engage in more information-sharing efforts, revisit patent term extension practice, "work with the FDA to understand how else the agencies' authorities and responsibilities overlap"—for example, with respect to "skinny labels" that carve out particular pharmaceutical uses—and finally remain open to discussing the FDA's concerns over "patent thickets," "evergreening," and "product hopping."[15] While the USPTO did expressly reiterate the FDA's concerns over these last three issues, its cursory recitation of an intention to "[r]emain open to discussing" them suggests it does not necessarily view these three issues as particularly actionable—at least absent intervening congressional action.

The second initiative the USPTO laid out is to improve procedures for obtaining a patent so that the USPTO issues "robust and reliable patents," specifically committing to introduce more examining time, give examiners more training and resources, enhance communication between examiners and the PTAB, consider enhancing the process for information disclosure statements submitted during prosecution, consider applying greater scrutiny to continuation applications in large families and/or the use of declaratory evidence to overcome rejections, revisit obviousness-type double patenting practices (which occur when a patentee seeks to secure a patent for an obvious variation of the innovation covered by

13. *Id.*

14. July 6, 2022, USPTO Responsive Letter to FDA, available at https://www.uspto.gov/sites/default/files/documents/PTO-FDA-nextsteps-7-6-2022.pdf.

15. *Id.* at 3–5.

another of their own patents), revisit procedures for third-party input during prosecution, conduct comparative analysis of the examination and issuance of pharmaceutical and biological patents in the United States as compared to other countries, and provide technical input on proposed legislative efforts.[16] The third initiative is to improve the process for challenging issued patents at the PTAB, including to consider whether to apply additional scrutiny in certain cases, whether to allow third-party input, and whether the USPTO should explore weighing the utility and integrity of the patent system when deciding whether to institute proceedings.[17] The fourth USPTO initiative is to improve public participation, which includes hearing more diverse viewpoints including by adding public interest representatives to the Patent Public Advisory Committee (PPAC), and to improve coordination with stakeholders and public interest groups.[18] Last, the USPTO sought to "[c]onsider and evaluate new proposals for incentivizing and protecting the investment essential for bringing life-saving and life-altering drugs to market while minimizing any unnecessary delay getting generic, biosimilar, and more affordable versions of those drugs into the hands of Americans who need them."[19]

Takeaways and Hot Takes

A key takeaway from the FDA and USPTO letter exchange is that the agencies will endeavor to exchange publicly available information more freely—for example, cross-training USPTO examiners in FDA resources to facilitate more efficient patent prosecution and prior art searching efforts. In practice, this could mean examiners reviewing FDA databases to ascertain state of the art or to locate data on approved drug products/labeling at a particular timepoint, which could serve as a novelty bar against a pending application seeking to claim an obvious variation of the same. Similarly, information exchange between the agencies could help hold organizations accountable for representations made to each. For example, patentees may argue to the USPTO that a method of use of a claimed drug product is novel or the clinical results "surprising" or "unexpected," while the same patentee may argue to the FDA that the drug product is known and the clinical results could be predicted or unremarkable warranting further study. But given the different standards at play between the FDA and the USPTO, more clear guidance is needed on

16. *Id.* at 5–7.
17. *Id.* at 7.
18. *Id.* at 7–8.
19. *Id.* at 8.

what companies and counsel may properly represent to each agency and how the agencies may share information without violating either agency's directives to protect commercial confidential information.

Beyond that, the FDA's letter homed in on a few particular patent issues it sees as crucial in "incentivizing innovation" without "unjustifiably delay[ing] generic drug and biosimilar competition" as directed by the Executive Order; while the USPTO expressed its intention to remain open to discussing these issues, it likely sees its hands as tied by the complex statutory regime that governs the patent system. For example, the FDA's concern over "patent thickets" arising out of continuation applications targeted at similar inventions runs headlong into an inventor's right to use continuation applications to claim inventions.[20] Indeed, even what seems like an improper practice of using a continuation application to claim a competitor's product falling within the scope of the pending application's disclosure is a common and legal strategy.[21]

Still, some think that the FDA should stay out of patent issues, a view perhaps fueled by the FDA's lack of appreciation for the dividing line between regulating patents and regulating the markets for patented products. Regardless, the FDA's expertise may be highly beneficial in the form of impact statements, for example, on what patents do to exclusivity periods. Such impact statements could help to shape USPTO decision-making as well as inform Congress to legislate effectively in this sphere. But critical thinking and decision-making on issues specific to patentability and patent practice may be best left up to the USPTO.

Best Practices in IP Law for Vaccines

Obtaining Patent Protection

The "enablement" requirement for patents (codified at 35 U.S.C. § 112) provides the source for the statutory requirement that a patent provides

20. *See* 35 U.S.C. § 120; 37 C.F.R. § 1.78(d).

21. *See, e.g.*, Kingsdown Med. Consultants, Ltd. v. Hollister Inc., 863 F.2d 867, 874 (Fed. Cir. 1988) ("It should be made clear at the outset of the present discussion that there is nothing improper, illegal or inequitable in filing a patent application for the purpose of obtaining a right to exclude a known competitor's product from the market; nor is it in any manner improper to amend or insert claims intended to cover a competitor's product the applicant's attorney has learned about during the prosecution of a patent application. Any such amendment or insertion must comply with all statutes and regulations, of course, but, if it does, its genesis in the marketplace is simply irrelevant.").

an adequate disclosure to enable a person of skill in the art to make and use the claimed invention without undue experimentation. The same provision (§ 112) also provides the "written description" requirement that the disclosure in the patent's specification would have been sufficient for a person of skill in the art to understand that the patentee possessed the full scope of the claimed invention. Both of these requirements are judged as of the priority date of the invention, which means that even if the patentee uses continuing applications to file new claims relating back to an earlier-filed specification, the earlier-filed written disclosure must still demonstrate enablement and written description support for the later-filed claims. In the same thread, advancements in the art that come after the priority date cannot be used to demonstrate adequate written description or enablement since those were not known to the person of skill in the art at the priority date. Finally, when patentee corresponds with the USPTO in seeking issuance of its patent, it creates the patent's "prosecution history," which often elucidates to the USPTO and the public how the patentee viewed the scope of its invention and further how the patentee and the USPTO understood the state of the art and knowledge of a person of skill in the art. In reviewing the prosecution history of an issued patent, the public is able to see what challenges the patentee overcame in reaching issuance of the patent. Because the legal landscape for patentability is affected by court decisions, recent court rulings can essentially moot findings or analyses in an older prosecution history.

Many messenger ribonucleic acid (mRNA) vaccine patents have prosecution histories going back ten years to when enablement under 35 U.S.C. § 112 was not as exacting of a standard, so the focus during prosecution then was just on obviousness of the invention—that is, whether there was known prior art that would render the claimed invention obvious to a person of skill in the art as of the priority date (35 U.S.C. § 103). But now that the law around enablement has shifted,[22] issued claims that were solid a decade ago may well be found invalid if scrutinized under current law. Similarly, patent subject matter eligibility (35 U.S.C. § 101) was a nonissue historically. In recent years, however, more strict court

22. *See, e.g.*, Wyeth & Cordis Corp. v. Abbott Laboratories, 720 F.3d 1380, 1385–86 (Fed. Cir. 2013); Enzo Life Sciences, Inc. v. Roche Molecular Systems, Inc., 928 F.3d 1340, 1345–48 (Fed. Cir. 2019); Idenix Pharmaceuticals LLC v. Gilead Sciences Inc., 941 F.3d 1149, 1160–63, 1165 (Fed. Cir. 2019). With the Supreme Court's recent grant of *certiorari* in case *Amgen et al. v. Sanofi et al.*, Case No. 21-757, it seems likely this body of law will continue to shift—but exactly how remains unclear.

decisions have come down that changed the landscape, demonstrating that claims to natural products are disfavored.[23]

Common solutions now for expanding a vaccine patent portfolio require looking beyond the basics. One option for avoiding the prohibition on claiming natural products is to mutate the antigens to change the properties of the protein enough to be patentable as a nonobvious variant. For example, in the context of a COVID vaccine, this could mean mutating the spike protein. Another solution is claiming combinations with specific adjuvants. An adjuvant is a substance added to a vaccine to help create a stronger immune response, which makes the vaccine work better.[24] In the 1920s, aluminum became the first approved adjuvant in the United States, and it remained the only one for over 70 years; since then, only a handful of adjuvants have been approved for clinical use, and the molecular mechanism by which adjuvants work in humans is still not well understood.[25] A third common way to prudently expand a vaccine patent portfolio is by exploring claims to delivery devices. For example, most COVID vaccines have been intramuscular injections, but other delivery routes were or should be considered—for example, intradermal, subcutaneous, intranasal, and intravenous injection.[26]

Regulatory Considerations: Incentives and Research Safe Harbor

In considering forward-looking policy, it remains crucially important to consider both what drives innovation and what motivates healthy competition in the marketplace. Both the BPCIA and the Hatch-Waxman Act represent complex regulatory IP frameworks that have for years influenced how innovators and market players dedicate resources; both the BPCIA and Hatch-Waxman Act provide insights relevant to best practices in IP law for vaccines.

---

23. *See, e.g.*, Mayo Collaborative Services v. Prometheus Labs., Inc., 566 U.S. 66 (2012) (holding that claims directed to a method of giving a drug to a patient, measuring metabolites of that drug, and with a known threshold for efficacy in mind, and deciding whether to increase or decrease the dosage of the drug, were not patent-eligible subject matter).

24. B. Pulendran, P.S. Arunachalam & D.T. O'Hagan. Emerging concepts in the science of vaccine adjuvants, *Nat. Rev. Drug Discov.* 20, 454–475 (2021). https://doi.org/10.1038/s41573-021-00163-y.

25. *Id.* at 454, 455.

26. Kyung Soo Park, Xiaoqi Sun, Marisa E. Aikins & James J. Moon. Non-viral COVID-19 vaccine delivery systems, *Advanced Drug Delivery Reviews*, 169, 137–51 (2021). https://doi.org/10.1016/j.addr.2020.12.008.

While still an open question, the BPCIA seems likely applicable to mRNA vaccines. This is because mRNA vaccines involve building on a biologic organism, which is more akin to developing an interchangeable insulin than a generic copy of a small molecule. Regardless of whether the BPCIA is strictly applicable to mRNA vaccines, lessons learned from the BPCIA are plainly relevant to understanding the incentives to innovate. When enacting the BPCIA, there was a large economic analysis undertaken that assessed how much money an innovator needs to incentivize him or her to make the needed biologic products. Vaccines are no exception. Even though used in a mass market, incentive to innovate is still necessary. Emerging from that research was the magic number of 12 years of exclusivity. This was put into practice in the BPCIA such that after an innovator is rewarded with 12 years of exclusivity for developing an approved biologic, the innovator cannot get another exclusivity period by simply adding a new indication or otherwise minimally changing the product. Instead, the innovator needs a significant enough change in the molecular structure of the biologic that it would change the safety or efficacy profile of it to obtain another 12 years of exclusivity.

Fortunately, innovators researching vaccines may still be protected from patent liability by the "safe harbor" provision of the Hatch-Waxman Act.[27] The safe harbor provision applies whenever an entity is working to develop a product regulated by the FDA; however, if an entity is just researching technology generally without a particular FDA use in mind, that would be outside the scope of the safe harbor provision and thus subject to liability for patent infringement.[28]

The precise contours of the safe harbor provision are still unknown, but the broad strokes have been shown through a series of court cases spanning the last few decades. In 1990, the U.S. Supreme Court held that the safe harbor provision extended not only to drugs but also to medical devices under investigation.[29] Then, in 2005 the Supreme Court discussed the safe harbor provision as broadly including any pre-clinical

---

27. 35 U.S.C. § 271(e)(1).

28. *See, e.g.*, Proveris Sci. Corp. v. Innovasystems, Inc., 536 F.3d 1256, 1265 (Fed. Cir. 2008) (safe harbor not applicable to research tools not subject to FDA approval); Momenta Pharms., Inc. v. Teva Pharms., 809 F.3d 610 (Fed. Cir. 2015) ("research tools or devices that are not themselves subject to FDA approval may not be covered" by the safe harbor provision); Isis Pharms., Inc. v. Santaris Pharma A/S Corp., 2012 WL 4111157, at *4 (S.D. Cal. Sept. 19, 2012) ("The Safe Harbor does not apply, however, when a biological compound is used to perform 'basic scientific research' or as a 'research tool.'").

29. Lilly & Co. v. Medtronic, Inc., 496 U.S. 661 (1990).

testing of patented compounds reasonably related to the submission of information to a regulatory agency, not just the late-stage approvals.[30] Finally, in 2012 the Federal Circuit held that the safe harbor provision also extended to protect activities relating to post-approval submissions, rather than only pre-approval.[31] While a central purpose of these IP regulatory frameworks is to bring more certainty to innovators and market entrants by allowing for a mechanism to decide patent disputes early, these broad-reaching regulatory frameworks provide little guidance for innovators to understand how patent rights may resolve after unforeseen emergencies such as a global pandemic.

Limited IP Waivers: WTO TRIPS

In 1995, the World Trade Organization (WTO) member states entered into the Agreement on Trade-Related Aspects of Intellectual Property Rights (TRIPS) that incorporates intellectual property rights obligations into the rules-based trading system.[32] Under TRIPS, most WTO members must respect minimum rules to protect patents, copyrights, and trademarks, and must do so domestically by enacting laws. While TRIPS provides some of the parameters for the IP protection, it is up to the individual country to determine what exactly that protection will entail. For example, TRIPS provides that members must make available patents "for any inventions, whether products or processes, in all fields of technology" that are novel, nonobvious, and useful[33]—but defining the contours of what exactly makes an invention any one of those three things is up to how the country construes those terms and writes its own laws protecting the same. For example, the nuances of novelty law in the U.S. patent system are different from those of the European patent system such that the effect of a given piece of art on patentability could be different in each jurisdiction,[34] yet both bodies of law deal in broad strokes with the requirement that an invention be novel.

30. Merck KGaA v. Integra Lifesciences I, Ltd., 545 U.S. 193 (2005).

31. Momenta Pharmaceuticals v. Amphastar Pharmaceuticals, Inc., 686 F.3d 1348 (Fed. Cir. 2012).

32. *See* Congressional Research Service Report, *World Trade Organization: "TRIPS Waiver" for COVID-19 Vaccines*, R47231, Aug. 31, 2022.

33. *See id.* at 3.

34. *See, e.g.*, Dale Bjorkman, Gilbert Voortmans & Lindsay M. Block. "'Made Available to the Public'—Understanding the Differences of the America Invents Act from the European Patent Convention in Its Definition of Prior Art," *Cybaris*®, 4(2), 191–218 (2013), available at https://open.mitchellhamline.edu/cybaris/vol4/iss2/1.

Against that backdrop, in 2001, the WTO member states made a ministerial agreement focused on compulsory licensing, which could be considered a patent waiver in the developing world. The latest ministerial agreement again focused on compulsory licensing, largely waiving the requirements for getting compulsory licensing during the COVID-19 pandemic—for example, waiving the requirement that the party first tried to get a voluntary license, waiving the requirement that vaccines be primarily manufactured for the domestic market, and allowing for export of vaccines to low-income countries.[35] These WTO declarations do not have immediate effect in member countries; the countries instead have to put their own laws into place to effectuate the agreements. The latter declaration says it will be in force for five years and can be renewed in the event that the COVID-19 pandemic continues, which throws significant uncertainty into reliance on that waiver to form the basis of a commercial decision on manufacturing or production.

Patent Pledges and IP Waivers: Enforceable Actions or Theater?

When an entity makes a voluntary public commitment that it will not exercise some or all of its patent rights, it is considered a "patent pledge." This is not a new concept, but it has received considerable attention during the COVID-19 pandemic, when many companies issued patent pledges seeking to help bring an end to the pandemic. While patent pledges are benevolent in theory, the big question now is their enforceability—leaving many to wonder: Do patent pledges have any teeth, or are they just pandemic public relations theater?

Moderna's Patent Pledges

In October 2020, Moderna Therapeutics made the following statement via press release regarding enforcement of its patents:[36]

> We feel a special obligation under the current circumstances to use our resources to bring this pandemic to an end as quickly as possible. Accordingly, while the pandemic continues, Moderna

35. *See* Congressional Research Service Report, *World Trade Organization: "TRIPS Waiver" for COVID-19 Vaccines*, R47231, Aug. 31, 2022, at 9–11.

36. Dan Shores. Breaking Down Moderna's COVID-19 Patent Pledge: Why Did They Do It?, *IPWatchdog* (Nov. 11, 2020), available at https://ipwatchdog.com/2020/11/11/breaking-modernas-covid-19-patent-pledge/id=127224/.

> will not enforce our COVID-19 related patents against those making vaccines intended to combat the pandemic. Further, to eliminate any perceived IP barriers to vaccine development during the pandemic period, upon request we are also willing to license our intellectual property for COVID-19 vaccines to others for the post pandemic period.

This statement is understood as a "patent pledge"—Moderna publicly pledged to not sue anyone over its mRNA vaccine patents during the pandemic, further pledging to license its IP in the post-pandemic phase. Over the ensuing year and a half, Moderna stayed true to its pledge as the world watched Moderna and competitors such as Pfizer and BioNTech launch mRNA vaccines to combat COVID-19; according to Moderna, the Pfizer and BioNTech vaccines use Moderna's patented technology.[37]

Then, in March 2022, Moderna issued an updated patent pledge, pledging to "never enforce" its patents for COVID-19 vaccines "against companies manufacturing in or for the 92 low- and middle-income countries in the Gavi COVAX Advance Market Commitment ("AMC"), provided that the manufactured vaccines are solely for use in the AMC 92 countries."[38] Moderna's updated pledge also clarified Moderna's position on where the rest of the world stands in relation to the COVID-19 pandemic and Moderna's prior pledge, stating in relevant part:[39]

> In non-AMC 92 countries, vaccine supply is no longer a barrier to access. In these countries, the Company expects those using Moderna-patented technologies will respect the Company's Intellectual property. Moderna remains willing to license its technology for COVID-19 vaccines to manufacturers in these countries on commercially reasonable terms. Doing so enables Moderna to continue to invest in research to develop new vaccines, prepare for the next pandemic, and meet other pressing areas of unmet medical need.

Moderna's updated patent pledge made clear its intention to shift away from the thrust of its initial patent pledge, moving its focus in non-AMC 92

37. Andrew Alexander. Caldwell Intellectual Property Law, Did Moderna Sink Its Own Ship by Making A "Patent Pledge"?, *JDSupra* (Oct. 14, 2022), available at https://www.jdsupra.com/legalnews/did-moderna-sink-its-own-ship-by-making-5067968/.

38. Moderna's Updated Patent Pledge, *Moderna* (Mar. 7, 2022), available at https://investors.modernatx.com/Statements--Perspectives/Statements--Perspectives-Details/2022/Modernas-Updated-Patent-Pledge/default.aspx.

39. *Id.*

countries toward licensing efforts. As discussed more in-depth below, Moderna followed this updated pledge with litigation against competitor Pfizer, confirming Moderna's essential revocation of its initial patent pledge.

Other COVID-19 Pandemic Patent Pledges

Moderna's patent pledges were not the only ones made during the COVID-19 pandemic. Some of the other patent pledges made during the pandemic are discussed below, varying from individual companies to coordinated pledges—but the question of enforceability remains the same.

Fortress and its subsidiary Labrador Diagnostics had filed a lawsuit in March 2020 against a French diagnostic company asserting infringement of diagnostic patents originally developed by Theranos and Elizabeth Homes.[40] Fortress and Labrador faced backlash after the defendant corporation announced it was developing diagnostic testing for COVID-19, leading Fortress and Labrador to back off the patent suit and pledge royalty-free licenses for its patented diagnostics technology for development of COVID-19 testing.[41] In 2020, AbbVie purportedly pledged to not enforce global patent rights on formulations of its HIV medication Kaletra® (lopinavir/ritonavir), which is an antiviral medication that was under investigation as a potential COVID treatment during earlier phases of the pandemic.[42] And in 2020, Medtronic went a step further, making its ventilator IP available to the public by actually sharing its design specifications and know-how to allow other companies to make and use their medical-grade ventilators.[43]

There have also been coordinated pledges during the COVID-19 pandemic. One, the Wellcome Trust Publisher's Pledge for copyrighted material opened up a mechanism for sharing intellectual property by

40. Craig Clough. Fortress Offers IP Rights To Fight COVID-19 After Backlash, *Law360* (Mar. 17, 2020), available at https://www.law360.com/articles/1254102/fortress-offers-ip-rights-to-fight-covid-19-after-backlash.

41. *Id.*

42. Kyle Blankenship. AbbVie gives up patent rights to HIV med Kaletra amid COVID-19 tests: report, *Fierce Pharma* (Mar. 23, 2020), available at https://www.fiercepharma.com/pharma/abbvie-gives-up-patent-rights-to-hiv-med-kaletra-amid-covid-19-tests-report.

43. Noel Courage. Companies are Not only Freely Sharing IP, They are Enabling Others to Copy Their Product (COVID-19), *Bereskin & Parr* (Apr. 14, 2020), available at https://www.bereskinparr.com/doc/companies-are-not-only-freely-sharing-ip-they-are-enabling-others-to-copy-their-product-covid-19; *see also* Medtronic Permissive License—Open Ventilator Files, *Medtronic*, available at https://www.medtronic.com/content/dam/medtronic-com/global/Corporate/covid19/documents/permissive-license-open-ventilator.pdf.

numerous publishers of scientific journals and proceedings, including the American Chemical Society, *British Medical Journal*, Elsevier, *New England Journal of Medicine*, and more.[44] Another coordinated pledge is the Open COVID Pledge, developed by a coalition of scientists, engineers, and legal experts and adopted by a range of organizations (including Amazon, Intel, Microsoft) holding in excess of 250,000 patents worldwide—all promising to make IP free of charge for use during the pandemic.[45]

Enforceability of Pandemic Patent Pledges?

Two primary questions arise when considering the enforceability of COVID-19 pandemic patent pledges: (1) what mechanism could be used to compel compliance with a patent pledge, should the pledging company renege on its promise? and (2) how does one determine the "end" of the pandemic where a company has pledged to not enforce its IP during the pandemic?

For the first question, the main legal theories suggested by the literature for enforcement of patent pledges are based on contractual theory. In the United States, enforcement of a contract requires an offer, acceptance, and consideration—while establishing all of these elements may be a barrier to enforcing a patent pledge in the United States under a straight contractual theory, these requirements are not uniform worldwide, meaning that a patent pledge could be enforceable in other countries directly as a contract. Arguably a patent pledge is an offer for a public license open to anyone who accepts it, thus sealing the deal and making an enforceable contract should consideration not be necessary (or should it be otherwise found). Beyond straight contractual theory, there is a related doctrine known as "promissory estoppel" that can be used to recover on the basis of a promise made in absence of an enforceable contract when one party reasonably relies on the promise to its own detriment. In that scenario, a party accused of infringing a patent subject to a prior patent pledge would argue that it reasonably relied on the pledge to not enforce the patent, and should the promisor be permitted to renege on its promise, that would unjustly harm the relying party.

For the second question, there also does not seem to be a straightforward answer. For example, in its complaint for patent infringement

44. J.L. Contreras, M. Eisen, A. Ganz et al. Pledging intellectual property for COVID-19, *Nat. Biotechnol.* 38, 1146–49 (2020). https://doi.org/10.1038/s41587-020-0682-1.

45. *Id.*

against competitor Pfizer,[46] Moderna took the position that the COVID-19 pandemic was over as of August 2022—but by public health standards, the pandemic was not yet over, and experts continue to hedge on projecting the end of the pandemic, despite the promise by the Biden administration that the official public health emergency ended on May 11, 2023. Where other companies have used similarly vague language in their patent pledges, it is possible we will see similar infringement suits crop up as parties become antsy to enforce their IP in what they assert to be a post-pandemic world.

Between the question of enforceability of patent pledges generally and this more particular question about the "end" of the pandemic contemplated by some pledges as the end of the pledge, many are left reasonably wondering whether patent pledges are real action that moves the ball forward in stopping the pandemic, or just public relations theater aimed to make us feel like the ball is moving. Further, in other spheres (e.g., small molecule, mechanical inventions), it is often easier to replicate or copy another product without having access to materials such as confidential know-how or trade secrets, but with biologic products and vaccines it is usually not that easy to make a copy or competing version; because of this, it is not clear that patent waivers are particularly motivating during the pandemic. For example, if a company invests significant time and resources into developing a product, it is possible the IP waiver could lapse by the time the product is commercialized. This means the company seeking to invest still needs to figure out whether it is worth ramping up huge amounts of resources and manufacturing capacity regardless of whether there is an IP waiver in place when embarking on the endeavor. This suggests that the power of a patent pledge lies not in the promise itself but in the actions undertaken alongside it to actually increase access to lifesaving technology.

Conclusion

While there remains a good deal of uncertainty in the path forward through and beyond the COVID-19 pandemic, it is clear that it will be incumbent on manufacturers, researchers, key opinion leaders, and legislators around the world to balance the public health and the need for appropriate incentives in view of current and potential future infectious

46. ModernaTX, Inc. et al v. Pfizer Inc. et al., Case No. 1:22-cv-11378 (D. Ma), filed Aug. 26, 2022.

diseases. Outside of the safe harbor provisions in the Hatch-Waxman Act that arguably apply to biologics such as vaccines, the Hatch-Waxman Act and BPCIA do not have other provisions tied to public health emergencies such as the COVID-19 pandemic to address both the regulatory and IP incentives necessary to encourage and reward the sharing of information during the public health emergency while providing for an orderly transition for patent enforcement once the emergency ends. Further, in view of the uncertainty tied to patent pledges and whether WHO will be able to enforce IP waivers worldwide, additional measures need to be considered to provide this balance of sharing/noninfringement during a public health emergency and coordinate the transition to a more definitive time for IP enforcement once the emergency ends. For these reasons, we recommend that regulators and legislators take a more proactive role to develop specific guidelines, regulations, or statutory provisions to better address the balance between innovation and collaboration during a public health emergency situation and how to transition that balance from an emergency to nonemergency situation to advance world health objectives.

Chapter 6

The Two Federal Vaccine Injury Compensation Programs: Successes and Failures and Proposals for Improvement

Peter H. Meyers[1]

Two federal vaccine injury compensation programs have been established in the United States. The National Vaccine Injury Compensation Program (NVICP)[2] began operating 35 years ago. It covers injuries from the childhood vaccines and the annual influenza vaccines. The second program is the Countermeasure Injury Compensation Program (CICP),[3] which covers injuries from COVID-19 and other vaccines. This program has been operating for 17 years. How have these two programs changed since their early years, and how successful have they been? This article discusses the main features of both programs and their successes and failures, and it recommends revisions to improve their operations.

1. I would like to thank Professor Sara Schotland for her substantial assistance with the article.

2. National Childhood Vaccine Injury Act of 1986, Pub. L. No. 99-660, 100 Stat. 3755 (codified as amended as 42 U.S.C. §§300aa-1 to -34).

3. Public Readiness and Emergency Preparedness Act of 2005 (PREP Act), Pub. L. No. 109-148, 119 Stat. 2818 (2005) (codified at 42 U.S.C. §§247d-6d to 6e).

The NVICP: Addressing Childhood Injury and Flu Vaccines

The NVICP was an innovative, pioneering federal no-fault tort reform program that has served as a model for several later compensation programs, including the September 11th Victims Compensation Fund.[4] This chapter will first investigate how the NVICP has evolved since it began and then consider what steps can be taken now to improve it.

Congress's stated purpose in passing the NVICP was to provide compensation "quickly, easily, and with certainty and generosity" to individuals injured by the childhood vaccines.[5] In the early years of the program those objectives were largely met, but today they are largely unfulfilled. So, what has changed and what should be done to again make it work the way Congress intended?

The Changing Role of the Vaccine Compensation Table

Let us look first at the key innovation in the law—the vaccine injury table—which was intended to be the centerpiece of this program. The vaccine injury table eliminated the need to prove that a vaccine caused an injury. To recover compensation, petitioners need only prove that they suffered an injury specified in the table and that the onset of the injury was within the time period specified in the table.[6] If a petitioner establishes this by a preponderance of the evidence, a presumption is created that the vaccine caused the injury, and the burden then shifts to the government to prove that some factor unrelated to the vaccine was likely the cause of the injury, and this cannot be a cause of idiopathic or unknown origin.[7] This is a relatively easy burden for petitioners to satisfy and a relatively easy issue for the special masters to decide, because the petitioner's medical records will often make this clear or, if necessary, a medical expert can show to the special master that these criteria have been satisfied.

In the early years of the program, more than 90 percent of the vaccine injury claims filed asserted table injuries, and these cases were resolved

---

4. *See* Peter H. Meyers, "Fixing the Flaws in the Federal Vaccine Injury Compensation Program," 63 Admin. L. Rev. 785, 792 (2011) (hereafter "Fixing the Flaws").

5. H.R. REP. NO. 99-908, pt. 1, at 3 (1986), reprinted in 1986 U.S.C.C.A.N. 6344, 6344.

6. 42 U.S.C. § 300aa-14(a).

7. 42 U.S.C. § 300aa-11(a)(1)(B).

relatively quickly and easily.[8] But over the years, the percentage of table injury cases in the program changed dramatically. By 2016, more than 90 percent of the cases filed in the program asserted injuries that were not listed in the table.[9] This imposes a much higher burden on petitioners to prove that their injuries were likely caused by or significantly aggravated by the vaccination. These cases are much more difficult to prove than table injury cases and take much longer to compile the necessary expert testimony and medical literature reviews.

There were two principal reasons for this change. First, the Secretary of Health and Human Services (HHS) amended the table in 1995 through an administrative rulemaking proceeding,[10] substantially narrowing the covered table injuries. Second, nine additional vaccines had been added to the Vaccine Act by 2016, often with no specified table injuries at all or only the table injury of anaphylactic shock.

Then, in 2017 the situation changed drastically again. SIRVA injuries—the acronym for shoulder injuries related to vaccine administration—were added to the vaccine table through an administrative rulemaking proceeding.[11] These injuries are viewed today as predominantly caused by the negligent administration of the vaccinations rather than reactions to the components of the vaccines.[12] Now, more than 50 percent of the claims filed after 2017 allege SIRVA injuries.[13] The Trump administration tried to eliminate SIRVA injuries from the vaccine table[14] but it did not act quickly enough, and the Biden administration quashed this change before it became final.

8. Stevens v. Sec'y of Health and Human Services, No. 99-594V, 2001 WL 387418, at *8 (Ct. of Fed. Cl. Mar. 30, 2001) (opinion of Chief Special Master Gary J. Golkiewicz).

9. Dee Lord, Chief Special Master, U.S. Court of Federal Claims, Evolving Caseload of the Office of Special Masters (Oct. 2010) (unpublished presentation) (on file with author) (hereafter "Evolving Caseload").

10. National Vaccine Injury Compensation Program Revision of the Vaccine Injury Table, 60 Fed. Reg. 7678, 7694 (Feb. 8, 1995) (codified at 42 C.F.R. § 100.3).

11. National Vaccine Injury Compensation Program: Revisions to the Vaccine Injury Table, 82 Fed. Reg. 6294 Jan. 19, 2017) (codified at 42 C.F.R. § 100.3).

12. National Vaccine Injury Compensation Program: Revisions to the Vaccine Injury Table, 86 Fed. Reg. 6249, 6256 (Jan. 21, 2021) (codified at 42 C.F.R. § 100.3).

13. National Vaccine Injury Compensation Program: Revisions to the Vaccine Injury Table, 86 Fed. Reg. 6249, 6256 (Jan. 21, 2021) (codified at 42 C.F.R. § 100.3).

14. National Vaccine Injury Compensation Program: Revisions to the Vaccine Injury Table, 86 Fed. Reg. 6249 (Jan. 21, 2021) (codified at 42 C.F.R. § 100.3).

The Changing Composition of Vaccine Injury Petitioners

A second major change in the program involves the type of claimants who are filing for compensation. Congress passed the statute primarily to protect children who were receiving school-mandated vaccinations, such as the diphtheria, pertussis, tetanus (DPT) shot and the measles, mumps, rubella (MMR) shot.[15] In the early years of the program, the overwhelming majority of claims were filed on behalf of children who had received these childhood vaccinations.[16]

But today the situation is dramatically different. Most vaccine injury claims are now filed for injuries to adults, for three principal reasons.[17] First, annual flu vaccines, which are taken by both adults and children, were added to the Act. Second, SIRVA injuries were added to the table. And third, according to many experts, the childhood vaccines available today such as the acellular pertussis vaccine are safer than the whole cell pertussis vaccine administered in the 1980s.[18]

The Problem of Delay

A third major change in the program is that cases are no longer proceeding expeditiously before the special masters. Congress intended that the cases proceed quickly, informally, and with less adversarial back and forth than in traditional litigation in the courts. In the early years of the program the cases largely proceeded in this manner,[19] but not today.

The Vaccine Act provides that cases shall generally be resolved within 240 days of filing,[20] and in the beginning of the program the cases were usually disposed of within that time period.[21] But today, typically it takes years to even schedule a hearing on the causation issue, let alone have the special master decide the causation issue and then address the damages issue in a later hearing.[22] And the Vaccine Rules and Guidelines adopted by the judges and special masters have made the proceedings much more formal and much more like other adversarial litigation in the courts.[23]

---

15. Fixing the Flaws, *supra* note 4, at 795.
16. *Id.*
17. Evolving Caseloads, *supra* note 9.
18. Katherine M. Edwards & Michael D. Deck, "Pertussis Vaccines," in Walter Orenstein, et al., eds., Plotkin's Vaccines (7th ed. 2017), at 711 *et seq.*
19. Fixing the Flaws, *supra* note 4, at 789.
20. 42 U.S.C. § 300aa-11(a)(1).
21. Bruesewitz v. Wyeth L.L.C, 562 U.S. 223, 228 (2011).
22. Fixing the Flaws, *supra* note 4, at 795.
23. *Id.* at 795–96.

The limited number of special masters is a major reason for the delays. The NVICP statute authorizes a maximum number of eight special masters,[24] and they are today overwhelmed by the large number of cases that have been filed and are pending before them. There are more than 4,000 cases currently pending before the eight special masters.[25] A bill that has been introduced in Congress to increase the number of special masters to a minimum of ten[26] would help substantially.

The special masters have taken steps to address the delay problem. They created procedures to expedite the SIRVA and other table injury claims and claims asserting quasi-table injuries. Pre-Assignment Review has been instituted by the chief special master, and a Special Proceedings Unit has been created to process these claims. While these steps have helped, additional measures should be taken to adopt rules and guidelines to further streamline and increase the informality of the procedures. Additional resources must also be allocated to increase the number of attorneys in the Justice Department and medical experts in the Department of Health and Human Resources who review these cases to further reduce the current backlogs.

Vaccine Manufactures' Liability Protections

While all the substantial changes described above were occurring in this vaccine injury compensation program over the past 35 years, one very important aspect of the program has remained the same. The compensation program was designed to primarily protect vaccine manufacturers from liability for vaccine injuries and shift this liability to the NVICP program.[27] In this respect, the program has been extremely successful. Vaccine manufactures have remained in the market producing vaccines, and have not abandoned it, and America has continued to have an adequate supply of the vaccines covered by the Act.[28]

The limited liability for manufacturers who produce vaccines covered by the Act was described in the U.S. Supreme Court case of *Bruesewitz v. Wyeth L.L.C.*[29] as follows:

---

24. 42 U.S.C. §300aa-12(c)(1).

25. Congressional Research Service, The National Vaccine Injury Compensation Program and the Office of Special Masters (Sept. 14, 2022).

26. H.R. 3655, 117th Cong., The Vaccine Injury Compensation Modernization Act of 2021.

27. Fixing the Flaws, *supra* note 4, at 841.

28. *Id.* at 788.

29. 562 U.S. 223 (2011).

> Manufacturers are generally immunized from liability for failure to warn if they have complied with all regulatory requirements (including but not limited to warning requirements) and have given the warning either to the claimant or the claimant's physician.[30]

The Act also expressly eliminates liability for a vaccine's unavoidable, adverse side effects:

> No vaccine manufacturer shall be liable in a civil action for damages arising from a vaccine-related injury or death associated with the administration of a vaccine after October 1, 1988, if the injury or death resulted from side effects that were unavoidable even though the vaccine was properly prepared and was accompanied by proper directions and warnings.[31]

The manufacturers are immunized from liability for punitive damages absent failure to comply with regulatory requirements, for "fraud," and for "intentional and wrongful withholding of information" or other "criminal or illegal activity."[32]

Since the Vaccine Act was passed, no vaccine manufacturer has been successfully sued for a vaccine injury caused by any vaccine covered by the Act. The manufactures' immunity from legal liability for vaccine injuries has been the one constant feature of this compensation program from its beginning until today.

Recommended Changes That Should Be Made in the NVICP

In this author's view, the NVICP has a number of flaws that should be addressed to make the program work better and more like the program that Congress intended when the program was adopted. More special masters should be authorized by statute and appointed to deal with the substantial backlog that currently exists. More funding should also go to supplement the number of attorneys in the Department of Justice and medical experts in the Department of Health and Human Services to process these cases more expeditiously. The NVICP statute should also be amended to adopt provisions that scholars have recommended to make it more petitioner friendly: giving the petitioners the benefit of the doubt in close cases, lengthening the statute of limitation to file the claim, allowing parents to sue for their

30. *Id.* at 229.
31. 42 U.S.C. § 300aa-22(b)(1).
32. *Id.*

own injuries when their children are injured by vaccines, and raising the caps on death benefits and pain and suffering benefits.[33]

The CICP: A Program to Address Pandemics and Bioterrorism Threats

The second federal vaccine injury compensation program covers vaccines created to deal with pandemics and bioterrorism threats—the Countermeasures Injury Compensation Program (CICP). This program covers injuries from vaccines given to address COVID-19. The program was passed by Congress back in 2005 to encourage the creation of vaccines and other countermeasures to combat a potential H1N1 avian flu pandemic and fears that bioterrorists might release anthrax, smallpox, or other toxins on the American public.[34]

Excessive Secrecy

From its very beginning, the CICP operated as an extremely secretive program within the Department of Health and Human Services.[35] CICP proceedings, unlike proceedings in the NVICP, which are litigated in the U.S. Court of Federal Claims, do not allow petitioners to have their cases decided after hearings before independent special masters but are decided instead in hidden proceedings before unknown HHS officials. Also unlike in the vaccine court, the CICP did not publish decisions granting or denying compensation, so the public and other petitioners never know what injuries are compensated and the reasons why claims are granted or denied.[36]

In the pre-COVID years, the CICP did not release any information on the number of vaccine injury claims filed, the number granted, the number denied, and the reasons why HHS made those decisions. The public was kept totally in the dark and never provided with this information. And persons filing claims in the program had no idea what criteria and key facts HHS was using to decide the cases. The program operated like a black hole—petitions for compensation were filed and entered the

33. *See* Fixing the Flaws, *supra* note 4, at 845–50.

34. *See* Sarah A. Lister, "Pandemic Influenzia: Domestic Preparedness Efforts," RL 33145 Cong. Research Serv. 32 (2005).

35. *See* Peter H. Meyers, "The Trump Administration's Flawed Decision on Coronavirus Vaccine Injury Compensation: Recommendations for Changes," 7 J. of Law and the Biosciences Issue 1 (Jan.–June 2020), Isaa082 (hereafter "Flawed Decision").

36. *Id.*

program, but no information about the operation of the program or the cases filed or the reasons for the decisions ever emerged into the light.

It was only in June 2020, in response to a Freedom of Information Act request I filed with HHS, that the agency finally released information to me about the number of pre-COVID vaccine injury cases filed, granted, and denied.[37] And the information provided was shocking.

It turned out that prior to COVID-19, the CICP had received 446 vaccine injury claims and granted only 39 of them, for asserted injuries from H1N1, anthrax, and smallpox vaccines.[38] That represented compensation granted in less than 10 percent of the filed claims, in sharp contrast to 70–78 percent of claims that have been compensated in recent years in the Vaccine Court program for childhood vaccines.[39] Even if some pre-COVID claims filed in the CICP were questionable or even bogus, a program that rejected over 90 percent of the claims filed cannot be considered a properly functioning compensation program.

And the CICP has never released any information on the reasons it granted and denied these claims for compensation. So even today we have no idea why these pre-COVID vaccine injury claims were decided the way they were. It is a horrible record.

Other Problems with the CICP

Unlike the vaccine court, the CICP does not allow judicial review of adverse decisions. And also unlike vaccine court cases, in CICP cases the government does not pay fees for attorneys and medical experts to assist the claimants in seeking to make their cases. As for decisions that were successful pre-COVID, only limited compensation was awarded, which did not include compensation for pain and suffering, future rehabilitation, or full lost wages. Only partial lost wages were allowed.[40]

So, how does the program operate now in the COVID era? Only slightly better. The procedures at HHS are still the same deficient procedures. Hearings before special masters or other independent decision-makers are still not allowed. Instead, unknown HHS officials still decide

37. Attachment to letter from Anthony Clemons, Government Information Specialist, Dept. of Health and Human Services, to Peter Meyers, Professor Emeritus, The George Washington University Law School, June 26, 2020 (on file with the author), at 1.

38. *Id.*

39. Health Resources and Services Administration, "Vaccine Injury Compensation Data," https://www.hrsa.gov/vaccine-compensation/data (updated Dec. 1, 2022) (last visited Dec. 22, 2022).

40. *See* Flawed Decision, *supra* note 35.

all petitions seeking compensation for COVID vaccines or other COVID countermeasure injuries in secret proceedings. The public know nothing about who decides these cases, how many individuals are involved, or the procedures or criteria they use in reaching their decisions.

The government still will not pay fees for attorneys and medical experts to assist claimants in making their case and still does not publish decisions granting or denying compensation, so the public and other petitioners never know what injuries are compensated and why. And no judicial review of adverse decisions is allowed.

There is one way in which there has been a marginal improvement. HHS now published on its website the number of COVID vaccine injury cases filed, granted, and denied, and the injury alleged for each case. The published statistics are appalling. As of December 1, 2022, the latest date for which statistics are available,[41] 7,624 claims for COVID vaccine injury or death have been filed, and only a single claim for injury has been partially compensated, involving an anaphylactic reaction to a COVID-19 vaccination. Ten other cases involving myocarditis and one case involving pericarditis have been determined to be eligible for compensation, but no compensation has yet been awarded in these cases as of this date. Thus, of the more than 7,000 vaccine injury cases filed in the CICP for COVID-19 vaccine injuries, only 12 cases have been determined to be eligible for compensation.[42] This reflects less than one quarter of i percent of the cases filed.

Vaccine Manufactures' Liability Protections

To encourage manufactures to create vaccines for pandemic and bioterrorism threats, Congress gave manufactures virtually 100 percent protection from legal liability for adverse effects of the vaccines. The manufactures can only be sued if they engage in "willful misconduct" (but not for negligent conduct or even gross negligence in making the vaccines).[43] This level of manufacturers' immunity from litigation is broader that the protection afforded under the NVICP, as described above. But just like the NVICP, no claim has ever been successfully brought to date for willful misconduct for vaccines covered by the CICP. While some might argue that the protection for manufactures is excessive, in my view it is

41. Health Resources and Services Administration, "Countermeasures Injury Compensation Program (CICP) Data," https://www.hrsa.gov.CICP-data (updated Dec. 1, 2022) (last visited Dec. 22, 2022).

42. *Id.*

43. 42 U.S.C. § 247d-6d(d)(1).

appropriate protection for manufacturers to insure they stay in the market and produce the needed vaccines. The risk of adverse publicity to their companies if they ever failed to use maximum care to ensure their vaccines are as safe as possible is sufficient, I believe, to protect against negligent conduct.

However, since individuals who have suffered injuries as a result of the vaccines cannot sue the manufacturer and have only one available remedy—to seek compensation in the CICP—it is very important that the CICP provide a meaningful opportunity to receive fair compensation for injuries caused by these vaccines. I do not believe it has ever done so.

Let us compare how the program operated in its early pre-COVID years with how the program operates today in dealing with asserted COVID-19 vaccine injuries.

Changes That Should Be Made in the CICP

In my view, the Countermeasures Injury Compensation Program has been a severe disappointment from its beginning to today. In recent years, the program has become slightly better in releasing limited information about the cases before it, but it is still a deeply flawed program that operates in almost total secrecy. One alternative would be to move the COVID-19 vaccine injury claims to the NVICP. Congress could do this by passing a statute, or the Secretary of HHS could do it through administrative action. Before a vaccine can be added to the NVICP by the Secretary of HHS, (1) it must be recommended for the routine administration to children or pregnant women by the CDC, (2) Congress must approve an excise tax for the vaccine, and (3) the Secretary of HHS must add it to the list of vaccines covered by the NVICP.[44] These measures can and should be adopted.

In the alternative, the CICP could be substantially improved by Congressional amendments to the statute and procedural changes that HHS can and should make. The CICP needs to become a more compassionate, transparent, and generous program. The statute and procedures should be modified to adopt provisions that scholars have recommended would make it more petitioner friendly:[45]

- Adopt open decision-making procedures that allow meaningful participation by petitioners.

44. *See* Dept. of Health and Human Services Rule, 86 Fed. Reg. 68423 (Dec. 2, 2021).

45. *See* Flawed Decision, *supra* note 35.

- Authorize independent special masters to decide compensation claims.
- Impose strict time limits for final decision-making.
- Adopt more generous limits on the compensation awards.
- Allow for judicial review of final agency decisions.
- Adopt a legal standard of proof more generous to petitioners.
- Extend the statute of limitation beyond one year to at least three or four years.

Chapter 7

Improving Mechanisms to Compensate Individuals for Vaccine Injuries

Anna Boltyanskiy, Megha Hoon, Bharath Palle, and John Winter

Introduction

The COVID-19 pandemic has highlighted the importance of globally coordinated vaccination programs, as well as the challenges to achieving this critical public health goal. As we saw with COVID-19, diseases travel quickly, reaching all corners of the earth in a matter of months.[1] Governments and vaccine manufacturers worked expeditiously to develop safe and effective vaccines, but vaccine hesitancy also quickly spread around the world. Global vaccination efforts that quell concerns about vaccine safety and ensure that those who do experience adverse side effects from vaccination are appropriately compensated are therefore vital.

Over the last several decades, vaccines have played a critical role in eradicating diseases such as smallpox, polio, diphtheria, rubella, and others.[2] The Centers for Disease Control and Prevention (CDC) estimates that four million deaths worldwide are prevented by childhood vaccination

1. Brakkton Booker, *The Coronavirus Crisis, The Coronavirus Has Reached Antarctica. Now It's On Every Continent*, NPR (Dec. 23, 2020), https://www.npr.org/sections/coronavirus-live-updates/2020/12/23/949552848/the-coronavirus-has-reached-every-continent-after-positive-cases-in-antarctica.

2. Mayo Clinic staff, *Herd immunity and COVID-19: What you need to know*, https://www.mayoclinic.org/diseases-conditions/coronavirus/in-depth/herd-immunity-and-coronavirus/art-20486808#:~:text=quickly%20become%20overwhelmed.-,Vaccines,causing%20illness%20or%20resulting%20complications (last visited Dec. 23, 2022).

each year and that 51 million deaths can be prevented through immunization between 2021 and 2030.[3] As these figures demonstrate, vaccines can play an important role in improving public health outcomes.

In addition, as compared with medicines that individuals take to treat specific ailments they are personally experiencing, vaccination benefits the general population, including those in the community who may not be able to get vaccinated.[4] When enough people are vaccinated against a disease, herd immunity is achieved, and the spread of contagious diseases slows.[5] Thus, a vaccine's full potential can be realized only when a high percentage of a community's members are vaccinated.[6] Accordingly, vaccine efficacy depends on a large portion of a population becoming vaccinated, and the social gain of a vaccine dose is considered to be greater than the private gain to the recipient. This is because the risk of vaccination is generally at the individual level, but the benefits flow to the general population. Similarly, this makes it difficult to assess the risks to those who get vaccinated.[7] Despite vaccines' proven effectiveness, mass vaccination faces two distinct and significant challenges.

On the side of production, vaccine development systems in the United States and throughout the world are lacking, in part because of the high costs of such systems, including the complex legal liability issues associated with vaccines that disincentivize vaccine development. Unless specifically protected by one of the liability protection mechanisms described in greater detail below, the risk of liability from vaccines is greater than medicines developed to treat specific conditions because courts traditionally are less inclined to give manufacturers the benefit of certain important defenses, such s the "learned intermediary" rule, in a

---

3. Centers for Disease Control and Prevention (CDC), *Fast Facts on Global Immunization*, https://www.cdc.gov/globalhealth/immunization/data/fast-facts.html (last visited Dec. 23, 2022).

4. U.S. Dept of Health & Human Services, *Vaccines Protect Your Community*, https://www.hhs.gov/immunization/basics/work/protection/index.html (last visited Dec. 23, 2022).

5. Mayo Clinic staff, *supra* note 2.

6. Jan Hoffman, *How Anti-Vaccine Sentiment Took Hold in the United States*, N.Y. Times (Sept. 23, 2019), https://www.nytimes.com/2019/09/23/health/anti-vaccination-movement-us.html.

7. *See* Bruesewitz v. Wyeth, 562 U.S. 223, 227 (2011) (noting that vaccination rates are a matter of social concern because "vaccines are effective in preventing outbreaks of disease only if a large percentage of the population is vaccinated"); Jennifer Keelan & Kumanan Wilson, *Designing a No-Fault Vaccine-Injury Compensation Program for Canada*, Munk School Briefings (Feb. 2011), at 7–8 (discussing herd immunity and its significance for compensation schemes).

mass immunization context.[8] In addition to the typical liability considerations such as the potential for unpredictable legal outcomes or large damages awards, vaccine manufacturers (and public health initiatives) also are impacted by public perception of the efficacy and safety of a vaccine.

On the side of administration, there has been an unsettling increase in vaccine hesitancy, a term for people who view vaccinations (and the associated scientific developments in the field of medicine) with skepticism or even outright hostility.

In this chapter, we propose solutions to tackle both of these challenges by altering the structure of incentives for both vaccine makers and the general public. We argue that increasing the funding for, and participation in, global vaccine-injury compensation schemes can provide an insurance system for the general public to overcome hesitancy and skepticism toward the safety and efficacy of vaccines as well as incentives to manufacturers to innovate swiftly, particularly in the context of a global health emergency.

From Vaccine Hesitancy to Vaccine Acceptance: The COVID-19 Scenario

The COVID-19 pandemic highlighted a curious paradox. Vaccines were developed and rolled out at an unusually rapid pace. The number of vaccines that were developed in response to the virus also dramatically increased.[9] At the same time, vaccine skepticism grew among segments of the population. Although a large number of vaccines became available

---

8. *See* Reyes v. Wyeth Laboratories, 498 F.2d 1264 (5th Cir. 1974) (finding that the "learned intermediary" rule does not apply in vaccination context; instead applying "mass immunization" exception whereby the manufacturer has a duty to warn of the risks of the vaccine when it knows or has reason to know that healthcare providers will not be in an intermediary position to evaluate the risks on an individual basis, including mass vaccination campaigns); *see also* Mazur v. Merck & Co., Inc., 964 F.2d 1348 (3rd Cir. 1992) (manufacturer could discharge its duty to warn by contracting with the CDC to distribute vaccine, informing the CDC of the risks of the vaccine, and relying on the CDC's guarantee that the vaccine would only be administered after providing a warning to recipients).

9. Three years after the COVID-19 pandemic broke out, the World Health Organization (WHO) estimates that there are 175 vaccines in clinical development with another 199 vaccines in pre-clinical development globally. *See* WHO, *COVID-19 vaccine tracker and landscape* (Dec. 13, 2022), https://www.who.int/publications/m/item/draft-landscape-of-covid-19-candidate-vaccines (last visited Dec. 23, 2022).

within a short span of time, an increasing number of people were reluctant or refused to be vaccinated. This troubling phenomenon is known as vaccine hesitancy. Although public levels of trust in vaccines vary by country—for example, public acceptance of vaccines is much greater in China than in Russia[10]—vaccine hesitancy is nevertheless a global issue. As such, diminishing public trust in vaccines represents a global challenge to public health. Vaccine hesitancy results in fewer people being vaccinated and this, in turn, decreases the efficacy of public vaccination campaigns.[11] In this section, we discuss the problem of vaccine hesitancy and the complex factors that have contributed to eroding public trust (at least in certain segments of the population) in vaccines and scientific experts. We then identify ways in which public compensation schemes can improve public trust in vaccines.

The concept of "vaccine hesitancy" is somewhat ambiguous in the medical literature.[12] Notably, the World Health Organization (WHO) includes the "inconvenience in accessing vaccines" within this concept.[13] In this chapter, we propose using an attitudinal model in which vaccine hesitancy characterizes the attitudes and beliefs that influence someone's decision to be vaccinated (or refuse vaccination). On this view, vaccine hesitancy is "a state of indecision and uncertainty that precedes a decision to become (or not become) vaccinated."[14] By distinguishing *attitudes* (the mental states that shape decisions toward vaccinations) from *accessibility* (the external state of development of the primary healthcare within a

10. Jeffrey V. Lazarus et al., *A global survey of potential acceptance of a COVID-19 vaccine*. 27 Nat. Med. 225 (2021), *available at* https://doi.org/10.1038/s41591-020-1124-9.

11. "Vaccine hesitancy is threatening the historical achievements made in reducing the burden of infectious diseases, which have plagued humanity for centuries." *Vaccine hesitancy: a generation at risk*, 3 The Lancet Child & Adolescent Health 281 (2019), *available at* https://doi.org/10.1016/S2352-4642(19)30092-6; *see also* Daniel Freeman et al., *COVID-19 vaccine hesitancy in the UK: the Oxford coronavirus explanations, attitudes, and narratives survey (Oceans) II*, Psychol. Med. (2020), *available at* https://pubmed.ncbi.nlm.nih.gov/33305716/.

12. Patrick Peretti-Watel et al., *Vaccine hesitancy: clarifying a theoretical framework for an ambiguous notion*, PLoS Curr. (2015), *available at* https://pubmed.ncbi.nlm.nih.gov/25789201/.

13. World Health Organization, *Ten Threats to Global Health in 2019*, https://www.who.int/news-room/spotlight/ten-threats-to-global-health-in-2019 (last visited Dec. 23, 2022).

14. Heidi J. Larson et al., *The Vaccine-Hesitant Moment*, 387 N. Engl. J. Med. (2022), *available at* https://www.nejm.org/doi/full/10.1056/nejmra2106441.

particular region), we can examine more clearly the processes that shape negative attitudes toward vaccines.

In 2019, the WHO identified vaccine hesitancy as among the ten biggest threats to global health, alongside other threats such as HIV, Ebola, Dengue, climate change, and weak primary healthcare.[15] Vaccine hesitancy, according to the WHO, "threaten[ed] to reverse progress made in tackling vaccine-preventable diseases."[16] The same report tied vaccine hesitancy to the sharp resurgence of measles in countries that had come close to eliminating the disease.[17] Although the report did not specifically identify any country, there were spikes in measles outbreaks in the United States in 2014 and again in 2018 to 2019.[18] A recent *Lancet* report concluded that vaccine hesitancy at least partly caused measles outbreaks to persist in the United States.[19] Vaccine hesitancy can in effect erode previous gains made through successful vaccination campaigns.[20]

Although skepticism and lack of trust in vaccines is not a new phenomenon, the modern opposition to vaccination (or the "antivaxxer" movement) can be traced to two events. First, in 1998, British physician Andrew Wakefield and his colleagues published a study in *Lancet* claiming that measles, mumps, and rubella (MMR) vaccines predispose children to developmental disorders. *Lancet* later retracted Wakefield's study on the ground that there was no causal link between the MMR vaccine and autism.[21] Nonetheless, Wakefield's study was widely publicized and now forms a cornerstone of the influential antivaxxer movement that emerged over the past two decades.[22] Then, the following year

15. World Health Organization, *supra* note 13; I Ullah et al., *Myths and conspiracy theories on vaccines and COVID-19: Potential effect on global vaccine refusals*, 22 Vacunas 93–97 (2021).

16. World Health Organization, *supra* note 13

17. *Id.*

18. Centers for Disease Control and Prevention, *Measles Cases and Outbreaks*, https://www.cdc.gov/measles/cases-outbreaks.html (last visited Dec. 23, 2022).

19. Lauren Gardner et al., *Persistence of US measles risk due to vaccine hesitancy and outbreaks abroad*, The Lancet Infectious Diseases (2020), *available at* https://doi.org/10.1016/S1473-3099(20)30522-3.

20. "Such is the dominance of anti-vaccine disinformation online that [it] has seriously diminished vaccine uptake worldwide, leading to a dark renaissance of once-virtually conquered diseases." David Robert Grimes, *Medical disinformation and the unviable nature of COVID-19 conspiracy theories*, 16 PLoS ONE (2021), *available at* https://doi.org/10.1371/journal.pone.0245900.

21. Jason L. Schwartz, *The First Rotavirus Vaccine and the Politics of Acceptable Risk*, 90 Milbank Quarterly 278, 286 (2012), *available at* https://doi.org/10.1111/j.1468-0009.2012.00664.x.

22. *Id.*

in 1999, the U.S. Food and Drug Administration (FDA) began to assess whether childhood vaccines contained thimerosal (a mercury-based preservative). As a precautionary measure, the U.S. Public Health Service and the American Academy of Pediatrics recommended removing thimerosal from vaccines.[23] Although there was no evidence of harm, there was a significant decrease in infant vaccination for vaccines containing thimerosal following this recommendation.

The main causes of vaccine hesitancy are primarily epistemic: false beliefs shape people's decisions not to be vaccinated.[24] In her recent book, the philosopher Maya Goldenberg characterizes vaccine hesitancy as a "complex set of social, historical, and personal anxieties resulting in the expression of poor public trust in science and the health professions."[25] The public either relies on scientifically unreliable sources of information about vaccines or adopts a position of skepticism toward reliable scientific authorities and experts.[26] Vaccine hesitancy has been observed globally—multiple studies conducted in different countries have shown that these false beliefs mostly pertain to the safety and efficacy of vaccines.[27] According to one recent study, "[t]he most commonly stated reason for

---

23. Centers for Disease Control and Prevention, *Thimerosal in vaccines: a joint statement of the American Academy of Pediatrics and the Public Health Service,* 48 MORB. MORTAL WKLY. REP. 563 (1999).

24. Roland Imhoff & Pia Lamberty, *A bioweapon or a hoax: The link between distinct conspiracy beliefs about the coronavirus disease (COVID-19) outbreak and pandemic behavior*, 11 SOC. PSYCHOL. AND PERSONALITY SCI. (2020), *available at* https://journals.sagepub.com/doi/pdf/10.1177/1948550620934692 ("Conspiracy mentality . . . has been connected to distrust in both science in general . . . and the biomedical system more specifically . . . . [P]eople who endorse a conspiracy worldview are particularly unlikely to trust the expert recommendations aimed at reducing infection rates."

25. MAYA J. GOLDENBERG, VACCINE HESITANCY: PUBLIC TRUST, EXPERTISE, AND THE WAR ON SCIENCE 18 (2021).

26. Joseph E. Uscinski et al., *Why do people believe COVID-19 conspiracy theories?* THE HARVARD KENNEDY SCHOOL MISINFORMATION REVIEW, https://misinforeview.hks.harvard.edu/article/why-do-people-believe-covid-19-conspiracy-theories/; *see also* Lorenzo Palamenghi et al., *Mistrust in biomedical research and vaccine hesitancy: the forefront challenge in the battle against COVID-19 in Italy*, 35 EUR. J. EPIDEMIOL. (2020); Jan Hoffman, *How Anti-Vaccine Sentiment Took Hold in the United States*, N.Y. TIMES (Sept. 23, 2019), https://www.nytimes.com/2019/09/23/health/anti-vaccination-movement-us.html; Karin Roberts, *When It Comes to Vaccines, Celebrities Often Call the Shots*, NBC NEWS (Oct. 28, 2018), https://www.nbcnews.com/health/health-care/when-it-comes-vaccines-celebrities-often-call-shots-n925156.

27. Dott F. Rosiello et al., *Acceptance of COVID-19 vaccination at different hypothetical efficacy and safety levels in ten countries in Asia, Africa, South America* (Dec. 2021), *available at* https://narraj.org/main/article/view/55.

vaccine refusal is concern about safety (side effects)."[28] Such attitudes shaped by false beliefs are spread evenly across political and socioeconomic factors.[29]

False beliefs about the safety and efficacy of vaccines—and skepticism toward reliable scientific authorities—are exacerbated by social media.[30] Although the COVID-19 pandemic saw a number of false claims about vaccines circulating on social media, the problem is broader. A recent review published in the *New England Journal of Medicine* concluded that a "cascade of new Internet-based and social media technologies, allowed widespread access to information, as well as misinformation, and fueled the viral spread of questioning about vaccines."[31] False claims circulating on social media, or on the internet more generally, contribute to a pervasive skepticism toward scientific authority. Vaccine hesitancy is often not tied to a single vaccine—concerns about the safety and efficacy of one vaccine can result in concerns about the safety of vaccination overall. For instance, a vaccine scare relating to the human papillomavirus (HPV) vaccine in Denmark was followed by a decline in MMR vaccination.[32] Vaccine-related concerns are also not tied to a specific country but instead have global implications. For example, when the Japanese government suspended its recommendation of the HPV vaccine, news of this suspension "prompt[ed] a viral global spread of HPV vaccine hesitancy."[33]

Vaccine hesitancy based on safety concerns indirectly leads to vaccines being less efficacious. So long as people perceive vaccines as unsafe, they are likely to be more hesitant about becoming vaccinated. This also undermines the efficacy of vaccines, since vaccines are not effective unless a critical mass of people are inoculated.[34] Thus, concerns about vaccine efficacy and safety perpetuate a self-fulfilling cycle with

28. Julio S. Solis Arce et al., *COVID-19 vaccine acceptance and hesitancy in low- and middle-income countries*, NATURE (July 16, 2021), *available at* https://www.nature.com/articles/s41591-021-01454-y.

29. Freeman et al., *supra* note 11.

30. *See* David Robert Grimes, *Medical disinformation and the unviable nature of COVID-19 conspiracy theories*, 16 PLoS ONE (Mar. 12, 2021), *available at* https://doi.org/10.1371/journal.pone.0245900.

31. Larson et al., *supra* note 14.

32. M Gørtz et al., *The contagious nature of a vaccine scare: how the introduction of HPV vaccination lifted and eroded MMR vaccination in Denmark*, VACCINE (2020).

33. Larson et al., *supra* note 14.

34. *See* Freeman et al., *supra* note 11 at 1 ("The success of a safe, efficacious, coronavirus 2019 (COVID-19) vaccine will depend on uptake; if there are individuals who are reluctant or unwilling to be immunized, uptake will be limited.").

considerable harm to global public health. Not only does vaccine hesitancy put the individual at greater risk of contracting the disease, but it also increases the risk of transmission for the larger community.

Studies have shown that emphasizing vaccine safety and efficacy and the prosocial benefits of vaccination in public health messages are important ways to counter vaccine hesitancy. For example, a recent study pointed out that, "By offering information . . . addressing the main doubts raised by hesitant people . . . , it was possible to increase participants' intention to vaccinate."[35] An emphasis on "clear, accurate messages regarding vaccine safety and efficacy . . . can help to boost the general public confidence in COVID-19 vaccination."[36] Successful campaigns to increase vaccination rates among the general public have relied on a range of interventions to "nudge people with positive intention to vaccinate into action, through prompts, reminders, and incentives."[37]

Creating transparent public health messages can overcome hesitancy across both demographic lines and national borders. A recent study conducted across low-income countries across South America, South Asia, and the Middle East "demonstrate[ed] . . . how communication about the COVID-19 vaccine safety and efficacy can affect its acceptance."[38] Mass marketing and public awareness campaigns are ways of increasing public trust in vaccines. As *Lancet* noted prior to the pandemic, "Only a collaborative effort between pediatricians, family doctors, parents, public health officials, governments, the technology sector, and civil society will allow myths and misinformation around vaccination to be dispelled."[39] The fundamental question, however, is how to rebuild the public's trust and faith in experts and institutions once it has been eroded.[40] This is a long-term process that raises philosophical questions about how to create a climate of mutual trust between scientific experts and the public within a democratic society.[41] As a philosopher recently observed, "To

---

35. Piero Ronzani et al., *Countering vaccine hesitancy through medical expert endorsement*, 40 VACCINE (2022), *available at* https://doi.org/10.1016/j.vaccine.2022.06.031; Rosiello et al., *supra* note 27 at 13.

36. *See* Rosiello et al., *supra* note 27; *see* Freeman et al., *supra* note 11.

37. GOLDENBERG, *supra* note 25 at 175.

38. Rosiello et al., *supra* note 27.

39. *Vaccine hesitancy: a generation at risk*, *supra* note 11.

40. Lorenzo Palamenghi et al., *Mistrust in biomedical research and vaccine hesitancy: the forefront challenge in the battle against COVID-19 in Italy*, 35 EUR. J. EPIDEMIOL. (2020).

41. PHILIP KITCHER, SCIENCE IN A DEMOCRATIC SOCIETY (2011); NAOMI ORESKES, WHY TRUST SCIENCE? (2019).

counter falling public trust in scientific institutions, public health agencies and experts must move their ideas and communications beyond false ideals of scientism and work to address vaccine hesitancy by responding to discrimination within their institutions, reforming their susceptibility to industry influence, and appealing to shared values and priorities with public stakeholders."[42]

Although public health and other educational campaigns can "sensitize, educate, and engage the public" toward scientific studies and developments, the basic concerns about the safety and efficacy of vaccines must still be engaged with directly.[43] A critical way of building trust is to take concrete steps to ensure that fears about vaccines, well-founded or not, are adequately addressed. In other words, public trust in scientists and institutions can be rebuilt not simply by educating the public but by supporting those scientific claims with effective guarantees to mitigate possible future harm. Having a swift, effective, and generous compensation scheme for those who may suffer side effects from vaccination may help in building that public trust. Such compensation funds would effectively function as insurance mechanisms for those who develop unintended side effects from vaccines.

Background on No-Fault Compensation Schemes and Liability Protection Programs

Effective mechanisms for compensating individuals who suffer from vaccine-related injuries are no-fault compensation schemes. No-fault compensation schemes provide a simplified process to qualify individuals who are injured as a result of a vaccine for compensation without having to establish liability or fault on the part of a specific manufacturer. No-fault compensation programs go together with manufacturer liability protection programs. Because individuals incur a risk to themselves by getting vaccinated, and given the increased fears regarding vaccine safety, the prospect of compensation can provide insurance to compensate for this risk and improve vaccination rates.[44] Compensation schemes

42. Goldenberg, *supra* note 25 at 169.

43. Palamenghi et al., *supra* note 40.

44. *See* Gareth Millward, *A Disability Act? The Vaccine Damage Payments Act 1979 and the British Government's Response to the Pertussis Vaccine Scare*, 30 Soc. Hist. Med. 429, 440–41 (2016), *available at* https://academic.oup.com/shm/article/30/2/429/2669669/; D'Errico et al., *"First Do No Harm." No-Fault Compensation Program for COVID-19 Vaccines as Feasibility and Wisdom of a Policy*

also ensure that vaccine manufacturers will continue to develop vaccines without fearing large and possibly ruinous compensation awards. Without protection from liability, manufacturers are disincentivized from expending the capital required to develop and manufacture vaccines.[45] In this section, we discuss two programs in the United States that provide compensation mechanisms to those injured from certain vaccines and liability protections to vaccine manufacturers: the Vaccine Injury Compensation Program (VICP) and the Countermeasures Injury Compensation Program (CICP).

The VICP

The VICP was created by the National Childhood Vaccine Injury Act of 1986 (NCVIA) as a response to a wave of pertussis vaccine litigation and the resulting concern that vaccine manufacturers would diminish or cease vaccine production.[46] In 1981, the Office of Technology Assessment issued a report for the House Interstate and Foreign Commerce Committee, proposing a compensation fund that granted some immunity to vaccine manufacturers.[47] The report suggested that a compensation program was necessary to encourage vaccination and to prevent manufacturers from leaving the vaccine market.[48] Thereafter, as reports emerged blaming the pertussis vaccine for causing encephalopathy, extensive litigation against the pertussis vaccine producers ensued. In the three years after a British researcher claimed that the pertussis vaccine caused permanent brain damage in 22 children, personal injury lawyers in the United States

---

Instrument to Mitigate Vaccine Hesitancy, VACCINES (BASEL) (Sept. 30, 2021), *available at* https://www.ncbi.nlm.nih.gov/pmc/articles/PMC8540114/.

45. W. Kip Viscusi et al., *A Statistical Profile of Pharmaceutical Industry Liability, 1976-1989*, 24 SETON HALL L. REV. 1418, 1419 (1994) ("[T]he net effect of the surge in liability costs ha[s] been to discourage innovation in the pharmaceutical industry."); Richard A. Epstein, *Legal Liability for Medical Innovation*, 8 CARDOZO L. REV. 1139, 1153 (1987) ("If in the aggregate the net gains are wiped out by the liability costs, then the product will no longer be made.").

46. Health Resources & Services Administration (HRSA), *About the National Vaccine Injury Compensation Program*, *available at* https://www.hrsa.gov/vaccine-compensation/about (last visited Dec. 23, 2022); James D. Cherry, *The 112-Year Odyssey of Pertussis and Pertussis Vaccines—Mistakes Made and Implications for the Future*, 8 J. OF THE PEDIATRIC INFECTIOUS DISEASES SOCIETY 334–41 (Sept. 2019), https://doi.org/10.1093/jpids/piz005.

47. *Compensation for Vaccine-Related Injuries*, Office of Technology Assessment (1981), 19–20.

48. *Id.* at 20.

filed 800 lawsuits against vaccine manufacturers.[49] The costs associated with defending these lawsuits were added to the price of the pertussis vaccine, which rose from $.011 per dose to $11.00 per dose between 1981 and 1986.[50] Further research revealed that the concerns about the pertussis vaccine were unwarranted, but the vaccine's public image was damaged beyond repair. Three manufacturers of the pertussis vaccine ceased production, leaving just one manufacturer in the market, Lederle. Eventually, Lederle, was faced with a vaccine injury claim that resulted in an award that was equivalent to more than half the value of the entire pertussis vaccine market in the United States.[51]

Facing this litigation onslaught, vaccine manufacturers "threatened to cause vaccine shortages and reduce vaccination rates."[52] In response, and out of concern for diminished vaccine access, Congress established the VICP as an alternative mechanism to traditional tort litigation.[53]

The VICP provides compensation for vaccine-related injuries or death for certain vaccines that are routinely administered to children and pregnant women.[54] Specifically, the VICP is limited to those vaccines that are enumerated on the statute-mandated Vaccine Injury Table (known as "the Table").[55] For a vaccine to be added to the Table, the CDC and the Health and Human Services (HHS) Secretary must recommend the vaccine for "routine administration to children" or "routine administration in pregnant women," which is a lengthy process.[56] If a vaccine is part of the Table, individuals can submit claims for compensation with the U.S. Court of Federal Claims, commonly referred to as the Vaccine

49. Paul A. Offit, *Why Are Pharmaceutical Companies Gradually Abandoning Vaccines?*, 24 HEALTH AFFAIRS 622 (2005), at 626–27.

50. Ken S. Rosenthal & Daniel H. Zimmerman, *Vaccines: All Things Considered*, 13 CLIN. VACCINE IMMUNOL. (2006), available at https://www.ncbi.nlm.nih.gov/pmc/articles/PMC1539119/.

51. *Id.* at 627.

52. HRSA, *supra* note 46.

53. Cherry, *supra* note 46.

54. HRSA, *supra* note 46; Kevin J. Hickey & Erin H. Ward, *Compensation Programs for Potential COVID-19 Vaccine Injuries*, CONGRESSIONAL RESEARCH SERVICE (Oct. 20, 2021), https://crsreports.congress.gov/product/pdf/LSB/LSB10584.

55. Vaccine Injury Table, 42 U.S.C. § 300aa-14 (2018).

56. Health Resources & Services Administration (HRSA), *Covered Vaccines*, https://www.hrsa.gov/vaccine-compensation/covered-vaccines (last visited Dec. 23, 2022).

Court.[57] The applicant must show that the vaccine caused or significantly aggravated an injury, or that he or she suffered an injury that is enumerated in the Table that grants the presumption that the injury was caused by the vaccination.[58] When causation is not proven, applicants may still receive payment in the form of a settlement that does not admit manufacturer fault.[59]

The VICP limits the possibility of civil lawsuits against vaccine manufacturers because claimants must go through the above-enumerated process before filing any civil action.[60] Further, the VICP ensures that vaccine manufacturers are not liable for vaccine injuries or deaths that result from "unavoidable side effects from properly prepared vaccines accompanied by proper directions and warnings."[61]

However, the VICP's protection against liability is not absolute. Once a claimant exhausts the VICP process by filing a claim and rejecting the decision of the Vaccine Court, he or she may file a civil lawsuit against the vaccine manufacturer or administrator.[62] Likewise, if the petition is determined to be noncompensable or is dismissed under the VICP, or the vaccine is not covered by the VICP, the applicant may also file a tort lawsuit in court.[63]

The VICP is funded by an excise tax of $0.75 per dose of a CDC-recommended, routinely administered vaccine.[64] The proceeds of this tax are placed into the Vaccine Injury Compensation Trust Fund (hereinafter "Trust Fund"), which is managed by the U.S. Department of the

57. Health Resources & Services Administration (HRSA), *Vaccine Compensation*, https://www.hrsa.gov/vaccine-compensation/how-to-file (last visited Dec. 23, 2022).

58. Federal Register, *National Vaccine Injury Compensation Program: Revisions to the Vaccine Injury Table*, https://www.federalregister.gov/documents/2017/01/19/2017-00701/national-vaccine-injury-compensation-program-revisions-to-the-vaccine-injury-table (last visited Dec. 23, 2022).

59. Health Resources & Services Administration (HRSA), *About the National Vaccine Injury Compensation Program*, https://www.hrsa.gov/vaccine-compensation/about (last visited Dec. 23, 2022).

60. Hickey & Ward, *supra* note 54.

61. *Id.*

62. Health Resources & Services Administration (HRSA), *Frequently Asked Questions*, https://www.hrsa.gov/vaccine-compensation/faq (last visited Dec. 23, 2022).

63. Health Resources & Services Administration (HRSA), *National Vaccine Injury Compensation Program*, https://www.in.gov/health/immunization/files/VICP.pdf.

64. HRSA, *supra* note 59.

Treasury.[65] From this Trust Fund, payments are made to compensate individuals for injuries or deaths stemming from a covered vaccine, with a cap of $250,000 for vaccine-related deaths and $250,000 for actual and projected pain and suffering for a vaccine-related injury.[66] There is no cap, however, on the other types of expenses that the VICP covers, such as nonreimbursable medical expenses, lost earnings, and attorneys' fees.[67]

While the VICP provides a mechanism for compensation and limits liability for manufacturers, it is far from perfect. For one, as noted above, vaccine manufacturers can still face civil lawsuits for vaccine-related injuries and deaths, creating a risk and burden for vaccine manufacturers that may discourage the development of new vaccines.[68] A recent multidistrict litigation (MDL) regarding Gardasil, a vaccine developed to treat HPV, demonstrates the liability risk that remains under the VICP.[69] As an HPV vaccine, Gardasil is included on the Table and covered under the VICP.[70] Accordingly, plaintiffs wanting to bring a claim related to loss or injury resulting from the administration of Gardasil had to first exhaust the claims process in the Court of Federal Claims. After a group of plaintiffs exhausted this process, they began filing claims in federal court and thereafter successfully created an unprecedented MDL, the first such litigation involving claims subject to the VICP. In this MDL, plaintiffs raise claims that they, or their minor children, developed postural orthostatic tachycardia syndrome and other injuries as an autoimmune reaction to the Gardasil vaccine. As Merck, the manufacturer of Gardasil and defendant in the action, argued to the Judicial Panel on Multi-District Litigation, allowing litigation to be consolidated and aggregated further burdens an already overwhelmed VICP[71] and raises concerns about liability disincentivizing vaccine development, as the consolidation and aggregation of claims artificially inflate the settlement value of the claims of existing and future plaintiffs. The "blackmail settlement" problem associated

65. 26 U.S.C. § 9510.

66. Health Resources & Services Administration (HRSA), *What You Need to Know About the National Vaccine Injury Compensation Program (VICP)* at 12, https://www.hrsa.gov/sites/default/files/hrsa/vicp/about-vaccine-injury-compensation-program-booklet.pdf.

67. *Id.*

68. Viscusi et al., *supra* note 45; Richard A. Epstein, *supra* note 45.

69. *In re* Gardasil Products Liability Litigation, No. MDL 3036, 2022 WL 3138681 (U.S. Jud. Pan. Mult. Lit. Aug. 4, 2022).

70. Health Resources & Services Administration (HRSA), *Vaccine Injury Table*, https://www.hrsa.gov/sites/default/files/hrsa/vicp/vaccine-injury-table-01-03-2022.pdf (last visited Dec. 23, 2022).

71. *Id.*

with consolidated mass torts was identified by Judge Henry J. Friendly almost 50 years ago.[72]

Further, with just eight special masters, the VICP's Vaccine Court is understaffed, which significantly delays the adjudication of claims.[73] The Government Accountability Office released a study in 2014 that found that most of the approximately 10,000 claims filed with the VICP since 1999 took several years to decide, with more than 1,000 claims still pending as of March 31, 2014.[74]

The VICP is also limited in its reach. The compensation mechanism only applies to the enumerated vaccines in the Table, and it can take months for a new vaccine to be added as the Table needs to be modified by "regulation after consulting with the Advisory Commission on Childhood Vaccines, posting a notice, and soliciting public comment."[75] Further, the VICP is largely restricted to domestic application, and only in limited circumstances can it be applied extraterritorially where there is a clear nexus to the United States.[76] As such, the VICP does not protect manufacturers from liability for vaccines administered internationally to non-U.S. residents.

The CICP and the PREP Act

Another no-fault compensation scheme in the United States is the CICP, which was created in 2010 pursuant to the U.S. Public Readiness and Emergency Preparedness Act (PREP Act). The PREP Act was enacted on December 30, 2005, in the wake of the severe acute respiratory syndrome (SARS) and avian flu epidemics, as an amendment to the Public Health Service Act.[77] It authorizes the HHS Secretary to issue a declaration in

72. Henry J. Friendly, Federal Jurisdiction: A General View 120 (1973).

73. *See* Eli Wolfe, *Federal vaccine court quietly pays out billions*, Salon.com (Dec. 23, 2018), https://www.salon.com/2018/12/23/federal-vaccine-court-quietyly-pays-out-billins_partner/; Tom Hals, *COVID-19 era highlights U.S. 'black hole' compensation fund for pandemic vaccine injuries*, Reuters (Aug. 21, 2020), https://www.reuters.com/article/us-health-coronavirus-vaccines-liability/covid-19-era-highlights-u-s-black-hole-compensation-fund-for-pandemic-vaccine-injuries-idUSKBN25H1E8.

74. Government Accountability Office, *Vaccine Injury Compensation* (Nov. 2014), https://www.gao.gov/assets/670/667136.pdf (last visited Dec. 23, 2022).

75. Health Resources & Services Administration (HRSA), *Frequently Asked Questions*, https://www.hrsa.gov/vaccine-compensation/faq#Covered (last visited Dec. 23, 2022).

76. 42 U.S.C. § 300aa–11(c)(1)(B) (2018).

77. Public Readiness and Emergency Preparedness Act, Pub. L. No. 109-148, 42 U.S.C. § 247d, 119 Stat. 2818 (2005).

the Federal Register providing immunity from tort liability for claims of loss or injury caused by countermeasures against diseases or other threats to public health emergencies. As relevant to vaccine manufacturers, the PREP Act provides immunity from liability to persons and entities involved in the manufacture, testing, distribution, administration, and use of "covered countermeasures."[78] A covered countermeasure under the PREP Act includes a drug, device, or biological product manufactured, used, designed, developed, modified, licensed, or procured to diagnose, mitigate, prevent, treat, or cure a pandemic or epidemic or limit the harm such a pandemic or epidemic might otherwise cause.[79]

The PREP Act's no-fault compensation scheme, the CICP, compensates individuals for serious physical injury or death directly caused by the administration or use of a "countermeasure," as defined by the HHS Secretary to include certain vaccines.[80] The CICP is "a regulatory process" managed by the Health Resources and Services Administration (HRSA), an agency within HHS, and unlike the VICP, does not have any adjudication component.[81] To apply for compensation, an individual must complete a form and submit medical evidence and other supporting documentation.[82] The CICP only compensates claims for serious injury and death, including reasonable medical expenses, lost income, and a set death benefit.[83] It does not provide compensation for emotional injury,

---

78. The Coronavirus Aid, Relief and Economic Security Act PL 116-136, § 3103 ("CARES Act"), enacted on March 27, 2020, amended the PREP Act to authorize nonmedical respiratory protective devices as covered countermeasures if they are approved by the National Institute for Occupational Safety and Health (NIOSH). If NIOSH approves a respiratory protective device, that device must still be subject to an emergency use authorization (EUA) issued by the FDA. The CARES Act also revised the covered person definition to limit liability for volunteer healthcare professionals—whether or not they have administered a covered countermeasure. Under the CARES Act amendments to the PREP Act, qualified healthcare volunteers are not liable for the provision of healthcare services during the present public health emergency with respect to COVID-19 (*id*. at § 3215).

79. 42 U.S.C. § 247d-6d(i)(1).

80. Health Resources & Services Administration (HRSA), *About the Countermeasures Injury Compensation Program*, https://www.hrsa.gov/cicp/about (last visited Dec. 23, 2022); Hickey & Ward, *supra* note 54.

81. Kevin J. Hickey & Erin H. Ward, *Compensation Programs for COVID-19 Vaccine Injuries*, Congressional Research Service (December 9, 2021), https://sgp.fas.org/crs/misc/R46982.pdf.

82. *Id.*

83. Hickey & Ward, *supra* note 54.

fear of injury, business losses, or pain and suffering damages, or award attorneys' fees.[84]

Protection from liability is provided for vaccine manufacturers regardless of the method in which the vaccine was sold or distributed, including through government contracts or by hospitals or pharmacies.[85] When a vaccine is administered outside the United States, the CICP only applies to otherwise eligible individuals at American embassies or military installations abroad or at North Atlantic Treaty Organization (NATO) installations.[86]

The CICP is funded by Congressional appropriations to the Covered Countermeasure(s) Process Fund (CCPF).[87] The CICP currently has a $422,035 limit on compensation for death and a $50,000 limit on lost employment income.[88] Since its establishment in 2010 and through November 2022, the CICP received 11,159 total claims and paid out 30 of them (less than 1 percent), totaling just over six million dollars in awards.[89] In 2021, it was reported that the average payment was approximately $207,000.[90] Tellingly, of the 262,908,216 people who have received at least one dose of a COVID-19 vaccine,[91] only 10,646 have alleged injuries or death relating to COVID-19 countermeasures, of which 7,582 alleged claims related to COVID-19 vaccines.[92] Nine of these claims have been deemed eligible for compensation, all of which relate to injuries or death from COVID-19 vaccines, and are awaiting submission of supporting documents.[93]

---

84. *Id.*

85. John D. Winter et al., *Toward a Global Solution on Vaccine Liability and Compensation*, 74 Food and Drug Law Journal 1, 11 (2019).

86. 42 U.S.C. § 110.3(f)(2) (2010).

87. Junying Zhao et al., *Reforming the countermeasures injury compensation program for COVID-19 and beyond: An economic perspective*, 9 J. Law Biosci. (2022).

88. Hickey & Ward, *supra* note 81 at 5; U.S. Department of Justice Bureau of Justice Assistance, *Benefits by Year*, https://bja.ojp.gov/program/psob/resources/benefits-by-year (last visited Dec. 23, 2022).

89. Health Resources & Services Administration (HRSA), *Countermeasures Injury Compensation Program (CICP) Data*, https://www.hrsa.gov/cicp/cicp-data#table-1 (last visited Dec. 23, 2022).

90. Jacquie Lee & Ian Lopez, *Covid-19 Vaccine Recipients Face Injury Payment 'Black Hole,'* Bloomberg Law (Mar. 23, 2021), https://news.bloomberglaw.com/pharma-and-life-sciences/covid-19-vaccine-recipients-face-injury-payment-black-hole.

91. USA Facts, *US Coronavirus vaccine tracker*, https://usafacts.org/visualizations/covid-vaccine-tracker-states (last visited Dec. 23, 2022).

92. HRSA, *supra* note 89.

93. *Id.*

The CICP has been heavily criticized, especially as compared to the VICP. For example, the CICP's compensation payments have been described as inadequate and lower than those of the VICP,[94] potentially due to the CICP's higher burden of proof,[95] shorter statute of limitations,[96] and the unavailability of compensation for pain and suffering damages. Further, unlike the VICP, the CICP does not allow applicants to appeal administrative decisions to a civil court. While this reduces liability for vaccine manufacturers, it limits the program's accountability and transparency.[97] In fact, the CICP does not provide any "guarantee of legal representation, a hearing, or a publicly available final decision,"[98] which limits the program's accessibility for lay people.[99] The CICP also has unusually high administrative costs that require reform.[100] In a study published in April 2022, scholars estimated that "[i]f administrative costs were added at the historical rate of 94%, the program would face about $317.94 million in total outlays, a 5,138% increase, 72.1 times its current balance, making the CICP highly likely unable to compensate for current COVID-19 claims."[101] Although the CCPF paid about $0.57 million in compensation in fiscal years 2017 through 2021, $8.64 million was spent on administrative costs in that same time frame. In other words, it costs the CCPF in administrative costs 15 times the amount paid out to compensate vaccine-related injuries.[102] Currently, claims for compensation due to injury or death caused by COVID-19 vaccines can only be

---

94. Maryanne Demasi, *Covid-19: Is the US compensation scheme for vaccine injuries fit for purpose?*, BMJ (Apr. 19, 2022), https://www.bmj.com/content/377/bmj.o919.

95. While for the VICP, causation must be proven by a preponderance of the evidence, the CICP "only allows claims for 'serious physical injury or death' arising via 'willful misconduct' in the administration of a countermeasure." Kimberly K. Henrickson, *Immunizing the Immunizers: How COVID-19 Vaccine Injury Claims and the CICP Will Increase Anti-Vaccine Sentiment in the United States and How HRSA Can Prevent It*, 77 FOOD AND DRUG LAW J. 93, 106.

96. "In the VICP, injured petitioners have until three years after the first symptom of the vaccine injury manifests to file a claim. Similarly, death claims must be filed within two years of the death and four years of when the first symptom of the vaccine injury that led to the death appeared. Under the CICP, however, claimants must file for benefits within one year after the administration of the countermeasure that led to the injury." *Id.* at 109.

97. Zhao et al., *supra* note 87.

98. Lee & Lopez, *supra* note 90.

99. Henrickson, *supra* note 95 at 108.

100. Zhao et al., *supra* note 87.

101. *Id.*

102. *Id.*

filed through the CICP,[103] but due to the CICP's limitations, scholars are advocating that all COVID-19 compensation claims should be handled by the VICP instead.[104]

Table 1 summarizes the differences between the VICP and CICP programs:[105]

Table 1 Comparison of Vaccine-Injury Compensation Programs: CICP v. VICP

	Countermeasures Injury Compensation Program (CICP)	Vaccine Injury Compensation Program (VICP)
Scope of Coverage	"Covered countermeasures" under the PREP Act, such as pandemic and epidemic products used to treat, mitigate, prevent, or cure COVID-19 (e.g., vaccines, PPE, treatments)	"Covered vaccines" are those recommended by CDC for routine administration to children or pregnant women, subject to a federal excise tax, and included on the Vaccine Injury Table
Covered Injuries	Death or serious physical injury that (1) warrants hospitalization or (2) led to a significant loss of function or disability	Death or an illness, injury, or condition that lasted more than six months or required inpatient hospitalization and surgical intervention and was associated with one or more vaccines in the Vaccine Injury Table, unless the cause was an adulterant or contaminant that was intentionally added to the vaccine
Process for Obtaining Compensation	Administrative process: file request form and supporting documentation with CICP to prove eligibility and compensation amounts	Judicial process ("vaccine court"): file a petition in the U.S. Court of Federal Claims
Available Benefits	Reasonable medical expenses, lost employment income, and death benefits	Nonreimbursed expenses related to the injury for the diagnosis, medical care, and various rehabilitation and recovery services; lost employment income; pain, suffering, and emotional distress damages; death benefits; attorneys' fees

103. HRSA, *supra* note 62.
104. Demasi, *supra* note 94.
105. Hickey & Ward, *supra* note 54.

	Countermeasures Injury Compensation Program (CICP)	**Vaccine Injury Compensation Program (VICP)**
Unavailable Benefits	Attorneys' fees, pain and suffering damages, and punitive damages	Punitive or exemplary damages
Benefit Caps	$50,000/year for lost employment income (lifetime cap is generally $379,000); standard death benefit of $370,376 for FY2021	$250,000 for death; $250,000 for pain and suffering and emotional distress
Filing Deadlines	Within one year of the administration of the covered countermeasure (or within one year of the issuance of a new Countermeasure Injury Table)	For injuries, within three years of the first symptom; for deaths, within two years of the death and four years of the first symptom
Standard of Proof	Must show the injury (1) meets the requirements on a Countermeasure Injury Table or (2) was a direct result of the administration or use of a covered countermeasure	Must show the person (1) received a vaccine on the Vaccine Injury Table; (2) sustained or significantly aggravated an illness, disability, injury, or condition, or died; (3) the illness, disability, injury, condition, or death is either listed in the Vaccine Injury Table in association with the vaccine and occurred within a set time period as specified in the table or was caused by the vaccine; (4) suffered the effects for more than six months or required inpatient hospitalization and surgery or died; and (5) has not previously collected an award for the injury or death
Initial Decision-Maker	CICP (as delegate of the Secretary of HHS)	U.S. Court of Federal Claims special master
Appeals and Judicial Review	Claimant may seek reconsideration of CICP decision to a qualified independent panel within 60 days; no further judicial or administrative review	Claimant may seek review of special master decision by U.S. Court of Federal Claims within 30 days of decision; claimant may seek review by the U.S. Court of Appeals for the Federal Circuit within 60 days of final judgment; claimant may accept the judgment or reject it and file a tort claim

	Countermeasures Injury Compensation Program (CICP)	Vaccine Injury Compensation Program (VICP)
Funding Source	Emergency appropriations to Covered Countermeasure Process Fund	Vaccine Injury Compensation Trust Fund based on excise tax of $0.75 per dose on "taxable vaccines"
Number of Claims Processed	Non-COVID-19 claims (2010 to 2021): 491 claims, of which 452 were determined ineligible and 29 compensated (6 percent) COVID-19 countermeasure claims (as of September 1, 2021): 2,392 claims, of which 1,031 claims (43 percent) relate to COVID-19 vaccines; most of these claims (99.9 percnt) remain in or pending review	24,441 petitions as of October 1, 2021, of which 20,300 have been adjudicated, 11,947 were determined ineligible, and 8,353 compensated (41 percent)
Process for Adding New Vaccines	Scope of "covered countermeasures" is determined by Secretary of HHS's PREP Act declarations (within statutory limits)	Secretary of HHS may add vaccines to the Vaccine Injury Table that are (1) subject to the excise tax and (2) recommended by the CDC for routine administration to children or pregnant women

Source: HRSA; CRS; 42 U.S.C. §§ 300aa-10 to 300aa-34; 42 U.S.C. § 247d-6d to -6e; 42 C.F.R. pt. 110.

International Compensation Programs

Historical Approaches to Limiting Vaccine Liability Outside the United States

Outside of the United States, there are no-fault compensation programs operating in 25 of the 194 WHO member states.[106] The specific mechanisms of these programs, and the extent to which they provide compensation and limit manufacturer liability, differ from country to country.

Sixteen European countries have no-fault compensation funds: Austria, Denmark, Finland, France, Germany, Hungary, Iceland, Italy, Latvia, Luxembourg, Norway, Russia, Slovenia, Sweden, Switzerland,

106. Randy G. Mungwira et al., *Economic and Immunisation Safety Surveillance Characteristics of Countries Implementing No-Fault Compensation Programmes for Vaccine Injuries*, 37 VACCINES 4370, 4372 (2019), *available at* https://doi.org/10.1016/j.vaccine.2019.06.018.

and the United Kingdom.[107] In most of these countries, the compensation funds were established through legislation and are administered by government departments. Claimants may seek compensation through no-fault schemes or through the courts in their country, but not both, meaning that the risk of liability remains for vaccine manufacturers in those countries. Importantly, these jurisdictions largely do not have the same tort system that exists in the United States, as the United States is unusual in how it combines both a robust tort system premised on jury trials and a highly litigious culture.[108] Thus, the fact that manufacturers can be sued in jurisdictions outside the United States does not result in the same level of litigation exposure as in the United States due to the unpredictability of personal injury jury awards in this country.[109] In addition, vaccine compensation awards are circumscribed in other countries. For instance, in France, applicants may receive compensation for disabilities and lost income stemming from state-mandated vaccinations through a state-managed compensation fund or through litigation.[110] Compensation

107. Randy G. Mungwira et al., *Global landscape analysis of no-fault compensation programmes for vaccine injuries: A review and survey of implementing countries*, 15 PLOS ONE (2020), *available at* https://www.ncbi.nlm.nih.gov/pmc/articles/PMC7241762/.

108. *See* Robert A. Kagan, Adversarial Legalism: The American Way of Law (2d ed. 2019); *see also* Ulrich Magnus, *Why Is US Tort Law so Different*, 1 JETL 102 (2010).

109. In his comparative study of how different jurisdictions deal with tort claims, the political scientist Robert A. Kagan concludes that the U.S. legal system is "enormously threatening to actual and potential defendants," because of the size and unpredictability of jury awards and the scope of discretion afforded juries to impose punitive damages. Kagan, *supra* note 108. Kagan points out that "American tort law appears to over-deter, inducing precautions that make products and services much more (and arguable unreasonably) expensive or that suppress the provision of products and services that would actually reduce the risk of harm." *Id.* at 16970. One of the examples that Kagan gives for this tendency of over-deterrence is the tort litigation that nearly resulted in manufacturers of the DPT vaccine to discontinue the vaccine. *Id.* By contrast, most civil law jurisdictions in Western Europe have broad-based social insurance schemes for compensating workers that are funded by various kinds of taxes. In those jurisdictions, "Tort law damages are limited to economic loss that are not covered by such medical and social insurance programs; noneconomic damages are legally specified and moderate in amount." *Id.* at 154.

110. *See* Clare Looker & Heath Kelly, *No-Fault Compensation Following Adverse Events Attributed to Vaccination: A Review of International Programmes*, Bull. World Health Org., 3 (Mar. 21, 2011), *available at* https://pubmed.ncbi.nlm.nih.gov/21556305/.

schemes in Denmark and the United Kingdom deduct any compensation payments made through the courts from the fund payout.[111]

No-fault vaccine compensation funds exist in eight Asian and Pacific countries/regions: China, Japan, New Zealand, Nepal, Republic of Korea, Taiwan, Thailand, and Vietnam.[112] The fund in Japan applies to all vaccines for diseases specified in Japan's Preventive Vaccination Act and TB Central Law,[113] and in Taiwan, all "routine and compulsory vaccines" are covered.[114] New Zealand's scheme, part of its broader abolition of most tort litigation, is administered through a statutory corporation called the Accident Compensation Corporation (ACC) and provides extensive coverage for any personal injury or death caused by "accident."[115]

Canada only has a vaccine injury compensation fund in the province of Quebec, which is known as the Compensation for Victims of Vaccination Program.[116] "[A]ny victim of bodily injury caused by a voluntary vaccination against disease" is eligible for compensation. Victim is defined as "the vaccinated person, a person having contracted the disease from a vaccinated person, the foetus of either such persons" and bodily injury includes "serious permanent physical or mental injury, or death."[117] A committee consisting of three physicians evaluates each claim to determine whether there is a probable causal link between the vaccine and the injury.[118]

---

111. *Id.*

112. Mungwira et al., *supra* note 107.

113. National Research Council (US) Division of Health Promotion and Disease Prevention, *Vaccine Supply and Innovation*, NATIONAL ACADEMIES PRESS (1985), *available at* https://www.ncbi.nlm.nih.gov/books/NBK216818.

114. Ping-Cheng Wang, *Updates on Vaccine Injury Compensation Program in Taiwan and Program Evaluation*, TAIWAN EPIDEMIOLOGY BULLETIN, *available at* https://www.cdc.gov.tw/En/File/Get/nDYkbF-ODBJh7hLtNk5TUQ.

115. The Treasury of New Zealand, *Accident Compensation Corporation*, https://www.treasury.govt.nz/information-and-services/commercial-portfolio-and-advice/commercial-portfolio/accident-compensation-corporation#:~:text=ACC%20provides%20comprehensive%2C%20no%2Dfault,they%20have%20had%20an%20accident; https://www.commonwealthfund.org/publications/journal-article/2006/feb/no-fault-compensation-new-zealand-harmonizing-injury (last visited Dec. 23, 2022).

116. *See* Public Health Act, Chapter VII, Division III, *available at* http://www2.publicationsduquebec.gouv.qc.ca/dynamicSearch/telecharge.php?type=2&file=/S_2_2/S2_2_A.html.

117. *Id.*

118. *See* Quebec Government, *Vaccine Injury Compensation Program, available at* https://www.quebec.ca/en/health/advice-and-prevention/vaccination/vaccine-injury-compensation-program/ (last visited Dec. 23, 2022).

COVAX No-Fault Compensation Scheme

Given the wide disparities in how compensation programs are applied around the world and the global impact of the COVID-19 pandemic, the need for a globally coordinated no-fault compensation scheme should be evident. During the height of the pandemic, it also became clear that vaccine access was inequitable across the world. For example, within the first year of the distribution of COVID-19 vaccines, high-income countries achieved vaccination rates of 75 to 80 percent, while low-income countries vaccinated less than 10 percent of their populations.[119]

COVAX was created as an attempt to remedy these problems. It is one of the three pillars of the Access to COVID-19 Tools (ACT) Accelerator and aims to "provid[e] innovative and equitable access" to COVID-19 vaccines.[120] To receive doses through COVAX, all participating countries must sign indemnity agreements with "manufacturers, donors, distributors and other stakeholders . . . against any losses they incur from the deployment and use of" COVID-19 vaccines.[121] As of November 25, 2022, 1.83 billion COVID-19 vaccine doses were delivered through COVAX to 146 countries.[122]

A key innovation of COVAX is its no-fault compensation mechanism for COVID-19 vaccine injuries—the first such program on a global level.[123] The compensation component of COVAX was operationalized in March 2021.[124] It was created and is co-led by the WHO, Global Alliance

---

119. Victoria Pilkington et al., *Global COVID-19 Vaccine Inequity: Failures in the First Year of Distribution and Potential Solutions for the Future,* Front. Public Health (Mar. 7, 2022), *available at* https://www.frontiersin.org/articles/10.3389/fpubh.2022.821117/full.

120. Vaccines Work, *COVAX Explained*, Gavi, *available at* https://www.gavi.org/vaccineswork/covax-explained (last visited Dec. 23, 2022).

121. Ariel Gorodensky & Jillian Kohler, *State capture through indemnification demands? Effects on equity in the global distribution of COVID-19 vaccines*, J. of Pharm. Policy and Pract. 15, 50 (2022), *available at* https://doi.org/10.1186/s40545-022-00442-y; Anju Ghangurde, *Claims Stream in under COVAX No-Fault Compensation Program*, Citeline (July 7, 2021), https://pharmaintelligence.informa.com/resources/product-content/claims-stream-in-under-covax-no-fault-compensation-program.

122. Marta Frackowiak et al., *Factbox: Vaccines Delivered under COVAX Sharing Scheme for Poorer Countries*, Reuters (Nov. 25, 2022), https://www.reuters.com/business/healthcare-pharmaceuticals/vaccines-delivered-under-covax-sharing-scheme-poorer-countries-2022-01-03/.

123. Vaccines Work, *The COVAX No Fault Compensation Programme: Explained,* Gavi, *available at* https://www.gavi.org/vaccineswork/covax-no-fault-compensation-programme-explained.

124. Ghangurde, *supra* note 121.

for Vaccines and Immunization (Gavi), and the Coalition for Epidemic Preparedness Innovations (CEPI), and relies on the United Nations Children's Fund (UNICEF) as its delivery partner.[125] ESIS, Inc.,[126] a Chubb[127] company, functions as its independent claims administrator.[128] The compensation program is funded by donor contributions on the basis of a $0.10 levy per dose for two-dose vaccines and a $0.20 levy per dose for single-dose vaccines.[129] In total, the compensation fund provides up to $150 million for compensation payments to eligible individuals in participating countries.[130]

To be eligible for compensation through the COVAX program, the applicant must be a resident of one of the 92 Advance Market Commitment (AMC) eligible economies[131] or be a "population of concern"[132] as

---

125. World Health Organization, *COVAX Working for global equitable access to COVID-19 vaccines*, https://www.who.int/initiatives/act-accelerator/covax (last visited Dec. 23, 2022).

126. "ESIS is an independent claims administrator with over 30 years' of relevant claims handling experience, and has secured regional centers around the world able to assist Program applicants in all 92 AMC Eligible Economies." COVAX AMC, *Frequently Asked Questions (FAQs) Relating to the COVAX No-Fault Compensation Program for AMC Eligible Economies*, https://covaxclaims.com/faqs/ (last visited Dec. 23, 2022).

127. Chubb is "the world's largest publicly traded property and casualty insurance company." Ghangurde, *supra* note 121.

128. COVAX AMC, *supra* note 126.

129. Ghangurde, *supra* note 121; World Health Organization, *COVAX No-Fault Compensation Program: Explained*, https://www.who.int/initiatives/act-accelerator/covax/no-fault-compensation/covax-no-fault-compensation-program-explained (last visited Dec. 23, 2022); Anna Rouw et al., *COVAX and the United States* (Feb. 18, 2021), https://www.kff.org/coronavirus-covid-19/issue-brief/covax-and-the-united-states/; Rakesh Raman, *How to Get Compensated for Covid Vaccine Injury,* RAMAN MEDIA NETWORK (July 20, 2021), https://www.ramanmedianetwork.com/how-to-get-compensated-for-covid-vaccine-injury/.

130. Hannah Balfour, *$150 million made available for COVID-19 vaccine adverse event compensation scheme,* EUROPEAN PHARMACEUTICAL REVIEW (Apr. 30, 2021), https://www.europeanpharmaceuticalreview.com/news/152687/150-million-made-available-for-covid-19-vaccine-adverse-event-compensation-scheme/.

131. "The list of 92 AMC-eligible economies includes all economies with Gross National Income (GNI) per capita under US$ 4,000 plus other World Bank International Development Association (IDA)-eligible economies." Gavi, *92 low- and middle-income economies eligible to get access to COVID-19 vaccines through Gavi COVAX AMC*, https://www.gavi.org/news/media-room/92-low-middle-income-economies-eligible-access-covid-19-vaccines-gavi-covax-amc (last visited Dec. 23, 2022).

132. Populations of concern include but are not limited to refugees, asylum seekers, stateless persons, internally displaced persons, minorities, detainees, and

defined by the Inter-Agency Standing Committee.[133] The applicant must also have been administered a vaccine in an AMC Eligible Economy that was delivered through a COVAX facility on or earlier than June 30, 2023.[134] The compensation fund applies only to vaccines that "either have received a WHO Emergency Use Listing (EUL) recommendation or prequalification (if applicable), following authorization from a 'functional or stringent' national regulatory authority of reference for vaccines[, o]r under exceptional circumstances, the vaccine should have received either a standard or conditional marketing authorization, or emergency use authorization, from a stringent regulatory authority of reference for vaccines and also needs to be included in Schedule 1 of the program."[135] Further, the vaccine must have resulted in a serious adverse event, defined as (1) a permanent total or partial impairment, (2) a congenital birth injury or illness with permanent total or partial impairment in an unborn or newborn child of a woman who received the vaccine, or (3) death.[136] The injury does not necessarily need to involve hospitalization or the extension of an existing hospitalization.[137]

There is no fee for applying for vaccine injury compensation under COVAX.[138] The application consists of (1) a publicly available application form; (2) invoices, receipts, or other proof of payment of any medical expenses; (3) a supporting evidence form; and (4) documentation from one or more registered healthcare professionals.[139] If the vaccine recipient has died, is a child, or is otherwise incapacitated, the person applying on his or her behalf must also provide a power of attorney or notarized statement.[140]

---

vulnerable migrants irrespective of their legal status. IASC Working Group on the Humanitarian Buffer, *Frequently Asked Questions: The COVAX Humanitarian Buffer* (May 16, 2022), https://interagencystandingcommittee.org/system/files/2022-05/Frequently%20Asked%20Questions-%20The%20COVAX%20Humanitarian%20Buffer%2C%2016%20May%202022.pdf.

133. Vaccines Work, *The COVAX Humanitarian Buffer Explained*, GAVI (Mar. 30, 2021), https://www.gavi.org/vaccineswork/covax-humanitarian-buffer-explained.

134. COVAX AMC, *supra* note 126.

135. Ghangurde, *supra* note 121.

136. World Health Organization, *supra* note 129.

137. COVAX AMC, *supra* note 126.

138. Anne Mazur et al., *COVAX no fault compensation program for COVID-19 vaccine injuries in 92 low and middle income countries*, 39 VACCINE (Dec. 3, 2021), *available at* https://www.ncbi.nlm.nih.gov/pmc/articles/PMC8552561/.

139. COVAX AMC, *supra* note 126; Mazur et al., *supra* note 138.

140. COVAX AMC, *supra* note 126.

Claims can only be submitted a minimum of 30 days after the vaccine was administered, unless the injury is death.[141] This 30-day waiting period allows registered healthcare professionals to ascertain whether the injury the applicant suffered was serious and makes the person eligible for compensation.[142] An applicant must submit his or her materials by the end of the Reporting Period, which is calculated based on the difference between the patient's vaccination date and that vaccine's "End Point" (within two years after the date that vaccine was put on the market in any country).[143] Claims will no longer be accepted after June 30, 2027.[144]

Submitting a claim does not automatically guarantee a compensation payment.[145] Rather, the application is "assessed by an independent review panel of nurses and an appeals panel of nurses and physicians, appointed by ESIS."[146] These panels are assisted by a scientific advisory committee of independent public health experts who stay apprised of new developments in COVID-19 vaccine safety.[147] In assessing the claim, the reviewers utilize the most probable cause standard—"[t]he most likely cause (based on the balance of probabilities) that a vaccine or its administration resulted in a claimed injury."[148]

If the claim is approved, compensation is calculated based on a formula that incorporates the cost of living in the country where the applicant resides.[149] Specifically, the formula multiplies the country's GDP per capita by 12, and then by a harm factor ranging from 0.1 to 1.5 depending on the nature of the injury and the level of impairment.[150] Additionally, a daily in-hospital benefit of $100 per day, up to a maximum of 60 days, will be paid for each day of hospitalization or prolongation of existing hospitalization.[151] If the applicant previously received any payments from another vaccine injury compensation program for the same injury, those

141. *Id.*

142. *Id.*

143. *Id.*

144. *Id.*

145. *Id.*

146. World Health Organization, *supra* note 129.

147. Vaccines Work, *supra* note 123.

148. Mazur et al., *supra* note 138; *Definitions under the COVAX no-fault compensation program for AMC eligible economies* (July 5, 2022), *available at* https://covaxclaims.com/wp-content/uploads/2021/03/COVAX-Compensation-Program-Definitions.pdf.

149. World Health Organization, *supra* note 129.

150. *Id.*

151. *Id.*

payments may be deducted from the COVAX compensation amount.[152] While applying for compensation is voluntary, if a claimant accepts the payment through the COVAX compensation scheme, that payment is "in full and final settlement of any claims to ensure [that] the same injury is not compensated twice."[153]

Like other vaccine compensation programs, COVAX acknowledges that individuals who receive a vaccine are undertaking a risk to themselves for the broader welfare of society and thus deserve compensation if they are injured in doing so.[154] COVAX's compensation scheme also aims to limit the financial exposure of AMC eligible economies by reducing the need to indemnify manufacturers.[155] "For the governments of AMC Eligible Economies, this kind of financial exposure could present too much risk for already-stretched health budgets, potentially delaying or even limiting the roll-out of COVID-19 vaccines to a large proportion of the global population."[156] Further, COVAX seeks to minimize the risk of litigation for manufacturers by providing an alternative method to obtain compensation outside of the court system.[157] This alternative to litigation also provides a benefit for applicants because pursuing compensation through the court system would be more time-consuming, complicated, and costly, and would involve a higher burden of proof and, thus, a more uncertain outcome.[158] Unlike in litigation, the amount of compensation through COVAX is not dependent on the abilities of the applicant's legal team and is instead based on a transparent, consistent formula.[159] Such an approach also provides uniformity and achieves equity across countries.[160]

COVAX's no-fault compensation program has limitations that must be accounted for in subsequent global vaccine injury compensation schemes. For one, compensation is restricted to the 92 AMC eligible economies, while approximately one-third of people experiencing

152. COVAX AMC, *supra* note 126.

153. Mazur et al., *supra* note 138; *see also* Lucy Parsons, *WHO agrees to no-fault compensation for rare serious side effects from COVAX-distributed vaccines*, PMLive (Feb. 23, 2021), https://www.pmlive.com/pharma_news/who_agrees_to_no-fault_compensation_for_rare_serious_side_effects_from_covax-distributed_vaccines_1363993.

154. World Health Organization, *supra* note 129.

155. *Id.*

156. *Id.*

157. *Id.*

158. *Id.*; Parsons, *supra* note 153.

159. Vaccines Work, *supra* note 123.

160. Mazur et al., *supra* note 138.

humanitarian crises are living outside of these countries.[161] Similarly, people who receive vaccines through the COVAX program are eligible for compensation, yet others living in the same country and who receive the same vaccine but through a different avenue would not be entitled to compensation.[162] Further, COVAX's compensation scheme has reduced but did not eliminate liability risk as the program does not include blanket liability waivers.[163]

There are also challenges to COVAX's setup and administration. Funding is a key difficulty to COVAX as a whole.[164] For example, while the program's overall funding target for 2020 to 2021 was $11.1 billion, it confronted a $7.2 billion funding gap.[165] Additionally, setting up COVAX required agreements and liabilities for financial and information flows between different organizations and imposed the risk of claims on global organizations and funders instead of manufacturers.[166] There is also a concern that the limited serious adverse event claims that have been filed may be due, at least in part, to limited awareness about the compensation fund among potential applicants.[167]

Despite these challenges and limitations, COVAX's no-fault compensation scheme is an achievement and a crucial model for future global vaccine injury compensation schemes. It succeeded in facilitating vaccine access for participants while limiting risk to manufacturers, produced a fair and efficient global system for applicants, and demonstrated how to set up a no-fault compensation system "without breaking the bank."[168] One comparative study of vaccination coverage in eighteen countries worldwide, ten of which were included in the COVAX no-fault compensation program, suggests that the compensation program potentially

161. Josh Michaud & Jennifer Kates, *The COVAX Humanitarian Buffer for COVID-19 Vaccines: Review and Assessment of Policy Implications*, KFF (Nov. 30, 2022), *available at* https://www.kff.org/global-health-policy/issue-brief/the-covax-humanitarian-buffer-for-covid-19-vaccines-review-and-assessment-of-policy-implications/.

162. Ghangurde, *supra* note 121.

163. Michaud & Kates, *supra* note 161.

164. Rouw et al., *supra* note 129.

165. *Id.*

166. CEPI, *COVAX: Key Learnings for Future Pandemic Preparedness and Response* (Sept. 2022), https://cepi.net/wp-content/uploads/2022/09/COVAX_Key-Learnings-for-Future-PPR_Sept-2022_FINAL_Updated-artwork.pdf.

167. *Id.*

168. *Id.*

contributed to increased vaccination coverage in those countries.[169] Seven out of the ten countries that participated in COVAX's vaccine injury compensation scheme had vaccination coverage of over 50 percent: Australia (80.3 percent), Argentina (80.18 percent), Brazil (69.99 percent), Egypt (69.73 percent), Colombia (65.58 percent), India (57.42 percent), and Indonesia (52.83 percent).[170] Pakistan had vaccination coverage of just under 50 percent, at 45.31 percent.[171] Two countries in the COVAX program were outliers and had very low vaccination coverage, Ethiopia (15.71 percent) and Nigeria (4.11 percent), which may be due to other factors, such as a poor medical infrastructure, that were not addressed by this study.[172] Overall, while more detailed data is needed, available information suggests that vaccine injury compensation programs are a promising way to encourage vaccination.[173]

Recommendations for a More Effective Compensation Regime

The Need for a Global No-Fault Compensation Scheme

The COVID-19 pandemic has shown that in today's age of globalization and international travel, viruses easily traverse national borders. Even as we optimistically and cautiously step toward a post-COVID world, epidemiologists predict that another pandemic-spurring virus is lurking around the corner.[174] To properly prepare for the inevitable next pandemic and incentivize vaccine development, creating a global no-fault compensation scheme must be prioritized. As discussed above, the availability of compensation funds and their related liability protections differ in critical ways in countries around the world. Without a coordinated global compensation system, an injured person will only be able to seek

169. Flavia Beccia et al., *COVID-19 Vaccination and Medical Liability: An International Perspective in 18 Countries*, 10 Vaccines (Aug. 7, 2022), https://www.ncbi.nlm.nih.gov/pmc/articles/PMC9415029/.

170. *Id.*

171. *Id.*

172. *Id.*

173. Stefano D'Errico et al., *"First Do No Harm". No-Fault Compensation Program for COVID-19 Vaccines as Feasibility and Wisdom of a Policy Instrument to Mitigate Vaccine Hesitancy*, 9 Vaccines (Sept. 30, 2021), https://www.ncbi.nlm.nih.gov/pmc/articles/PMC8540114/.

174. Kristen Rogers, *There Will Be Another Pandemic, Infectious Disease Experts Say. Here Are 6 Ways We Can Prepare for It*, CNN (June 1, 2022), https://www.cnn.com/2022/06/01/health/prepare-for-next-pandemic-life-itself-wellness/index.html.

compensation from the court system in his or her country (assuming a robust and reasonably accessible one exists), leading to slow and unpredictable results for individuals and potentially greater liability risk for manufacturers.

Such a global no-fault compensation scheme can be modeled off of COVAX but should address all mandatory or recommended vaccines, beyond COVAX's exclusive focus on COVID-19 vaccines. Crucially, the COVID-19 pandemic contributed to the inequity in vaccine access in countries around the world by "strain[ing] health systems" and diminishing global vaccination rates for other necessary vaccines.[175] In fact, "25 million children miss[ed] out on vaccination in 2021, 5.9 million more than in 2019 and the highest number since 2009."[176] In response, the international public health community, led by the WHO, is seeking to implement a global strategy known as Immunization Agenda 2030 for vaccines and immunization for the decade 2021 to 2030.[177] This agenda should incorporate within it a global no-fault compensation scheme based on COVAX, where participating countries that receive vaccines are also eligible to apply for compensation for related vaccine injuries or death.

Another possibility for a global compensation fund is modeling it off of the PREP Act and the CICP. Vaccine manufacturers could work with a third-party intermediary to provide immunity for all member states and compensation to those injured by eligible vaccines. However, European countries that already have funds that compensate vaccine injuries are unlikely to accept a PREP-like model if it provides less compensation than is currently available for other vaccines.[178]

No matter how it is organized, a global no-fault compensation fund will likely face severe funding challenges. Unlike a national vaccine compensation program such as the VICP in the United States, which is funded by way of an excise tax and handled by the Department of Treasury, there is no clear mechanism for funding an international program. While COVAX is funded by donor contributions on the basis of a set levy per dose, as noted above, COVAX is confronting a $7.2 billion funding gap.[179] Further, if a global compensation scheme is created that

175. WHO, *Immunization Coverage* (July 14, 2022), https://www.who.int/en/news-room/fact-sheets/detail/immunization-coverage.

176. *Id.*

177. *Id.*

178. Duncan Fairgrieve et al., *Products in a Pandemic: Liability for Medical Products and the Fight against COVID-19*, 11 European Journal of Risk Regulation 1, 35 (May 20, 2020), https://doi.org/10.1017/err.2020.54.

179. *See supra* note 129.

incorporates countries with vastly different GDPs, any contribution will have to account for those countries' financial status and ability to pay into the fund for the fund to be equitable.

Reforms to the VICP and the CICP

Both the VICP and the CICP programs require significant reforms. Scholars have questioned the ability of the CICP to compensate for vaccine-related injuries from the COVID-19 claims due to inadequate congressional appropriations. To make matters worse, the CICP's administrative costs are likely to take up most of the congressional outlays, and only an estimated 6 percent of those outlays will be used to compensate victims of vaccine-related injuries.[180] These problems will likely get worse in the coming years.

The problems, however, are not intractable. To function effectively, these programs must offer the certainty of rapid, fair, and accessible compensation outside the usual avenue of the U.S. litigation system. There are no publicly available audit reports of the CICP as of November 2022. Therefore, it is imperative that the federal government conduct a performance-related audit of the CICP and find ways to address the disproportionately high administrative costs associated with this program.[181] Although the VICP has a better track record than the CICP in compensating claimants, even the VICP's damages caps have not been revisited in nearly 40 years.[182] Making these VICP and CICP damage awards more generous is crucial to restoring public confidence in these systems and to justly compensating vaccine-related injuries. In addition, the CICP should be expanded to compensate claims for damages associated with pain and suffering.

Finally, we recommend that the funding for both the VICP and the CICP be substantially increased to both ease the administrative burden and ensure that these programs have sufficient funds to compensate vaccine-related injuries. One way to fund these programs is by increasing the $0.75 per vaccine administered excise tax. Alternatively, Congress

---

180. Zhao et al., *supra* note 87.

181. *Id.*

182. The average award payment for vaccine-related injuries under the VICP was $824,463, and today the average award is $585,000. *Compare* Health Resources & Services Administration (HRSA), *National Vaccine Injury Compensation Program*, https://www.in.gov/health/immunization/files/VICP.pdf (last visited Dec. 23, 2022) *to* Peter Loftus & Susan Pulliam, *People Harmed by Coronavirus Vaccines Will Have Little Recourse*, WALL ST. J. (Oct. 12, 2020), https://www.wsj.com/articles/people-harmed-by-coronavirus-vaccines-will-have-little-recourse-11602432000.

could apportion more funds on an ad hoc basis to the VICP and the CICP to afford these programs the ability to pay out compensation awards and cover administrative costs.

Tap the Vaccine Injury Trust Fund

Finally, we recommend reallocating part of the surplus in the Trust Fund, the funding mechanism for the VICP, to help address gaps in the VICP and CICP identified above, or to fund other global vaccine compensation programs. As noted above, the Trust Fund is funded through a $0.75 excise tax for each dose of vaccines recommended by the CDC for routine administration in children.[183] The only allowable expenditures out of the Trust Fund are for payment of compensation awards for vaccine-related injury under the VICP and related administration expenses.[184] The total compensation that has been paid out over the life of the VICP program is approximately $4.9 billion, which represents payments for 9,254 compensated awards since 1989.[185]

The Trust Fund currently has a surplus of more than $4 billion, which could be redirected, in part, to other compensation schemes.[186] Based on HRSA reports, the Trust Fund makes significant income from excise tax revenue and interest that far exceeds the amount needed to satisfy compensation awards and fees in a given year. For example, in fiscal year 2022, the Trust Fund received $322,664,764 in revenue from the excise tax, earned $61,064,353 in interest income, and paid out $230,015,959 in payments for settlements and fees, with a balance of $4,315,879,705 by the end of the fiscal year.[187] This represents a roughly $160 million surplus from fiscal year 2022 alone. The numbers in the preceding year showed a similar trend: $312,902,784 in excise tax revenue, $50,534,187

183. Health Resources & Services Administration (HRSA), *About the National Vaccine Injury Compensation Program*, https://www.hrsa.gov/vaccine-compensation/about#:~:text=What%20Is%20the%20Vaccine%20Injury,or%20after%20October%201%2C%201988 (last visited Dec. 23, 2022); *see also* 26 U.S.C. § 9510(b)(1).

184. 26 U.S.C. § 9510(c).

185. Health Resources & Services Administration (HRSA), *Data & Statistics*, https://www.hrsa.gov/sites/default/files/hrsa/vicp/11-01-22-VICP-Stats-508%20Compliant.pdf (last visited Dec. 23, 2022).

186. *Vaccine Injury Trust Fund, FY 2023* (Nov. 30, 2022), https://treasurydirect.gov/ftp/dfi/tfmb/dfivi1122.pdf.

187. Health Resources & Services Administration (HRSA), *National Vaccine Injury Compensation Program (VICP) Update* (Dec. 1, 2022), https://www.hrsa.gov/sites/default/files/hrsa/advisory-committees/vaccines/dicp-update-dec-2022.pdf.

in interest on investments, and $244,333,985 in payments for settlements and fees, with an ending balance of $4,177,377,384.[188,189]

Accordingly, we would propose amending the legislation that controls the Trust Fund to allow for the surplus amounts to be transferred to other vaccine compensation schemes discussed here,[190] such as the CICP, or to global organization, such as the COVAX program. Given the importance of global vaccination efforts to prevent worldwide spread of disease, the United States has an important interest in funding global vaccination efforts.[191] The surplus in the Trust Fund is a significant sum that could be put toward that effort.

Conclusion

Vaccination is a highly effective medical intervention for preventing the spread of diseases. According to recent WHO estimates, vaccination prevents 3.5–5 million deaths annually.[192] For this reason, vaccination "is a key component of primary health care and an indisputable human right."[193] Ensuring successful vaccination programs is not simply a matter of good policy—it is vital for securing global justice. One only needs to think of the devastation of the COVID-19 pandemic, in which over

188. Health Resources & Services Administration (HRSA), *The National Vaccine Injury Compensation (VICP) Division of Injury Compensation Programs (DICP) Program Update* (Dec. 2, 2021), https://www.hrsa.gov/sites/default/files/hrsa/advisory-committees/vaccines/december-2021-dicp-update.pdf; Health Resources & Services Administration (HRSA), *Data and Statistics* (Dec. 1, 2022); https://www.hrsa.gov/sites/default/files/hrsa/vicp/vicp-stats-12-01-22.pdf.

189. Assuming the COVID 19 vaccines are eventually added to the Table and are covered under the VICP, the tax revenue going to the Trust Fund will increase, though the amount that will need to be paid out in compensation awards for COVID-19 vaccine-related claims is unknown. Nonetheless, the net impact of adding COVID-19 to the Table will need to be taken into account in analyzing how much of the Trust Fund's surplus can be prudently transferred.

190. The Trust Fund was created by an act of Congress pursuant to 26 U.S.C. § 9510. That legislation provides that net revenues received from the excise tax on vaccines on the Table are appropriated into the Trust Fund, and that the money in the Trust Fund shall only be available to pay for compensation awards or administrative expenses in administering the VICP. This statute would need to be amended to permit the Trust Fund to transfer money to other compensation schemes.

191. *See supra* Introduction.

192. World Health Organization, *Vaccines and immunization*, https://www.who.int/health-topics/vaccines-and-immunization#tab=tab_1 (last visited Dec. 23, 2022).

193. *Id.*

6.5 million people died, to grasp the importance of mass vaccination programs.

Future successful vaccination programs will depend on the ability of governments to produce effective vaccines rapidly in response to emerging threats and the willingness of the public within each country impacted by the threat to uptake those vaccines. Due to the significance of vaccination programs in any effective system of primary health medicine, it is alarming that vaccine coverage has dropped over the past several years.[194] This exposes communities to greater risk of transmission for contagious diseases.

Crucial to increased uptake of vaccines is a greater trust in medical experts and scientific institutions. One strategy for creating a positive incentive structure is creating a global fund to compensate members of the public who suffer injuries after receiving vaccines. Meeting the challenges of future global health crises also depends on making effective innovations relating to vaccine development. Providing protection from civil liability to vaccine manufacturers creates positive incentives for making those innovations. Ultimately, a just and efficient system of global health can only be built on community participation.[195] It is not sufficient for scientists, researchers, physicians, and governments to work together to advance scientific knowledge. Members of the public must be able to trust and rely on scientific institutions and experts, so that those innovative scientific solutions can be deployed as effective medical interventions within an equitable public health system.

---

194. *Id.*

195. GOLDENBERG, *supra* note 25.

Chapter 8

The Elusive Self-Administering Vaccine: Understanding the Legal and Regulatory Hurdles

Richard Hughes IV, William Walters, and Jessika Tuazon

Despite the apparent demand in the wake of the COVD-19 pandemic, the nation's vaccine delivery infrastructure is not yet perfectly poised to enable self-administration of vaccines. Elsewhere in medicine, self-administration of medication is nothing new. Those, for example, living with diabetes, psoriasis, Crohn's disease, arthritis, allergies, and a host of other chronic conditions may self-administer medication, from the comfort of their own home, which often requires the use of needles or syringes.

As this article will review, a great deal of preclinical research studies—and even a few successful Phase I clinical trials—have explored the feasibility of self-administrable vaccine delivery systems. Though there are currently no self-administrable vaccines approved by the U.S. Food and Drug Administration (FDA), self-administered vaccines could take many forms other than the traditional subcutaneous needle delivery, including subcutaneous auto-injectors, mucosal and intranasal delivery options such as FluMist, orally delivered vaccine pills, and vaccine patches that deliver the vaccine intradermally. Unsurprisingly, studies[1] have found patients have a clear preference for the more painless delivery options, including patches, pills, and mists. Self-administrable vaccines

1. *See, e.g.*, Brenda L. Coleman, Allison J. McGeer, Scott A. Halperin, Joanne M. Langley, Yassein Shamout, Anna Taddio, Vibhuti Shah & Shelly A McNeil, *A randomized control trial comparing immunogenicity, safety, and preference for self- versus nurse-administered intradermal influenza vaccine*, Vaccine (Sept. 28, 2012), https://pubmed.ncbi.nlm.nih.gov/22902784/.

are still a long way from reaching the market but ultimately hold great promise for increased access and uptake.

The COVID-19 pandemic highlighted many vaccine access inequities that persist when attempting to vaccinate as many people as possible, as quickly as possible. In the United States, vaccination rates varied by income,[2] race, and ethnicity;[3] globally, the inequities among wealthy and low-income nations were stark.[4] But these inequities are not unique to the COVID-19 pandemic. Every year, vaccine inequities hamper efforts to vaccinate against preventable illnesses such as influenza that disproportionately affect minority populations.

Equity and access issues already proliferate in the current system for vaccine delivery. A self-administered vaccine is no panacea for access challenges, but a more robust suite of delivery options stands to maximize vaccine access equity and adherence. For example, a self-administered vaccine could be delivered to immunocompromised patients who are unable to travel to a doctor's office or pharmacy, and it could be used at greater rates by individuals who prefer the convenience of self-administering or a painless delivery system. Self-administered vaccines could also be sent through the mail to individuals who live in rural and remote areas.

Once clinically viable, nearly every aspect of our vaccine delivery system would need to evolve to facilitate self-administration. Before self-administrable vaccines can be made widely available to the public, there are a number of legal, policy, and regulatory barriers that must be addressed. To help streamline market entry and rapidly deploy self-administering vaccines as broadly and equitably as possible, we characterize the pathways for delivery of self-administered vaccines and identify the barriers in need of resolution. These include how vaccines are prescribed and dispensed to patients; who can prescribe them; the

---

2. *See* Zijing Cheng & Yue Li, *Racial and ethnic and income disparities in COVID-19 vaccination among Medicare beneficiaries*, J. Am. Geriatr. Soc. (June 7, 2022), https://www.ncbi.nlm.nih.gov/pmc/articles/PMC9348368/#:~:text=74%25%20of%20respondents%20earning%20an,rate%20among%20Medicare%20beneficiaries%20nationally.

3. *See* Nambi Ndugga, Latoya Hill, Samantha Artiga & Sweta Haldar, *Latest Data on COVID-19 Vaccinations by Race/Ethnicity*, Kaiser Family Foundation (July 14, 2022), https://www.kff.org/coronavirus-covid-19/issue-brief/latest-data-on-covid-19-vaccinations-by-race-ethnicity/#:~:text=Across%20the%2036%20states%20for,for%20Black%20people%20(59%25).

4. *Vaccine Equity*, World Health Organization, https://www.who.int/campaigns/vaccine-equity.

physical delivery systems of the vaccines themselves; how the used vaccines and delivery systems are disposed of after use; and how to monitor whether the vaccines were actually self-administered, including tracking of any complications.

The Promise of Vaccine Self-Administration: Can It Disrupt the Traditional Patient Vaccination Model?

Today, patients access vaccines across many different settings of care. Each patient's vaccination journey can follow a variety of paths most convenient for that patient, though continued fragmentation across our healthcare system means that vaccines may not be available in every healthcare setting or to every patient.

Physicians' offices have historically been primary vaccination sites, and pediatricians play a central role today in childhood vaccination. As vaccines for adults or targeting particular at-risk populations have become more common in recent decades, family practice and specialty practitioners have increasingly become immunizers. Today, patients have a broad array of choices for where to receive a vaccination, including retail or community pharmacies, public health clinics, Federally Qualified Health Centers, and rural health clinics.

The retail or community pharmacy setting, in particular, has become an increasingly common vaccination setting. In recent decades, all states have expanded pharmacists' scope of practice to allow them to administer vaccines.[5] Some states still require pharmacists to have a prescription from a physician, a standing order, or protocol to administer certain vaccines, while others grant inherent authority to pharmacists to administer vaccines.[6] Increasingly rare, "brown bagging" is a vaccine delivery scenario wherein a pharmacist is unable to prescribe or administer a particular vaccine independently, and therefore, a physician or allied health professional prescribes the vaccine and sends the patient to the pharmacy, and the patient returns to the prescribing provider's office for the administration of the vaccine. These fragmented approaches to delivery are known to result in patient attrition.

5. *See, e.g.*, Loren Bonner, *Pharmacists' expanded scope of practice here to stay?*, PharmacyToday (June 10, 2022), https://www.pharmacytoday.org/article/S1042-0991(22)00580-1/fulltext.

6. *See id.*

In recognition of these challenges, vaccine access has become increasingly de-medicalized as states have further expanded the ability of pharmacists to administer vaccines without a prescription. The advent of the seasonal flu vaccine and the H1N1 and even more so the COVID-19 pandemics have served as major catalysts of pharmacy-based vaccination.[7] As a result, patients who wish to receive a flu shot or a COVID-19 vaccination can generally choose from a number of different vaccination sites, ranging from their doctor's office, their local pharmacy, an employer-provided clinic in the workplace, a local health center, or others.

In addition to choosing *where* to get certain vaccines, some patients may also be able to choose *how* the vaccine is delivered. While the traditional intramuscular vaccination remains the most prevalent delivery method for the flu vaccine, live attenuated influenza vaccines delivered via intranasal mist, such as FluMist, are available for qualifying patients.[8]

The as-of-yet-unfulfilled promise of self-administered vaccines is increased vaccine access and uptake. Elsewhere in medicine, self-administration of medication is nothing new. Those living with diabetes, psoriasis, Crohn's disease, arthritis, allergies, and a host of other chronic conditions self-administer medication, often via needles or syringes, in the comfort of their own home. Similarly, women undergoing in vitro fertilization (IVF) may have to self-administer various hormones using a subcutaneous or intramuscular injection to increase the odds of successfully becoming pregnant.

The necessity of self-management of chronic conditions spurred development of additional delivery methods to simplify the self-administration of medication. Many treatments for chronic conditions have embraced auto-injectors as a simpler method of self-administration as compared to a traditional syringe. A typical auto-injection device is simply placed on the patient's skin and pressed down or activated in some other way, and the device then automatically injects and delivers the medication into the patient, often with some sort of clicking noise and auto-retraction when

7. *See* Richard Hughes IV, Daniel Nam, Nick Diamond, Colleen Hopkins, Neil Rosacker & Manuel Aviña, *The Pharmacist's Role In COVID-19 Response Efforts*, Health Affairs (July 23, 2020), https://www.healthaffairs.org/do/10.1377/forefront.20200721.162747.

8. Typically to qualify an individual would not be pregnant; would not have certain chronic such as asthma, heart disease, or kidney disease; and would be between 2 and 40 years old. *See Live Attenuated Influenza Vaccine [LAIV] (The Nasal Spray Flu Vaccine)*, The Centers for Disease Control and Prevention, https://www.cdc.gov/flu/prevent/nasalspray.htm.

the medication is fully delivered.[9] While patient training is still required, most auto-injectors are designed to be simple to use while also ensuring adequate medication delivery.

Patients with psoriasis and psoriatic arthritis, for example, may self-administer biologics at home after receiving instruction from a healthcare professional, such as their doctor, who might oversee the patient's first self-administered dose during an office visit, or a nurse or a pharmacist, who might instruct and oversee the first dose remotely over a phone or video call. Likewise, individuals living with type 1 diabetes who use various at-home use devices such as insulin pumps to self-administer insulin and continuous glucose monitors might be taught to use such devices by their doctor during an office visit or by another healthcare provider employed by the manufacturer of the device during an office visit or at home via video call.

Changes to the patient experience over the past several years, including the increasing rise in access to, and use of, telehealth services and self-administered diagnostic tests for infectious diseases during the COVID-19 pandemic, suggest a growing public interest in, and demand for, alternative, at-home options for vaccinations. This could entail making vaccinations available to patients for self-administration at home through a variety of modalities, whether through the involvement of one or more healthcare providers or, eventually, with an option that allows patients to access such vaccinations over the counter.

The COVID-19 pandemic shifted how Americans conceptualize healthcare visits. By necessity, patient homes and vehicles became recognized as healthcare settings during the pandemic. In fact, the Centers for Medicare and Medicaid Services (CMS) issued a rule that provides enhanced reimbursement for in-home COVID-19 vaccine administration.[10] Meeting people where they are increases the prospect of more equitable vaccine access and uptake and may also help to contribute to herd immunity by providing a more desirable mode of delivery to many who may be resistant to the current options available.

---

9. There are, of course, wide variations between auto-injection devices used to deliver different medications, but this description is meant to capture the general concept.

10. *See* Medicare and Medicaid Programs; CY 2023 Payment Policies under the Physician Fee Schedule and Other Changes to Part B Payment and Coverage Policies, 87 Fed. Reg. 69,404 (Nov. 18, 2022) (to be codified at 42 C.F.R. Parts 405, 410, 411, 414, 415, 423, 424, 425, and 455) (codifying the enhanced reimbursement for in-home COVID-19 vaccine administration).

Progressing toward self-administration of vaccines is not without challenges, as it will necessarily require building consensus among various healthcare providers already engaged in vaccine administration today. Self-administered vaccines are a double-edged sword, where allowing patients this option may increase access to important vaccines and patient compliance, but the element of convenience shifts patients away from traditional medical models. This raises important questions about the degree to which we involve the healthcare professional versus entirely patient-driven vaccination.

Understanding Potential Self-Administration Modalities, Their Feasibility, and Their Acceptability

To develop our explanation of potential self-administrable modalities, we identified a number of drug delivery categories that have been approved by the FDA for self-administration[11] or are otherwise known, based on simple public trade searches and a limited review of clinical trials (on ClinicalTrials.gov), to be under investigation for potential self-administration or at-home administration by a caregiver. The product categories and clinical trials that we highlight below are intended to illustrate different modes of prospective vaccine delivery and are not intended to be an exhaustive or systematic survey of possible modalities.

An integral component of the feasibility of self-administered vaccines is determining whether patients have an interest in or desire to self-administer a vaccine. Intuitively, the less painful the delivery system, the more likely it would be for the delivery system to be accepted by patients. We would expect industry and patient receptivity to the concept of self-administered vaccines to be informed by the frequency with which a patient would be expected to self-administer such products (e.g., whether the vaccination to be delivered is recommended once or twice a year versus once or twice a lifetime). Throughout the remainder of this chapter, we will focus on only four principal product categories, their potential feasibility and acceptability among patients, how they stand to reshape vaccine delivery, and the various known legal and regulatory steps and challenges for their market entry. These categories are, ranked by order

11. The product categories identified include drugs (which may require the use of a separate medical device (e.g., a separately packaged syringe) to administer) and combination products (which may be approved in a single- or multi-dose drug-device delivery system (e.g., an auto-injector)).

of perceived feasibility, syringes, auto-injectors, microneedle patches, and nasal or mucosal vaccines.

Drugs or Biologics Administered via Syringes

The most familiar method of self-administration—though likely not the most preferred by patients—is self-injection via syringe. The traditional syringe requires drawing medication from a vial into the syringe, meaning the patient is responsible not only for dosing accurately but also for manually measuring that dose and ensuring the medication drawn from the vial is replaced with air to prevent a vacuum from forming and harming the rest of the medication.[12]

Depo-Provera®, a long-acting injectable contraceptive that provides protection against pregnancy for three months, is the only known example of a self-administered prophylactic injectable.[13] While no mention is made in the label itself, Centers for Disease Control and Prevention (CDC) guidelines include self-administration of a low-dose subcutaneous product formulation in a patient-provider shared decision-making context.[14] The product is packaged as a prefilled syringe that simplifies dosing and is delivered via injection.[15] This system has also been used in lower- and middle-income countries for provider-administered vaccines for years.[16]

To help patients self-inject with syringes, there are products such as ShotBlocker®, which helps patients self-inject medication by confusing the sensory signals surrounding the injection site with many small, sharp contact points that imitate the injection.[17] These devices also help pinch the injection site for proper delivery. Even with a device like a ShotBlocker, intended to reduce pain, and even for individuals living with chronic conditions such as type 1 diabetes, for whom self-administration of medication is a way of life, the manual insertion of syringes is generally not

12. *See Drawing medicine out of a vial*, Medline Plus (Jan. 29, 2022), https://medlineplus.gov/ency/patientinstructions/000530.htm.

13. *See Highlights of Prescribing Information*, U.S. Food & Drug Administration, https://www.accessdata.fda.gov/drugsatfda_docs/label/2010/020246s036lbl.pdf.

14. *See Injectables*, The Centers for Disease Control and Prevention, https://www.cdc.gov/reproductivehealth/contraception/mmwr/spr/injectables.html#selfadministration.

15. *See Home-based administration of depo-subQ in the Uniject injection system*, PATH (July 2011) https://media.path.org/documents/RH_depo_subq_home_deliv.pdf.

16. *See Vaccines in the UnijectTM Injection System*, PATH (Aug. 2013), https://media.path.org/documents/TS_update_uniject_vaccine.pdf.

17. *ShotBlocker®*, Bionix, https://bionix.com/shotblocker.html.

a preferred option. Patient considerations and desire to self-administer medications in order to manage a life-threatening chronic condition—for instance, managing type 1 diabetes in a way that prevents serious complications of living with the disease, which can include diabetic ketoacidosis, diabetic neuropathy, and retinal neuropathy, to name a few—are inarguably very different than patients' calculus in determining whether or not to self-administer a vaccine to prevent a condition they do not yet have.

Auto-Injectors

Pens, jets, and related injectors are combination products[18] that can provide an alternative approach to deliver drugs or biological products, and may enhance safety, improve dosing accuracy, and increase patient compliance, particularly in self-administration contexts.[19] Commonly used auto-injectors include epinephrine injection, or EpiPens,[20] and insulin pump infusion sets used to manage diabetes.[21] Though used exclusively to treat anaphylaxis or allergic emergencies, EpiPens are approved for self-delivery (to the extent the individual in anaphylaxis is physically capable of delivering the medication).[22] Insulin pump infusion sets work in the same way as an intravenous line, but without requiring a vein. Instead, a small catheter is placed by auto-injecting a needle into subcutaneous fat, subsequently removing the needle, and leaving the catheter to deliver appropriate dosages of insulin for several days.

---

18. Combination products are therapeutic and diagnostic products that combine drugs, devices, and/or biological products. Combination products are composed of any combination of a drug and a device; a biological product and a device; a drug and a biological product; or a drug, device, and a biological product. *See Frequently Asked Questions about Combination Products*, U.S. Food & Drug Administration, *available at* https://www.fda.gov/combination-products/about-combination-products/frequently-asked-questions-about-combination-products#CP.

19. *See Guidance for Industry and FDS Staff: Technical Considerations for Pen, Jet, and Related Injectors Intended for Use with Drugs and Biological Products*, U.S. Food & Drug Administration, *available at* https://www.fda.gov/files/about%20fda/published/Technical-Considerations-for-Pen--Jet--and-Related-Injectors-Intended-for-Use-with-Drugs-and-Biological-Products.pdf.

20. EpiPen, *available at* https://www.epipen.com/en.

21. *See Insulin Pumps: Relief and Choice*, The American Diabetes Association, https://diabetes.org/healthy-living/medication-treatments/insulin-other-injectables/insulin-pumps-relief-and-choice.

22. *EpiPen Highlights of Prescribing Information*, National Institutes of Health, https://dailymed.nlm.nih.gov/dailymed/fda/fdaDrugXsl.cfm?type=display&setid=7560c201-9246-487c-a13b-6295db04274a#section-15.

Likewise, many individuals living with type 1 diabetes use insulin pens, which are a precursor to the insulin pump and come preloaded with much more insulin than is needed for any single dose, and replaceable, single-use needle cartridges.[23] A typical insulin pen will have a measuring mechanism to allow the patient to measure the proper dosage of insulin for injection.

There are many more types of auto-injector modalities approved by the FDA; the examples highlighted above are just a few common examples of those used frequently across ages and populations to self-administer medication.

Microneedle Patches

A survey of microneedle-based vaccines published in the *Journal of Biosafety and Biosecurity* identified five types of microneedles that could deliver a vaccine: solid microneedles, coated microneedles, hollow microneedles, dissolving microneedles, and hydrogel-forming microneedles.[24] Delivery methods range from hollow microneedles, which act as an array of traditional, albeit smallerm, syringes through which a vaccine is delivered, to coated microneedles, where the vaccine is dissolved off of the needles once they have penetrated the skin.[25] Dissolving microneedles employ needles that themselves dissolve, releasing the vaccine contained within the patch.[26] While different kinds of microneedles have advantages and disadvantages, the general approach for all types of microneedles is the same: instead of one relatively large needle, many much smaller needles are affixed to an adhesive and deliver a vaccine.[27] The survey found that, once proven safe and effective, microneedle patches could likely increase biosecurity by providing a means of self-vaccination against various bioterrorism agents and viruses, such as anthrax, Ebola, influenza, smallpox, and COVID-19.[28]

---

23. *See Insulin Pens*, The American Diabetes Association, https://diabetes.org/tools-support/devices-technology/insulin-pens.

24. Zhiying Jin, Baohua Zhao, Wei Wan, Yue Li, Xuexin Bai, Chenyi Hu, Jing Wang, Yanwei Li, Wenwen Xin, Lin Kang, Hao Yang, Jinglin Wang & Shan Gao, *Application of microneedle-based vaccines in biosecurity*, 4 J. of Biosafety & Biosecurity 75 (June 2022), https://www.sciencedirect.com/science/article/pii/S258893382200005X#b0125.

25. *See id.*

26. *See id.*

27. *See id.*

28. *See id.*

A search of studies on ClinicalTrials.gov using the terms "microneedle" and "vaccine" yielded 20 results.[29] Most trials examining vaccine self-administration and vaccine patches—as well as studies examining the use of needle-free vaccine patches to deliver a room-temperature stable COVID-19 vaccine—are still in their early stages.[30] Early findings suggest microneedle patches may be a viable delivery method, though additional evidence is needed to support regulatory approval of such products.

A clinical trial published in 2012 and supported by the National Institutes of Health investigated the immunogenicity, safety, and patient preference for a self-administered intradermal microinjection influenza vaccine, as compared to the same intradermal vaccine administered by a nurse.[31] The patient group was randomly selected and given an instruction sheet that described how to self-administer the vaccine. Of the 114 who self-administered the vaccine, 106 were able to do so successfully on their first try. Further, there was no difference in immunogenicity between the self- and nurse-administered groups, and the self-administered group even reported less pain involved with vaccination, despite increased redness post-vaccination.[32] Seventy percent of individuals across both groups preferred intradermal vaccination to intramuscular vaccination.[33]

Although the results of this clinical trial are limited, the 93 percent success rate of the patient group that self-administered an intradermal flu vaccine is an encouraging sign that patients could be taught to self-administer vaccines. This is especially true considering intradermal self-administration is likely on the more complicated and more invasive end of the spectrum of self-administrable modalities. Researchers have been exploring the possibility of cutaneous drug and vaccine delivery for years.[34] One possible delivery method this could establish is a vaccine

29. *ClinicalTrials.gov*, National Institutes of Health, https://clinicaltrials.gov/ct2/results?cond=&term=microneedle+vaccine&cntry=&state=&city=&dist= (accessed Dec. 12, 2022).

30. *See id.*

31. Coleman et al. *supra* note 1.

32. *See id.*

33. *See id.*

34. *See, e.g.*, Nicola Luigi Bragazzi, Andrea Orsi, Filippo Ansaldi, Roberto Gasparini & Giancarlo Icardia, Fluzone® intra-dermal (Intanza®/Istivac® Intra-dermal): An updated overview, Hum. Vaccin. Immunother. (May 31, 2016), https://www.ncbi.nlm.nih.gov/pmc/articles/PMC5085005/.

patch with dissolving microneedles that would deliver the vaccine into the skin, essentially a prophylactic Band-Aid.[35]

An earlier study, published in 2014, examined patient usability and acceptability of microneedle patches as a possible method of self-vaccination. In a randomized, repeated measures study of 91 adults, 70 were given microneedle patches to self-administer via thumb pressure, and the rest used a "snap device," a form of auto-injection device that would automatically snap the patch onto the skin.[36] Over three applications, the snap device registered a 93–96 percent application success rate.[37] Further, when self-administration was offered to study participants, their intent to vaccinate increased from 45 percent to 65 percent.[38] While this study did not test a vaccine, it provided strong foundational support suggesting a vaccine patch may be an effective delivery method that may improve patient vaccination acceptance and uptake.

Flu patches have been tested in various forms but are generally similar, if not identical, to one study supported by NIH's National Institute of Biomedical Imaging and Bioengineering (NIBIB) and the National Institute of Allergy and Infectious Diseases (NIAID), which analyzed patches containing 100 microneedles that delivered the flu vaccine into the skin before dissolving within minutes.[39] The researchers found similar responses between groups of participants who received the flu vaccine via flu shot given by a healthcare provider and via vaccine patch applied by a healthcare provider.[40] Importantly, even participants who

35. *See, e.g.*, Dimitrios G. Koutsonanos, Richard W. Compans & Ioanna Skountzou, *Targeting the skin for microneedle delivery of influenza vaccine*, Adv. Exp. Med. Biol. (May 18, 2019), https://www.ncbi.nlm.nih.gov/pmc/articles/PMC6525635/.

36. James J. Norman, Jaya M. Arya, Maxine A. McClain, Paula M. Frew, Martin I. Meltzer & Mark R. Prausnitz, *Microneedle patches: Usability and acceptability for self-vaccination against influenza*, 32 Vaccine 1856 (Apr. 1, 2014), https://www.sciencedirect.com/science/article/pii/S0264410X1400139X.

37. *See id.*

38. *See id.*

39. *See* Nadine G. Rouphael, Michele Paine, Regina Mosley, Sebastien Henry, Devin V. McAllister, Haripriya Kalluri, Winston Pewin, Paula M. Frew, Tianwei Yu, Natalie J. Thornburg, Sarah Kabbani, Lilin Lai, Elena V. Vassilieva, Ioanna Skountzou, Richard W. Compans, Mark J. Mulligan & Mark R. Prausnitz, *The safety, immunogenicity, and acceptability of inactivated influenza vaccine delivered by microneedle patch (TIV-MNP 2015): a randomised, partly blinded, placebo-controlled, phase 1 trial*, Lancet (Aug. 12, 2017), https://pubmed.ncbi.nlm.nih.gov/28666680/; *see also Microneedle patch for flu vaccine*, NIH Research Matters (July 25, 2017), https://www.nih.gov/news-events/nih-research-matters/microneedle-patch-flu-vaccine.

40. *See* Rouphael et al., *supra* note 40.

self-administered their own vaccine patch had robust immune responses.[41] This demonstrates both that vaccines patches are likely an effective vaccine delivery option and that self-administration is not likely to reduce efficacy because of improper use.

The closest approved analogue to microneedle patches today is transdermal nicotine replacement therapy for smoking cessation. Commonly known as nicotine patches, these products are placed on the skin and deliver nicotine steadily throughout the day.[42] Nicotine patches come in a variety of doses and are generally simple to use, and some are available over the counter without a prescription.[43]

Nasal or Mucosal Sprays

Nasal sprays are commonly used as delivery systems, particularly for colds and allergies. Many allergy treatments delivered as a nasal spray are available over the counter without a prescription. A nasal spray typically involves inserting the product nozzle upright into a nostril and gently pressing down on the nozzle to release medication into the nostril. Like transdermal nicotine patches, certain nasal sprays are simple to use as delivery systems and are already available over the counter and without a prescription for colds and allergies.

Traditionally, emergency treatment for individuals living with diabetes involved either an intramuscular or subcutaneous injection of glucagon, delivered either by powder, which needed to be mixed with a provided liquid before drawn into the needle and delivered, or by liquid via prefilled syringe. In 2019, the FDA approved the first severe hypoglycemia treatment that can be administered without an injection.[44] A powder delivered through the nose, Baqsimi, was a sea change for emergency care for individuals living with diabetes—particularly children.[45] Because Baqsimi is an emergency treatment used when an individual with diabetes is unresponsive or otherwise unable to consume glucose

41. *See id.*

42. *See How to Use Nicotine Patches*, The Centers for Disease Control and Prevention, https://www.cdc.gov/tobacco/campaign/tips/quit-smoking/quit-smoking-medications/how-to-use-quit-smoking-medicines/how-to-use-a-nicotine-patch.html.

43. *See Nicotine Patches*, CVS Pharmacy, https://www.cvs.com/shop/health-medicine/stop-smoking/nicotine-patches.

44. *FDA approves first treatment for severe hypoglycemia that can be administered without an injection*, U.S. Food & Drug Administration (July 24, 2019), https://www.fda.gov/news-events/press-announcements/fda-approves-first-treatment-severe-hypoglycemia-can-be-administered-without-injection.

45. Baqsimi, *available at* https://www.baqsimi.com/.

to treat hypoglycemia, it is typically not self-administered. The delivery, however, is viewed by many to be simpler than using a prefilled syringe and does not require a healthcare provider to administer it. As such, most parents and schoolteachers are able to deliver Baqsimi with minimal instruction. In the case of a hypoglycemic emergency, Baqsimi is simply placed into the nose, and a button is pressed to deliver the glucagon, the same way any nasal spray medication used to treat allergies is delivered.[46]

Every year many individuals opt to receive their flu vaccine as a nasal spray in lieu of the traditional intramuscular injection.[47] While intranasal mist options are not available to everyone, it may be a preferable alternative to intramuscular injection for some, particularly for children and their parents. Whether child or adult, for those approved to receive it, a nasal spray is a painless option to receive a vaccination and can generally be delivered wherever the traditional flu shot can be delivered. This option continues to require a prescription from, administration by, and supervision under a healthcare professional and does not permit self-administration by the patient.

Mucosal delivery systems entail the use of a mist spray or powder in the nasal cavity. Mucosal vaccines in development have the potential to induce both mucosal immunity—providing localized nasal protection against intruding viral threats—and the broader systemic immunity of traditional vaccines.[48] Because they are delivered through the nose as a mist spray or powder, mucosal delivery systems could trigger increased mucosal immunity, which would help protect against COVID-19 and other respiratory infections by improving immunity at the source of infection.[49] A clinical trial evaluating a mucosal delivery of the COVID-19 vaccine does not reference self-administration,[50] but because of the ease of mucosal delivery, as discussed above, once approved, a mucosal delivery system should be further evaluated as an option for the self-administration of vaccines.

46. *See id.*
47. FluMist Quadrivalent, *available at* https://www.flumistquadrivalent.com/.
48. *See, e.g.*, Jingen Zhu, Swati Jain, Jian Sha, Himanshu Batra, Neeti Ananthaswamy, Paul B. Kilgore & Emily K. Hendrix, *A Bacteriophage-Based, Highly Efficacious, Needle- and Adjuvant-Free, Mucosal COVID-19 Vaccine*, mBio (July 28, 2022), https://journals.asm.org/doi/10.1128/mbio.01822-22?_ga=2.202521105.1613266017.1670192628-1543394282.1670192628.
49. *See id.*
50. *See id.*

An Underlying Patchwork: The Legal and Regulatory Landscape for Vaccine Self-Administration

Successful market entry of and access to self-administering vaccination technologies is dependent on a multitude of regulatory requirements. In this section, we will describe the FDA and state legal and regulatory requirements and reporting considerations that apply to self-administered vaccines.

FDA Approval and ACIP Recommendation

In the United States, all drugs,[51] biologics,[52] and combination products[53] require FDA approval before they can be placed on the market and used by humans. In order to obtain FDA approval of a vaccine, vaccine sponsors or manufacturers must demonstrate to the FDA that the product is safe and effective for its intended use. Through its evaluation process, the FDA will review the scientific, pharmacological, and clinical information

51. The term "drug" means "(A) articles recognized in the official United States Pharmacopoeia, official Homoeopathic Pharmacopoeia of the United States, or official National Formulary, or any supplement to any of them; and (B) articles intended for use in the diagnosis, cure, mitigation, treatment, or prevention of disease in man or other animals; and (C) articles (other than food) intended to affect the structure or any function of the body of man or other animals; and (D) articles intended for use as a component of any articles specified in clause (A), (B), or (C). . . ." 21 U.S.C. § 321(g).

52. The term "biological product" means "a virus, therapeutic serum, toxin, antitoxin, vaccine, blood, blood component or derivative, allergenic product, protein, or analogous product, or arsphenamine or derivative of arsphenamine (or any other trivalent organic arsenic compound), applicable to the prevention, treatment, or cure of a disease or condition of human beings." 42 U.S.C. § 262(i)(1).

53. A combination product includes "(1) A product comprised of two or more regulated components, i.e., drug/device, biologic/device, drug/biologic, or drug/device/biologic, that are physically, chemically, or otherwise combined or mixed and produced as a single entity; (2) Two or more separate products packaged together in a single package or as a unit and comprised of drug and device products, device and biological products, or biological and drug products; (3) A drug, device, or biological product packaged separately that according to its investigational plan or proposed labeling is intended for use only with an approved individually specified drug, device, or biological product where both are required to achieve the intended use, indication, or effect and where upon approval of the proposed product the labeling of the approved product would need to be changed, e.g., to reflect a change in intended use, dosage form, strength, route of administration, or significant change in dose; or (4) Any investigational drug, device, or biological product packaged separately that according to its proposed labeling is for use only with another individually specified investigational drug, device, or biological product where both are required to achieve the intended use, indication, or effect." 21 C.F.R. § 3.2(e).

submitted in support of the product, including data obtained from clinical trials involving human participants, to determine whether the product meets the FDA's requirements for marketing approval.

The FDA considers any combination of a drug or biological product and a device used to deliver that drug or biological product a *combination product*.[54] Examples of combination products include devices coated with a drug or biologic and prefilled drug delivery systems, both of which are potential modalities of vaccine self-administration discussed above.[55] Receiving FDA approval is a complicated process that can take several years. Efforts to bring any form of self-administered vaccine to market appear to still be in the early stages of development. While some clinical trials for self-administrable modalities have been conducted or are underway, none appear to have progressed further than Phase I, where a novel intervention is tested in a small group of people. From there, it must be tested in increasingly larger groups (Phases II and III) so its safety and effectiveness can be monitored and analyzed before it is made available to the public. New modalities of already existing vaccines will need to be evaluated as combination products, and the FDA must find that no efficacy or safety is sacrificed by delivering the vaccine in a novel way. Investigators using an already FDA-approved vaccine should be prepared to provide specific or additional data regarding the safety and efficacy of the delivery mechanism. Vaccine patches and self-administered vaccines still have a long way to go before receiving FDA approval, and it remains to be seen whether there may be new opportunities to accelerate the approval timeline for self-administrable vaccines in light of ongoing public health concerns, such as the COVID-19 pandemic and the 2022 winter "triple-demic" of respiratory syncytial virus (RSV), influenza, and COVID-19.[56]

Drugs or Biologics Administered via Syringe

The FDA has a long history of approving vaccines that require a healthcare professional to prepare a syringe and/or administer a vaccine directly to the patient. Vaccines must undergo a rigorous review of laboratory and clinical data to demonstrate to the FDA that the safety, efficacy, purity,

---

54. *See Frequently Asked Questions about Combination Products*, U.S. Food & Drug Administration, https://www.fda.gov/combination-products/about-combination-products/frequently-asked-questions-about-combination-products#CP.

55. *See id.*

56. *See* Amy Schoenfeld Walker, *Just How Bad Is the "Tripledemic"?*, N.Y. Times (Dec. 16, 2022), https://www.nytimes.com/interactive/2022/12/16/us/covid-flu-rsv-tripledemic-data.html.

and potency of such products warrant approval of the drug for the submitted intended use.[57] Although the FDA has approved a number of *drug products* for self-administration and/or injection by a caregiver using a syringe, as discussed above, we have not identified any FDA vaccine approvals for patients to independently prepare a vaccine using a syringe and self-administer the vaccine.

Auto-injectors

While a complete survey of self-administration techniques and products is outside of the scope of this chapter, it bears noting that the FDA *has* approved drug injector products for administration by a healthcare provider or self-administration by a patient or a caregiver. Approved injectors include products designed to provide an accurate method of injecting a dose of a drug or biological product contained in a cartridge, reservoir, or syringe through an automatically or manually inserted hypodermic needle or through a high-velocity jet. Injectors may be designed for a single use or multiple uses, and they may be disposable or reusable. Injectors (which are typically regulated as combination products) are subject to different regulatory requirements depending, for example, on their intended use, technological characteristics, proposed labeling, and packaging. There are three basic usage groups of injectors: those intended for use with a wide range of drugs and biological products; those intended for use with a certain class or family of drugs or biological products, or with a specific product line; and (iii) those intended for use with a specific drug or biological product (e.g., (a) prefilled with the drug or biological product, (b) co-packaged with the drug/biological product, or (c) separately distributed but labeled for use together).[58]

Microneedle Patches

To date, no microneedle patches intended to deliver a drug or biologic have been approved by the FDA. There are a number of microneedle patch products currently in development, including ones in clinical trials and ones intended for the delivery of vaccines, but none have received approval from the FDA. To date, products that utilize microneedles have been cleared or approved by the FDA as medical devices (e.g.,

57. *See Vaccines*, U.S. Food & Drug Administration, *available at* https://www.fda.gov/vaccines-blood-biologics/vaccines.

58. *See Guidance for Industry and FDS Staff*, *supra* note 19.

microneedling devices intended for dermatologic uses)[59] intended to improve the appearance of facial scars, facial wrinkles, and abdominal scars, but, importantly, have not been cleared or approved to deliver a drug or biologic.

Nasal Sprays

The FDA has approved one intranasal vaccine for use in specific eligible populations, FluMist, which requires a prescription and must be administered by a healthcare provider. Should future clinical evidence demonstrate an adequate safety profile for self-administration of an intranasal vaccine, it is plausible that the FDA would approve such use.

It is also foreseeable that self-administered vaccines—especially patch or intranasal modalities—could someday be offered over-the-counter (OTC). Like prescription products, the FDA also requires a New Drug Application (NDA) or Biologics License Application (BLA) submission for new OTC products. By way of example, while some nicotine replacement therapy products are available by prescription only, transdermal nicotine patches have been reclassified from a prescription medication to an OTC product by the FDA. Currently, prescription nicotine replacement therapy is available only under the brand name Nicotrol and is available both as a nasal spray and as an oral inhaler. Access to Nicotrol is restricted to patients over the age of 18, which must be verified at the pharmacy counter. Restricting access to certain OTC products based on age may help facilitate appropriate use of self-administered vaccines while assuaging potential stakeholders about the de-medicalization of vaccinations.

Once approved by the FDA, the Advisory Committee on Immunization Practices (ACIP)—an advisory committee to the CDC—will review the vaccine and issue a recommendation for its use based on a number of factors, including the evidence of its safety and efficacy, patient and provider feasibility and acceptability, patient age and medical conditions, contraindications, and cost effectiveness.[60] Importantly, should the ACIP recommend a vaccine, health plans and insurers in most markets are required to provide first dollar coverage for the vaccine, that is coverage without cost sharing. The ACIP also determines whether a recommended

59. *See, e.g.*, Microneedling Devices, U.S. Food & Drug Administration, *available at* https://www.fda.gov/medical-devices/aesthetic-cosmetic-devices/microneedling-devices (last updated Aug. 15, 2021).

60. *Recommended Adult Immunization Schedule*, The Centers for Disease Control and Prevention, https://www.cdc.gov/vaccines/schedules/downloads/adult/adult-combined-schedule.pdf.

vaccine will be provided through the Vaccines for Children program to Medicaid and uninsured children.

The States as Arbiters of Access: Scope of Practice

States have long been the regulators of health professions, determining the legal scope of practice of healthcare professionals, including physicians, pharmacists, and other advanced practice and allied health professionals. While the approval of prescription products rests with the FDA, states traditionally determine who may assess a patient's eligibility for the product, who may prescribe the product, and who may dispense or administer it. As discussed above, the de-medicalization of vaccination through the expansion of pharmacist scope of practice has vastly expanded access to vaccines. So too will states determine who may prescribe and dispense self-administered vaccines.

Because self-administered vaccines will be dispensed to patients, pharmacists are likely to play a central role in delivery. Depending on the modality and product format, physician offices may stock self-administering products or prescribe or refer patients to a pharmacy to obtain the product. State scope of practice laws will greatly influence the ability of a patient to access vaccines in the pharmacy setting.

Today, all states permit pharmacists to administer vaccines, and though this authority varies as to specific vaccines, 17 states permit pharmacists to prescribe vaccines without the need for a protocol or order from another provider.[61] Notably, during the COVID-19 pandemic, the Secretary of the U.S. Department of Health and Human Services (HHS) exercised his authority under the Public Readiness and Preparedness (PREP) Act to preempt state law and permit qualified pharmacists and pharmacy interns to administer vaccines without a prescription, including all ACIP-recommended vaccines to children ages 3 to 18, COVID-19 vaccines to all persons age 3 and older, and the seasonal influenza vaccine to all persons ages 19 and older.[62] Certain states allow pharmacists

---

61. *See Pharmacist Administered Vaccines*, American Pharmacist Association (Aug. 2022), https://naspa.us/wp-content/uploads/2021/01/Pharmacist-Immunization-Authority-December-2022.pdf.

62. *See Third Amendment to Declaration under the Public Readiness and Emergency Preparedness Act for Medical Countermeasures against COVID–19*, Department of Health and Human Services (Mar. 17, 2020), https://www.hhs.gov/sites/default/files/third-amendment-declaration.pdf; *Guidance for Licensed Pharmacists and Pharmacy Interns Regarding COVID-19 Vaccines and Immunity under the PREP*

to dispense or administer other products either independently or under a physician's standing order or collaborative practice agreement, including contraceptives, naloxone, tobacco cessation products, pre-exposure prophylaxis (PrEP) for HIV, and antivirals.[63]

Other analogue products with invasive routes of administration continue to favor physician prescription requirements in state law. Due to the potential for unintended self-harm, for example, all insulin pumps and infusion sets require a prescription from a physician.[64] Insulin pumps are "contraindicated for people unwilling or unable to perform a minimum of four fingerstick blood glucose meter tests per day and for people unwilling or unable to maintain contact with their healthcare professional."[65] Prescription requirements for epinephrine auto-injectors vary by state. For example, California requires a prescription by a licensed healthcare professional—physicians, nurse practitioners, and physician's assistants—with no exceptions.[66]

Presumably, self-administering vaccines would produce fewer safety challenges—certainly patches or sprays would produce fewer challenges than self-administration via injection—which would mitigate potential safety concerns necessitating a prescription. This would more easily persuade state lawmakers to permit pharmacists to prescribe and dispense the product without the involvement of a physician. While this would not fully supplant the role of physicians as vaccinators, it would facilitate ease

---

Act, Department of Health and Human Services (Sept. 3, 2020), https://www.hhs.gov/sites/default/files/licensed-pharmacists-and-pharmacy-interns-regarding-covid-19-vaccines-immunity.pdf; *Tenth Amendment to Declaration Under the Public Readiness and Emergency Preparedness Act for Medical Countermeasures Against COVID–19*, Department of Health and Human Services: Office of the Secretary, https://www.phe.gov/Preparedness/legal/prepact/Pages/10th-Amendment.aspx.

63. *See Pharmacist Administered Vaccines*, *supra* note 61; *See Pharmacist Prescribing: Hormonal Contraceptives*, National Alliance of State Pharmacy Associations (Sept. 1, 2022), https://naspa.us/resource/contraceptives/; *Pharmacist Prescribing: "Test and Treat,"* National Alliance of State Pharmacy Associations (Oct. 10, 2022), https://naspa.us/resource/pharmacist-prescribing-for-strep-and-flu-test-and-treat/; *Pharmacist Prescribing: HIV PrEP and PEP*, National Alliance of State Pharmacy Associations (Dec. 9, 2022) https://naspa.us/resource/pharmacist-prescribing-hiv-prep-and-pep/

64. *See Summary of Safety and Effectiveness Data for Medtronic MiniMed 670G Insulin Pump System*, U.S. Food & Drug Administration, https://www.accessdata.fda.gov/cdrh_docs/pdf16/p160017b.pdf.

65. *Id.*

66. Ca. HS § 1797.197a; T. 22 §100044.2; Ca. Bus. and Prof. Code § 2636.1; Ca. Bus. and Prof. Code § 3502.1.

of access across settings and especially in the pharmacy where patients are accustomed to picking up products for home use.

Ensuring Patient Education and Safety

An adjacent consideration is that of patient education and safety. Immunizing providers today undertake several very important steps before vaccine administration, including reviewing a patient's immunization history, assessing the need for vaccination based on the ACIP's immunization schedule, screening for any particular medical contraindications or precautions (e.g., pregnancy, acute illness, latex sensitivity, or egg allergies), and educating the patient about the vaccine.[67] Under the National Childhood Vaccine Injury Act, providers must provide a patient with a Vaccine Information Statement prior to administering any vaccine dose.[68] States may also impose requirements for patient education and supervision for certain products. For example, monitoring requirements for epinephrine auto-injectors also vary by state, but in California, patients must be provided a manufacturer's product information sheet.[69]

For the typical insulin pump, monitoring requirements are set at the federal level and include maintaining regular contact with a healthcare professional and frequently monitoring blood glucose levels. Further, while not required, device companies and/or physicians and health practices often offer instructional sessions on how to use the device and infusion sets.

Clinical steps to educate and ensure the safety of the patient will remain essential even with the advent of self-administered vaccines, which means that vaccine self-administration will remain somewhat and appropriately tethered to the healthcare delivery system. How these steps are carried out between provider and patient is likely to change to facilitate the desired convenience of self-administration. Access at the pharmacy counter and telehealth are likely facilitators of both safety and convenience. Considering increased telehealth capabilities within the healthcare system stemming from the COVID-19 pandemic, offering telehealth tutorials on self-administration could be a simple strategy to recommend a patient receive a vaccine and assess eligibility and contraindications, prescribe the vaccine, ensure effective delivery and monitor for adverse

---

67. *See Vaccine Administration*, The Centers for Disease Control and Prevention, https://www.cdc.gov/vaccines/hcp/admin/admin-protocols.html.

68. National Vaccine Childhood Injury Act *as codified at* 42 U.S.C. § 300aa-26.

69. Ca B & P § 4119.4.

events. Some contraindications or precautions may continue to require a face-to-face encounter with a healthcare professional. This could perhaps mean dropping into a pharmacy and self-administering on-site or with the assistance of a pharmacist or pharmacy technician. Much evidence generation is still needed to ascertain circumstances requiring more or less clinical management in vaccine self-administration.

Immunization Reporting and Post-Marketing Surveillance

Following vaccination, the vast majority of patients simply return home. Some individuals do experience adverse reactions to vaccinations, most of which are minor—injection site soreness, headache, or fatigue. Several post-marketing surveillance systems are maintained to monitor for the occurrence of adverse events. The FDA and CDC conduct both passive and active surveillance[70] and co-manage the Vaccine Adverse Event Reporting System (VAERS).[71] Both healthcare professionals and vaccine manufacturers are required to submit certain types of adverse reactions through VAERS, should they become aware of such an event. Individuals who experience adverse reactions are also encouraged to report the event themselves. Notably, VAERS is a passive reporting system, in that it only accepts reports and does not actively seek out individuals who have experienced adverse events. Reports to VAERS do not establish a causal relationship between vaccination and the reported adverse event. The ability of patients to report to VAERS provides a ready system for reporting of adverse events following vaccine self-administration.

FDA and CMS have also developed various active surveillance systems relying on claims data to identify safety signals, underscoring the importance of capturing self-administration events in claims data.[72] In particular, the Vaccine Safety Datalink (VSD) relies on electronic health record (EHR) data from eight integrated health systems across

70. *See COVID-19 Vaccine Safety Surveillance*, U.S. Food & Drug Administration (Dec. 7, 2021), https://www.fda.gov/vaccines-blood-biologics/safety-availability-biologics/covid-19-vaccine-safety-surveillance.

71. *Vaccine Adverse Event Reporting System*, The Department of Health & Human Services, https://vaers.hhs.gov/.

72. *See COVID-19 Vaccine Safety Surveillance*, *supra* note 70.

the country to collect safety information that is further studied to better understand rare and serious adverse events.[73]

Indeed, capturing vaccine self-administration events is essential for assuring patient safety, for understanding adverse events potentially associated with a vaccine, and for public health surveillance purposes. Today, a variety of methods are used to capture immunization events, including Immunization Information Systems (IIS), EHR, claims data, and tools such as the CDC's National Immunization Survey. Tracking vaccination status using these methods is essential to ensuring the vaccination of individual patients and provider reimbursement for vaccine product and administration, and to understanding population level uptake and herd immunity.

IIS are centralized reporting systems maintained by almost all U.S. jurisdictions that include information regarding immunizations administered within the state.[74] There are known challenges in the ability of IIS to capture all vaccinations, particularly where administration occurred outside of the health system or in a setting that is unable to report to an IIS.[75] This exemplifies the foreseeable challenge of capturing vaccine self-administration events in IIS. Pharmacies, now major vaccination sites, have increasingly integrated IIS reporting into the clinical workflow.[76] Pharmacy reporting to IIS may become more essential as dispensing sites for self-administered vaccines.

---

73. *Vaccine Safety Datalink (VSD)*, The Centers for Disease Control and Prevention, https://www.cdc.gov/vaccinesafety/ensuringsafety/monitoring/vsd/index.html.

74. *See* Lynn Gibbs Scharf, Rebecca Coyle, Kafayat Adeniyi, Janet Fath, LaTreace Harris, Stuart Myerburg, Mary Beth Kurilo & Elizabeth Abbott, *Current Challenges and Future Possibilities for Immunization Information Systems*, Academic Pediatrics (May 2021), https://www.sciencedirect.com/science/article/pii/S1876285920305842.

75. *See* Holly C. Groom, Bradley Crane, Allison L. Naleway, Eric Weintraub, Matthew F. Daley, Kris Wain, Mary Beth Kurilo, Rachael Burganowski, Malini B. DeSilva, James G. Donahue, Sungching C. Glenn, Kristin Goddard, Michael L. Jackson, Elyse O. Kharbanda, Ned Lewis, Yingbo Lou, Marlene Lugg, Erica Scotty, Lina S. Sy, Joshua T.B. Williams & Stephanie A. Irving, *Monitoring vaccine safety using the vaccine safety Datalink: Assessing capacity to integrate data from Immunization Information systems*, Vaccine (Jan. 2022), https://www.sciencedirect.com/science/article/pii/S0264410X2101656X?casa_token=pKX-cBNRLCAAAAAA:v-yZWOktJm3w9dOjtJ4vWQ3EO-Z6ShCo2AQIZUYs3pJdZmrNcV05sV_YCzzeZKCfQceJf0g7i9g.

76. *See* Tessa J. Hastings, David Ha, Brent I. Fox, Jingjing Qian, Joni Lakin & Salisa C. Westrick, *Increasing use of immunization information systems for routine vaccinations in independent community pharmacies: A randomized controlled trial*, Journal of the American Pharmacists Association (July 2022), https://www.sciencedirect.com/science/article/pii/S1544319122000632.

Patient attestation, too, will be an especially important future tool to ensure timely and accurate reporting of these events. If a patient receives a self-administrable vaccine from a mail-order pharmacy, patient reporting becomes all the more essential. For children, proof of vaccination for purposes of school entry will also need to be accounted for in reporting the self-administration of vaccines. Similar concerns will arise for adults in situations where proof of vaccination is required for employment. A telehealth encounter could be used to document the event, though simplified and patient-friendly reporting options should be explored. For example, a text messaging system could serve as both a reminder/recall system to encourage vaccination and to prompt the patient to confirm the administration event. Likewise, a web portal or smartphone application integrated with IIS or EHR could facilitate patient attestation. Analyses of patient portal utilization have been associated with better clinical outcomes and satisfactory family experiences in reporting events for patient safety monitoring.[77] A particular consideration when designing a patient reporting instrument should be confirmation of the successful administration to avoid potential missed vaccination when self-administration fails.

The Last Mile: Distribution, Storage and Handling, Disposal

The vaccine distribution chain can present challenges of its own, particularly where ultra-low-temperature storage is required as with some currently licensed COVID-19 vaccines. Refrigeration or freezing requirements that begin during manufacture and end once the vaccine is injected into a patient and room-temperature stability considerations are the norm for traditional vaccines. Yet, the cold chain concern for shipments directly to the patient has been solved many times before elsewhere in medicine and, more recently, home meal delivery. Many biologics used to treat psoriasis, for example, are delivered in refrigerated boxes with ice and cold packs that keep the medication at the proper temperature until received by a patient. For Medicare beneficiaries, a signature is required when the

77. *See* Cesar Baeta, Edwin Owolo, Antoinette Charles, Zoey Petitt, Emily Poehlein, Chad Cook, Jacob Sperber, Rory Goodwin, Melissa Erickson & Cindy Green, *P92. The association between patient portal utilization and clinical outcomes*, 22 The Spine Journal S170 (Sept. 2022), https://www.sciencedirect.com/science/article/abs/pii/S1529943022006325.

beneficiary receives durable medical equipment through the mail.[78] For the product that does require cold chain, much progress has been made to assure product stability upon arrival, including innovative vaccine vial monitors that provide a simple visual indicator if the vaccine has been subjected to unsafe temperature variation.[79] Though these monitors are not used in the United States today, they are widely used throughout the remainder of the world.

Many of the, albeit early stage, clinical trials discussed above have tested room-temperature stable vaccines, which possibly eliminate the need for arduous temperature stability requirements in shipment. Still, assuring the product is stored safely prior to use will remain a consideration. For example, EpiPen has outlined specific storage recommendations (e.g., temperature, sun exposure) in the product's patient information and instructions.[80]

State regulatory oversight of distribution will also apply to self-administrable vaccine products. Distributors of pharmaceutical and biological products must generally obtain wholesale or distributor licenses in all states where they ship drug product (and a smaller number of states also require licenses for shipping medical devices). In addition, pharmacies must have pharmacy licenses in the states where they are located and in the states where they ship product.

Finally, sharps disposal is another area of regulation relevant to self-administered vaccines. Sharps disposal is regulated at the state level, including the definition for what constitutes a sharp, but the FDA provides recommendations on what to do in the absence of state regulation.[81] Some states, but not all, provide a definition of "sharps" in their statutes and/or regulations. For example, California defines "Home-generated sharps waste" as "hypodermic needles, pen needles, intravenous needles, lancets, and other devices that are used to penetrate the skin for the deliv-

78. *See Proof of Delivery Documentation Requirements*, MLN Matters, Centers for Medicare and Medicaid Services (Jan. 17, 2019), https://www.cms.gov/Outreach-and-Education/Medicare-Learning-Network-MLN/MLNMattersArticles/Downloads/SE19003.pdf.

79. *See Vaccine Vial Monitor*, World Health Organization, https://cdn.who.int/media/docs/default-source/immunization/supply-chain/vvm-infographic.pdf?sfvrsn=1a00c5b2_92&download=true.

80. *Patient Information and Instructions for Use*, National Institutes of Health, https://dailymed.nlm.nih.gov/dailymed/fda/fdaDrugXsl.cfm?type=display&setid=7560c201-9246-487c-a13b-6295db04274a#section-15.

81. *Sharps Disposal Containers*, U.S. Food & Drug Administration, https://www.fda.gov/medical-devices/safely-using-sharps-needles-and-syringes-home-work-and-travel/sharps-disposal-containers; *see also* https://safeneedledisposal.org/.

ery of medications derived from a household, including a multifamily residence or household."[82] This definition is generally indicative of the type of definition a state will provide, if any, but may be slightly more detailed than most.

For the states that do not provide a definition of sharps, the FDA recommends, "Sharps is a medical term for devices with sharp points or edges that can puncture or cut skin," and provides the following examples:

- "Needles—hollow needles used to inject drugs (medication) under the skin
- "Syringes—devices used to inject medication into or withdraw fluid from the body
- "Lancets, also called 'fingerstick' devices—instruments with a short, two-edged blade used to get drops of blood for testing. Lancets are commonly used in the treatment of diabetes.
- "Auto Injectors, including epinephrine and insulin pens—syringes pre-filled with fluid medication designed to be self-injected into the body
- "Infusion sets—tubing systems with a needle used to deliver drugs to the body.
- Connection needles/sets—needles that connect to a tube used to transfer fluids in and out of the body. This is generally used for patients on home hemodialysis."[83]

While injectable vaccines are clearly implicated under these definitions, a microneedle would also likely be considered a sharp, as it is designed to puncture the skin and deliver medication. With that said, the dissolving varieties of the needles were likely not considered when this definition was written and would constitute a gray area. Given that each state defines what is a sharp or needle differently, upon FDA approval of a microneedle patch, this could be an area in which new state regulations are promulgated.

The FDA requires used sharps to be placed in a sharps disposal container. FDA-cleared sharps containers are generally available through pharmacies, medical supply companies, healthcare providers, and online. These containers are made of puncture-resistant plastic with leak-resistant

82. CA Health & Safety Code § 117671 (2017).

83. *Safely Using Sharps (Needles and Syringes) at Home*, at Work and on Travel, U.S. Food & Drug Administration, https://www.fda.gov/medical-devices/consumer-products/safely-using-sharps-needles-and-syringes-home-work-and-travel.

sides and bottoms. They also have a tight fitting, puncture-resistant lid. If an FDA-cleared container is not available, a heavy-duty plastic household container, such as a laundry detergent container, can be used as an alternative.[84] The FDA recommends SafeNeedleDisposal.org, which provides an overview of how to dispose of sharps in each state.

Sharps disposal requirements may also vary by state.[85] Some states make it illegal to dispose of home-generated sharps waste in the trash or recycling containers, and require that sharps waste be transported to a collection center in an approved sharps container. Many states, including California, Illinois, and New York, impose a mix of requirements on the home use of sharps ranging from disposing of those sharps in a labeled sharps container and not mixing sharps waste with other trash and recycling to requiring used sharps to be destroyed. Additionally, many specialty medications are accompanied with mail-back programs or container services.[86]

Conclusion

Vaccine self-administration, while promising, is still for the most part in the early stages of clinical study. As we have outlined, a self-administrable vaccine product could take the form of many current delivery modalities. These modalities differ greatly in the degree of invasiveness, which will affect patient tolerability, feasibility, and acceptability.

There are many lessons that can be gleaned from the experience with the analogous products identified above and their use in chronic disease management. The familiarity patients and healthcare providers of varying levels of practice have with patient self-administration in a disease management context can provide a foundation for the self-administration of vaccines. However, we would underscore the differing patient incentives when comparing chronic disease management to prophylaxis. Less invasive modalities are more likely to constitute feasible options and garner patient acceptance.

---

84. *Id.*

85. *See Home-generated Sharps: Statewide Laws and Regulations Addressing Collection and Disposal*, Legislative Analysis and Public Analysis Association (Nov. 2019), https://legislativeanalysis.org/wp-content/uploads/2019/11/Summary-of-State-Legislation-and-Regulaion-Related-to-Sharps-Disposal.pdf.

86. *See, e.g.*, SafeNeedleDisposal.org, https://safeneedledisposal.org/solutions/pharmaceutical-programs/.

The community of immunization providers and stakeholders should begin to discuss the necessary shifts in our healthcare delivery and public health systems to facilitate vaccine self-administration. The patient convenience and comfort afforded by self-administration that could overcome vaccine reluctance is at natural tension with traditional medical models. As outlined, healthcare providers will continue to play an important role in assuring appropriate vaccination and patient safety. As clinical study progresses toward demonstrating the safety and efficacy of self-administrable vaccine candidates, patient, provider, and other stakeholder attitudes regarding self-administration should be evaluated.

Chapter 9

Steps to Stringency: California's Vaccine Laws

Nicole Strombom

Introduction

Vaccine policy varies throughout the United States. This chapter provides a brief background on vaccination policy authority on the federal, state, and local levels and then provides an in-depth look at recent vaccination policy within California. California has seen several policy changes related to vaccinations over the last decade, championed by Dr. Richard Pan, a pediatrician turned politician.[1] The case study of California shows the progression toward more stringent vaccination laws and the push back that occurs when public health measures limit individual choice.

Background

Federal Vaccination Authority

Vaccinations are considered one of the biggest scientific discoveries; with vaccinations, humans can pre-expose themselves to viruses and establish

1. Angela Hart, *'He Stood His Ground': State Senator Will Leave Office as Champion of Tough Vaccine Laws*, California Healthline (2022), https://californiahealthline.org/news/article/state-senator-richard-pan-champion-tough-vaccine-laws/ (last visited Dec. 29, 2022); *Q&A: Despite pushback, physician lawmaker stands up for vaccines*, American Medical Association, https://www.ama-assn.org/delivering-care/public-health/qa-despite-pushback-physician-lawmaker-stands-vaccines (last visited Dec. 29, 2022).

a pattern for how to defeat an infection before the body is attacked during an outbreak.[2] Vaccines are a line of defense in keeping the public healthy.[3] Within the United States, the authority to regulate vaccinations occurs on multiple levels. The federal government has the authorities provided to it within the U.S. Constitution; these powers include the regulation of food and drugs, which is performed by the Food and Drug Administration (FDA) under the authority of the executive branch.[4] Article I of the U.S. Constitution includes the Commerce Clause, which limits trade within the United States and between the United States and foreign countries.[5] This means that the federal government has the authority to determine what type of vaccines are marketed within the United States.[6] Further, the U.S. federal government does not have an enumerated power to mandate public health measures (e.g., vaccinations to all individuals), but the government can mandate vaccinations to those under its jurisdiction (including federal employees and military personnel).[7]

State and Local Vaccination Authority

State

States have authority, based on the Tenth Amendment, to make policy decisions on anything that is not discussed or prohibited in the U.S. Constitution.[8] Public health and safety are not discussed within the

2. *Counting the impact of vaccines*, WHO, https://www.who.int/news-room/feature-stories/detail/counting-the-impact-of-vaccines (last visited Dec. 29, 2022); *A Brief History of Vaccination*, WHO, https://www.who.int/news-room/spotlight/history-of-vaccination/a-brief-history-of-vaccination (last visited Dec. 29, 2022).

3. *Counting the impact of vaccines*, *supra* note 2.

4. Center for Biologics Evaluation and Research, *Vaccines*, FDA (2022), https://www.fda.gov/vaccines-blood-biologics/vaccines (last visited Dec. 29, 2022); *The Constitution of the United States: A Transcription*, National Archives (2015), https://www.archives.gov/founding-docs/constitution-transcript (last visited Dec. 29, 2022).

5. *The Constitution of the United States*, *supra* note 4.

6. *Center for Biologics Evaluation and Research*, *supra* note 4; *The Constitution of the United States*, *supra* note 4.

7. *The Constitution of the United States*, *supra* note 4; *VERIFY: No, the federal government can't mandate vaccines to the general public. Here's why*, WFAA.COM (2021), https://www.wfaa.com/article/news/local/verify-no-the-federal-government-cant-mandate-vaccines-to-the-general-public/287-9f537a12-1472-47a4-8a8d-9e8c107b03c8 (last visited Dec. 29, 2022).

8. *The Constitution of the United States*, *supra* note 4; *The Bill of Rights: A Transcription*, National Archives (2015), https://www.archives.gov/founding-docs/bill-of-rights-transcript (last visited Dec. 29, 2022).

Constitution; states have the authority to regulate public health and safety.[9] The power to regulate for public health and safety is commonly called the police power and means that states can legislate vaccine policies because these policies are for the good of the public's health.[10] Nolo's Plain-English Law Dictionary describes police powers as:

> [t]he fundamental right of a government to make all necessary laws. In the United States, state police power comes from the Tenth Amendment to the Constitution, which gives states the rights and powers "not delegated to the United States." States are thus granted the power to establish and enforce laws protecting the welfare, safety, and health of the public.[11]

States' police power to mandate vaccinations for public health was upheld in the 1905 *Jacobson v. Massachusetts* case.[12] Jacobson did not want to comply with a state-level requirement, implemented on the local level, to receive the smallpox vaccine and was issued a fine.[13] In response, Jacobson pursued a lawsuit against the State of Massachusetts; the U.S. Supreme Court heard the case and held that a state has a police power that can be used to protect the public health and safety of its citizens.[14]

School-based vaccine mandates are included within the police power.[15] In 1922, the Supreme Court heard *Zucht v. King* and dismissed the claim that school-based vaccine mandates were unconstitutional, providing the rationale that these requirements protect public health.[16] An

9. *The Constitution of the United States*, *supra* note 4; *The Bill of Rights*, *supra* note 8.

10. *police powers*, LII/Legal Information Institute, https://www.law.cornell.edu/wex/police_powers (last visited Dec. 29, 2022).

11. *Police Powers Definition*, WWW.NOLO.COM, https://www.nolo.com/dictionary/police-powers-term.html (last visited Dec. 29, 2022).

12. Jacobson v. Massachusetts, *197 U.S. 11 (1905)*, Justia Law, https://supreme.justia.com/cases/federal/us/197/11/ (last visited Dec. 29, 2022); *Jacobson v. Massachusetts,* Oyez, https://www.oyez.org/cases/1900-1940/197us11 (last visited Dec. 29, 2022).

13. Jacobson v. Massachusetts, 197 U.S. 11 (1905), *supra* note 12; Jacobson v. Massachusetts, *supra* note 12.

14. Jacobson v. Massachusetts, 197 U.S. 11 (1905), *supra* note 12; Jacobson v. Massachusetts, *supra* note 12.

15. Kevin M. Malone & Alan R. Hinman, *Vaccination Mandates: The Public Health Imperative and Individual Rights*, *in* Law in Public Health Practice 338 (Richard A. Goodman et al. eds., 2d ed. 2007), https://academic.oup.com/book/36355/chapter/319882359 (last visited Dec. 29, 2022).

16. *Id.*; Zucht v. King, 260 U.S. 174 *(1922)*, Justia Law, https://supreme.justia.com/cases/federal/us/260/174/ (last visited Jan. 3, 2023).

individual's right to an education does not supersede a state's right to protect public health.[17] In many states, including California, those who are homeschooled are excluded from school-based vaccine requirements.[18]

Preemption

Preemption occurs when a higher policymaking authority limits what policy or policy parameters a lower policymaking authority can make.[19] Three types of preemption exist: (1) floor preemption, (2) ceiling preemption, and (3) entire space preemption. Floor preemption sets a lower limit that a lower policymaking authority must stick to; the lower policymaking authority can make more stringent standards than the floor but cannot make lower standards. A minimum wage is an example of floor preemption.[20] Ceiling preemption is an upper limit that a lower policymaking authority must stick to. Rental pricing caps are an example of ceiling preemption because the price must be lower than the cap. Entire space preemption means there is no room for the lower policymaking authority to legislate in the policy area. An example of entire space preemption is a state saying that no local entity may have a mask mandate.[21] When a higher-level policymaking authority has not preempted a policy area, the lower-level policymaking authority is not limited in what policies it can adopt—except for policies that are constitutionally legal at both the federal and state level.

Local

Local governments can legislate in the same areas as states if the policies adopted are not preempted. Each state may reserve authority over certain police powers within the state's constitution or subsequent laws. Police powers extend to local governments to ensure that those closest to a public health and/or safety issue can manage the issue.[22] At the local

17. Malone & Hinman, *supra* note 15.

18. *Do Homeschoolers Need to Be Vaccinated? (We Have The Answer)*, How Now Homeschooling, https://hownowhomeschool.com/do-homeschoolers-need-to-be-vaccinated-weve-got-the-answer/ (last visited Jan. 3, 2023).

19. *preemption*, LII/Legal Information Institute, https://www.law.cornell.edu/wex/preemption (last visited Dec. 29, 2022).

20. *Preemption 101*, National League of Cities, https://www.nlc.org/wp-content/uploads/2020/11/Preemption_101.pdf (last visited Dec. 29, 2022).

21. *Preemption and the COVID-19 Pandemic*, National League of Cities, https://www.nlc.org/wp-content/uploads/2020/11/COVID-19_Preemption_Report.pdf (last visited Dec. 29, 2022).

22. *Police Powers—Municipal*, US Legal, https://municipal.uslegal.com/police-powers/ (last visited Dec. 29, 2022).

level, police powers can be utilized in forming ordinances.[23] In terms of vaccination policy, preemption is key because a local entity may want stringent vaccination ordinances but be thwarted by a later-adopted state policy that limits local efforts by utilizing entire space preemption.

Vaccines

When vaccines were first discovered in the 1700s, the debate about receiving a vaccination or not began.[24] School-based vaccination mandates began in the 1850s with Massachusetts as the earliest adopting state.[25] California adopted its first school vaccination mandate in 1889, which was amended in 1911 to allow for exemptions.[26] The March of Dimes provided a wave of support for vaccines (1955) with a means to avoid the ramifications of polio.[27] In 1998, the now-debunked research that purported to connect Autism spectrum disorder to vaccinations was published; this paper was rescinded—in 2010—and Dr. Andrew Wakefield lost his medical license.[28] Despite this paper being rescinded, parents continue to associate vaccines with adverse health outcomes, which impacts vaccine efficacy.[29] The Centers for Disease Control and

23. *Id.*

24. *A Brief History of Vaccination*, *supra* note 2.

25. Malone & Hinman, *supra* note 15.

26. Merrie Monteagudo, *From the Archives: San Diego schools fought smallpox vaccine mandates in 1908*, The San Diego Union-Tribune, Sept. 28, 2021, https://www.sandiegouniontribune.com/news/local-history/story/2021-09-28/from-the-archives-san-diego-schools-fought-smallpox-vaccine-mandates-in-1908.

27. *Our History*, March of Dimes, https://www.marchofdimes.org/about-us/celebrate-our-history (last visited Dec. 29, 2022); *Polio Elimination in the United States*, Centers for Disease Control and Prevention (2022), https://www.cdc.gov/polio/what-is-polio/polio-us.html (last visited Dec. 29, 2022).

28. Aderbal Sabra, Joseph A. Bellanti & Angel R. Colón, *Ileal-lymphoid-nodular hyperplasia, non-specific colitis, and pervasive developmental disorder in children*, 352 The Lancet 234 (1998), https://linkinghub.elsevier.com/retrieve/pii/S0140673605778375 (last visited Dec. 29, 2022); Laura Eggertson, *Lancet retracts 12-year-old article linking autism to MMR vaccines*, 182 CMAJ E199 (2010), https://www.ncbi.nlm.nih.gov/pmc/articles/PMC2831678/ (last visited Dec. 29, 2022); Alice Park, *Doctor behind vaccine-autism link loses license*, Time, May 2010, https://healthland.time.com/2010/05/24/doctor-behind-vaccine-autism-link-loses-license/ (last visited Dec. 29, 2022).

29. Eggertson, *supra* note 28; Matthew Motta & Dominik Stecula, *Quantifying the effect of Wakefield et al. (1998) on skepticism about MMR vaccine safety in the U.S.*, 16 PLOS ONE e0256395 (2021), https://journals.plos.org/plosone/article?id=10.1371/journal.pone.0256395 (last visited Dec. 29, 2022); T*he Vaccine-Autism Myth Started 20 Years Ago. It Still Endures Today*, Time, Feb. 28, 2018, https://time.com/5175704/andrew-wakefield-vaccine-autism/ (last visited Dec. 29, 2022).

Prevention (CDC) and FDA monitor vaccine safety; reports on specific vaccines are available and include side effects.[30] Although vaccine safety information is available, the debate on whether to vaccinate one's children or not continues and leads to the spread of disease in school settings.

California Political Will

California is known to be left leaning.[31] Democrats have controlled California politics since the 2000s with a majority in the Senate and Assembly.[32] The last Republican governor of California was Arnold Schwarzenegger from 2003 to 2011.[33] The 2012 election saw Democrats gain a supermajority in both houses and gain the governor seat.[34] The Democrat supermajority was lost in 2013, 2014, and 2017.[35] The 2016,

30. *U.S. Vaccine Safety—Overview, History, and How It Works*, CDC, (2020), https://www.cdc.gov/vaccinesafety/ensuringsafety/history/index.html (last visited Dec. 29, 2022).

31. Tyler Kingkade, Alicia Victoria Lozano & David Ingram, *California has a reputation for progressive politics. Don't tell that to the state's progressives*, NBC News (2020), https://www.nbcnews.com/politics/2020-election/california-has-reputation-progressive-politics-don-t-tell-state-s-n1243023 (last visited Jan. 2, 2023); *California's Political Geography 2020*, Public Policy Institute of California, https://www.ppic.org/publication/californias-political-geography/ (last visited Jan. 2, 2023); Charles R. Kesler, *California Has Become the Far Left Coast*, WSJ, https://www.wsj.com/articles/california-has-become-the-far-left-coast-11551917067 (last visited Jan. 2, 2023).

32. *Party control of California state government*, Ballotpedia, https://ballotpedia.org/Party_control_of_California_state_government (last visited Jan. 2, 2023).

33. *Schwarzenegger declares California fiscal emergency*, Reuters, https://www.reuters.com/article/us-economy-california/schwarzenegger-declares-california-fiscal-emergency-idUSTRE66R5FE20100728 (last visited Jan. 2, 2023); *California's debt triples in Schwarzenegger's 7 years*, Ballotpedia, https://ballotpedia.org/California%27s_debt_triples_in_Schwarzenegger%27s_7_years (last visited Jan. 2, 2023); *Former Governors—California*, National Governors Association, https://www.nga.org/former-governors/california/ (last visited Jan. 2, 2023).

34. Adam Nagourney, *With a Supermajority, California Democrats Begin to Make Plans*, The New York Times, Dec. 17, 2012, https://www.nytimes.com/2012/12/17/us/politics/for-california-democrats-supermajority-is-a-new-challenge.html (last visited Jan. 2, 2023); *Former Governors—California*, *supra* note 33.

35. Associated Press, *California Democrats temporarily lose Assembly supermajority*, The Mercury News (2017), https://www.mercurynews.com/2017/12/11/california-democrats-temporarily-lose-assembly-supermajority/ (last visited Jan. 2, 2023); Jessica Calefati, *Scandals cost California Democrats supermajority in Senate*, The Mercury News (2014), https://www.mercurynews.com/2014/03/03/scandals-cost-california-democrats-supermajority-in-senate/ (last visited Jan. 2, 2023); Laird

2018, 2020, and 2022 elections resulted in Democrats gaining supermajors in both houses.[36] A supermajority means Democrats can pass progressive legislative measures with little opposition. Additionally, Republicans hold less than 50 percent of local legislative positions (mayors or city council members); this means little local pushback occurs when implementing progressive legislation on the local level.[37]

California Vaccine Legislative Champion Dr. Richard Pan

With a Doctor of Medicine degree from the University of Pittsburg and a Master's in Public Health from Harvard, Dr. Pan served as an Associate Professor of Pediatrics at the University of California, Davis.[38] In 2010, with the passage of the Affordable Care Act, Dr. Pan saw the need for a politician with medical experience to join California's Assemble (lower house), ran for office, and won.[39] While serving his second term in the California Assembly, 2013–2014, Dr. Pan served as the Chair of the Assembly Health Committee.[40] The 2014 election saw Dr. Pan make a successful bid for a California Senate seat, and he served in the

Harrison, *Democrats Lose Supermajority in California Senate*, KQED, https://www.kqed.org/news/89936/resignation-emperils-democrats-supermajority-in-california-senate (last visited Jan. 2, 2023).

36. *California Democrats Capture Legislative Supermajorities*, https://www.capradio.org/85717 (last visited Jan. 2, 2023); Patrick McGreevy, *Democrats win back a supermajority in California's Legislature*, Los Angeles Times (2018), https://www.latimes.com/politics/la-pol-ca-democrats-supermajority-california-legislature-20181112-story.html (last visited Jan. 2, 2023); Nicole Nixon, *Democrats Look To Expand Their Supermajority In California's Statehouse*, https://www.capradio.org/158373, CapRadio (last visited Jan. 2, 2023); 2020 California legislative session, Ballotpedia, https://ballotpedia.org/2020_California_legislative_session (last visited Jan. 2, 2023); *California State Senate elections, 2022*, Ballotpedia, https://ballotpedia.org/California_State_Senate_elections,_2022 (last visited Jan. 2, 2023); *California State Assembly elections, 2022*, Ballotpedia, https://ballotpedia.org/California_State_Assembly_elections,_2022 (last visited Jan. 2, 2023).

37. Kesler, *supra* note 31.

38. *Richard Pan*, Ballotpedia, https://ballotpedia.org/Richard_Pan (last visited Dec. 29, 2022); Vivian Ho, *The California senator fighting for the strictest vaccination laws in the US*, The Guardian, Aug. 29, 2019, https://www.theguardian.com/us-news/2019/aug/28/richard-pan-california-vaccines-strictest-law (last visited Dec. 29, 2022).

39. *Richard Pan*, *supra* note 38; *H.R.3590 - 111th Congress (2009–2010): Patient Protection and Affordable Care Act*, Congress.gov, https://www.congress.gov/bill/111th-congress/house-bill/3590 (last visited Jan. 2, 2023).

40. *Richard Pan*, *supra* note 38.

Senate until he hit California's 12 years in the state legislature term limit (December 2022).[41] During his time in the Senate, Dr. Pan was Chair of the Senate Health Committee from 2019 to 2022.[42] Throughout his time in California politics, Dr. Pan was a champion for more stringent vaccine legislation. For his efforts, Dr. Richard Pan was named a vaccine hero by *TIME*.[43] With backing from several large associations (including the American Medical Association in most cases), support from his staff, and support from many constituents, Dr. Pan authored six pieces of vaccine legislation.[44]

California's School Mandated Vaccine Law

School policies are an area left to the state and local level by the U.S. Constitution.[45] Here, state laws can preempt local school board policies. School-based vaccination requirements exist within all 50 states.[46] However, what vaccinations are required and vaccination exemption types available are inconsistent between states.[47] Throughout the last decade, California saw significant changes to school mandated vaccine law, which resulted in one of the nation's most stringent set of guidelines.[48]

41. *Id.*; *Elected Officials*, California State Assembly, https://clerk.assembly.ca.gov/legislative-information/elected-officials (last visited Jan. 3, 2023).

42. *Richard Pan*, *supra* note 38.

43. Jeffrey Kluger, *Meet the Heroes and Villains of Vaccine History*, TIME, https://time.com/3977055/vaccine-heroes-villains/ (last visited Dec. 29, 2022).

44. *Q&A: Despite pushback, physician lawmaker stands up for vaccines*, AMERICAN MEDICAL ASSOCIATION (2021), https://www.ama-assn.org/delivering-care/public-health/qa-despite-pushback-physician-lawmaker-stands-vaccines (last visited Apr. 7, 2023); *SGR advocate among four Dr. Nathan Davis Award winners*, AMERICAN MEDICAL ASSOCIATION (2014), https://www.ama-assn.org/practice-management/medicare-medicaid/sgr-advocate-among-four-dr-nathan-davis-award-winners (last visited Apr. 7, 2023).

45. *Federal Role in Education*, U.S. DEPARTMENT OF EDUCATION (2021), https://www2.ed.gov/about/overview/fed/role.html (last visited Apr. 7, 2023).

46. *Vaccination Laws*, CDC (2023), https://www.cdc.gov/phlp/publications/topic/vaccinationlaws.html (last visited Apr. 7, 2023).

47. *U.S. vaccine mandates in schools, state by state*, REUTERS, https://www.reuters.com/graphics/HEALTH-CORONAVIRUS/BIDEN/zgpombrajpd/ (last visited Dec. 29, 2022); *Vaccination Laws*, *supra* note 46.

48. *U.S. vaccine mandates in schools, state by state*, *supra* note 47.

Chapter 821, Statutes of 2012 (AB 2109, 2011–2012 Legislative Session)

Dr. Pan saw, in practice, the deleterious effects preventable diseases have when populations choose not to vaccinate.[49] Pertussis (whooping cough) was increasing nationwide and causing the death of infants (who were too young to be vaccinated).[50] Young siblings, teachers' children, and pregnant teachers were at risk of acquiring whooping cough infection from disease spread in classrooms. Therefore, as a first step into vaccine law, Dr. Pan sought to strengthen school vaccine requirements, increasing herd immunity and limiting the continued spread of whooping cough.[51]

When AB 2109 was introduced, California offered three exemptions to school mandated vaccines (1) personal belief exemptions, (2) religious exemptions, and (3) medical exemptions.[52] AB 2109 provided a mild policy change by ensuring parents seeking a philosophically based exemption (called a personal belief exemption) to school mandated vaccinations sought medical advice and were informed about vaccinations prior to receiving an exemption.[53] Parents seeking a personal belief exemption would need to provide a signed statement from a healthcare practitioner to ensure they were aware of the potential consequences and harm that could result from not vaccinating their children.[54] Within AB 2190, a broad definition of healthcare practitioner was utilized and included physicians, nurse practitioners, physician assistants, osteopathic physicians, naturopathic doctors, and school nurses.[55]

---

49. *Q&A: Despite pushback, physician lawmaker stands up for vaccines*, *supra* note 1.

50. *Pertussis outbreak spurs reconsideration of vaccination rules*, American Council on Science and Health (2012), https://www.acsh.org/news/2012/08/21/pertussis-outbreak-spurs-reconsideration-of-vaccination-rules (last visited Jan. 3, 2023); James D. Cherry, *Epidemic Pertussis in 2012—The Resurgence of a Vaccine-Preventable Disease*, 367 New England Journal of Medicine 785 (2012), https://doi.org/10.1056/NEJMp1209051 (last visited Jan. 3, 2023).

51. *Pertussis outbreak spurs reconsideration of vaccination rules*, *supra* note 50; *AB-2109 Communicable disease: immunization exemption*, California Legislative Information, https://leginfo.legislature.ca.gov/faces/billHistoryClient.xhtml?bill_id=201120120AB2109 (last visited Dec. 29, 2022).

52. *AB-2109 Communicable disease: immunization exemption*, *supra* note 51.

53. *Pertussis outbreak spurs reconsideration of vaccination rules*, *supra* note 50; *AB-2109 Communicable disease: immunization exemption*, *supra* note 51.

54. *AB-2109 Communicable disease: immunization exemption*, *supra* note 51.

55. *Id.*

While AB 2109 did not eliminate any vaccination exemptions offered in California, AB 2109 faced backlash and strong opposition.[56] Opposition included the Pacific Justice Institute, Child and Family Protection Association, Health Advocacy in the Public Interest, and National Vaccine Information Center.[57] Support was garnished from the California Medical Association, American Academy of Pediatrics, and California School Health Centers Association.[58] AB 2109 became law as Chapter 821, Statutes of 2012 with implementation starting January 1, 2014.[59]

During Chapter 821's implementation phase, the required exemption document was produced and included a checkbox stating, "I am a member of a religion which prohibits me from seeking medical advice or treatment from authorized health care practitioners."[60] The language included on the document created a loophole to the intentions of Chapter 821. The problematic implementation of Chapter 821 was based on a directive from Governor Jerry Brown to California's Department Public Health; the included language provides an easy means for parents to avoid discussing exempting their children from mandated school vaccinations with a healthcare practitioner.[61]

Chapter 35, Statutes of 2015 (SB 277, 2015–2016 Legislative Session)

Chapter 821 did not strengthen California's public health vaccine policies as planned.[62] California vaccine rates remained low, jeopardizing herd immunity.[63] The lack of herd immunity resulted in a well-publicized

56. Kingkade et al., *supra* note 31; *AB-2109 Communicable disease: immunization exemption*, *supra* note 51.

57. *AB-2109 Communicable disease: immunization exemption*, *supra* note 51; Dawn Richardson, *CA Bill Restricting Personal Belief Vaccine Exemption Heats Up*, National Vaccine information Center, https://www.nvic.org/newsletter/jul-2012/ca-bill-restricting-personal-belief-vaccine-exemption-heats-up (last visited Jan. 3, 2023).

58. *AB-2109 Communicable disease: immunization exemption*, *supra* note 51.

59. *Id.*

60. Nancy Shute, *How A California Law To Encourage Vaccination Could Backfire*, NPR, Nov. 9, 2013, https://www.npr.org/sections/health-shots/2013/11/09/243937869/how-a-california-law-to-encourage-vaccination-could-backfire (last visited Jan. 3, 2023).

61. *Id.*

62. *Id.*

63. Jane Meredith Adams, *California kindergarten vaccination rates reach all-time high in aftermath of new law*, EdSource, https://edsource.org/2017/california

measles outbreak that began in Disneyland.[64] In response, Dr. Pan introduced SB 277 in 2015.[65]

SB 277 eliminated both personal belief exemptions and religious exemptions for school mandated vaccinations.[66] SB 277 faced a high threshold of legislative barriers and was sent to the California Senate Health Committee, California Senate Education Committee, California Senate Judiciary Committee, California Senate Appropriations Committee, and California Assembly Health Committee; those supporting and opposing the bill showed up in mass for bill hearings.[67] Those opposing SB 277 wore red to committee hearings and on days that they protested against the bill.[68] Despite fierce opposition, SB 277 overcame every committee hurdle.[69] On June 29, 2015, SB 277 passed out of California's legislature and was subsequently signed by Governor Jerry Brown as Chapter 35, Statutes of 2015.[70]

To prevent Chapter 35 from being enacted, a lawsuit was filed; however, the California Second Appellate District's Court of Appeals upheld the law.[71] Further—as a result of this legislation—Dr. Pan faced a recall that failed.[72] After Chapter 35's implementation, a decrease in those entering kindergarten without vaccinations occurred after the first year; however, in the second year of implementation, the rate of those entering kindergarten without vaccinations increased.[73] In response to eliminating

-kindergarten-vaccination-rates-reach-all-time-high-in-aftermath-of-new-law/580170 (last visited Jan. 4, 2023).

64. *Measles*, California Department of Public Health, https://www.cdph.ca.gov/Programs/CID/DCDC/Pages/Immunization/measles.aspx (last visited Jan. 4, 2023).

65. *Id.*; SB-277 Public health: vaccinations, California Legislative Information, https://leginfo.legislature.ca.gov/faces/billHistoryClient.xhtml?bill_id=20152 0160SB277 (last visited Jan. 4, 2023).

66. SB-277 Public health: vaccinations, *supra* note 65.

67. SB-277 Public health: vaccinations, *supra* note 65.

68. Thousands of Californians Protest SB-277 at the Sacramento State Capitol, Jennifer Margulis (2015), https://www.jennifermargulis.net/protestors-say-proposed-law-is-bad-for-californias-kids/ (last visited Jan. 4, 2023).

69. *SB-277 Public health: vaccinations, supra* note 68.

70. *Id.*

71. Dorit Reiss, *California Court of Appeal Rejects Challenge to Vaccine Law*, Bill of Health (2018), https://blog.petrieflom.law.harvard.edu/2018/07/30/california-court-of-appeal-rejects-challenge-to-vaccine-law/ (last visited Dec. 29, 2022).

72. *Richard Pan recall, California State Senate (2015)*, Ballotpedia, https://ballotpedia.org/Richard_Pan_recall,_California_State_Senate_(2015) (last visited Dec. 29, 2022).

73. Paul L. Delamater et al., *Elimination of Nonmedical Immunization Exemptions in California and School-Entry Vaccine Status*, 143 Pediatrics e20183301

personal belief exemptions and religious exemptions for school mandated vaccinations, medical exemptions increased.[74]

Chapters 278 and 281, Statutes of 2019 (SB 276 & SB 714, 2019–2020 Legislative Session)

After the elimination of personal belief exemptions and religious exemptions for school mandated vaccinations, some medical exemptions were issued with questionable merit and outside clinical guidelines.[75] With medical exemptions as the only means to avoid school mandated vaccinations, California saw a tripling of medical exemptions.[76] Therefore, working with the medical board, Dr. Pan introduced SB 276.[77] SB 276 requires medical exemptions be granted by the California Department of Public Health based on information submitted by a child's physician.[78] CDC guidelines are to be followed by the California Department of Public Health in allowing medical exemptions to school mandated vaccinations.[79] SB 276 became Chapter 278, Statutes of 2019.[80]

As a result of authoring SB 276, Dr. Pan faced political opposition and personal violence. During opposition protests, protesters wore shirts

(2019), https://publications.aap.org/pediatrics/article/143/6/e20183301/37129/Elimination-of-Nonmedical-Immunization-Exemptions (last visited Jan. 3, 2023).

74. *Lorena Gonzalez and Dr. Richard Pan Combat Fake Medical Exemptions*, Assembly Democratic Caucus (2019), https://asmdc.org/press-releases/lorena-gonzalez-and-dr-richard-pan-combat-fake-medical-exemptions (last visited Dec. 29, 2022); Ho, *supra* note 38.

75. Barbara Feder Ostrov, *Medical board slams California doctor for exempting kids from school vaccinations*, CalMatters, Sep. 5, 2020, http://calmatters.org/health/2020/09/california-doctor-school-vaccination-exemptions/ (last visited Jan. 4, 2023).

76. Adams, *supra* note 63; *Lorena Gonzalez and Dr. Richard Pan Combat Fake Medical Exemptions*, *supra* note 75.

77. Ostrov, *supra* note 76.

78. *Lorena Gonzalez and Dr. Richard Pan Combat Fake Medical Exemptions*, *supra* note 75; *Bill Text—SB-276 Immunizations: medical exemptions*, California Legislative Information, https://leginfo.legislature.ca.gov/faces/billNavClient.xhtml?bill_id=201920200SB276 (last visited Jan. 3, 2023); *Bill Analysis—SB-276 Immunizations: medical exemptions*, California Legislative Information, https://leginfo.legislature.ca.gov/faces/billAnalysisClient.xhtml?bill_id=201920200SB276 (last visited Jan. 4, 2023).

79. *Lorena Gonzalez and Dr. Richard Pan Combat Fake Medical Exemptions*, *supra* note 75.

80. *Bill Text—SB-276 Immunizations: medical exemptions*, *supra* note 79.

and displayed posters of blood on Dr. Pan's face.[81] Dr. Pan faced a second recall that failed.[82] In August 2019, Dr. Pan was physical assaulted by an antivaccine activist who was live on Facebook.[83] The antivaccine activist was charged with misdemeanor battery, and a restraining order was issued.[84]

After passage of SB 276 into law, SB 714 was introduced as a clean-up bill to SB 276 and became Chapter 281, Statutes of 2019.[85] This means that SB 276 needed some language changed to be effective, and the language was included in SB 714. To do this, SB 714, was gutted and amended, which is a process where the original purpose of a bill is removed and the language to make the bill fit a new purpose is inserted. Here, the original bill dealt with Knox-Keene Health Care Service Plans (this was the case in April–May 2019); the bill was amended in September 2019.[86] Both laws, Chapters 278 and 281, became effective January 1, 2021, and their effect on vaccination rates is currently unknown.[87]

---

81. *Q&A: Despite pushback, physician lawmaker stands up for vaccines*, *supra* note 1.

82. *Richard Pan recall, California State Senate (2019-2020)*, Ballotpedia, https://ballotpedia.org/Richard_Pan_recall,_California_State_Senate_(2019-2020) (last visited Dec. 29, 2022).

83. *Q&A: Despite pushback, physician lawmaker stands up for vaccines*, *supra* note 1; *Anti-Vaccine Activist Shoves Sen. Richard Pan*, FOX40 (2019), https://fox40.com/news/local-news/anti-vaccine-activist-shoves-sen-richard-pan/ (last visited Dec. 29, 2022).

84. *Anti-Vaccine Activist Shoves Sen. Richard Pan*, *supra* note 84; Sen. Richard Pan Granted Restraining Order against Anti-Vaccine Activist, CBS News Sacramento, https://www.cbsnews.com/sacramento/news/richard-pan-anti-vaccine-activist-restraining-order/ (last visited Dec. 29, 2022).

85. *Bill Text—SB-714 Immunizations*, California Legislative Information, https://leginfo.legislature.ca.gov/faces/billTextClient.xhtml?bill_id=201920200SB714 (last visited Jan. 4, 2023); *Bill Analysis—SB-714 Immunizations*, California Legislative Information, https://leginfo.legislature.ca.gov/faces/billAnalysisClient.xhtml?bill_id=201920200SB714 (last visited Dec. 29, 2022).

86. *Bill Analysis—SB-714 Immunizations*, *supra* note 86; *Bill History—SB-714 Immunizations*, California Legislative Information, https://leginfo.legislature.ca.gov/faces/billHistoryClient.xhtml?bill_id=201920200SB714 (last visited Jan. 4, 2023).

87. *Bill Text—SB-276 Immunizations: medical exemptions*, *supra* note 79; *Bill Text—SB-714 Immunizations*, *supra* note 86.

COVID-19-Related Vaccine Law Changes in California

Chapter 737, Statues of 2021 (SB 742, 2021–2022 Legislative Session)

During the COVID-19 pandemic, vaccinations became contentious throughout the United States. Harassment, bullying, and attacks on clinics occurred. In California, a vaccine clinic at Dodger's Stadium was disrupted due to a mob.[88] In response, SB 742 was introduced to ensure those seeking vaccination are protected from harassment or intimidation.[89] SB 742 prohibits obstructing or interfering with a vaccination site and makes doing so a crime.[90] SB 742 became law in California as Chapter 737, Statues of 2021.[91]

Chapter 729, Statues of 2021 (SB 510, 2021–2022 Legislative Session)

Throughout the COVID-19 pandemic, the federal government prohibited cost sharing associated with COVID-19 vaccination.[92] SB 510 codifies, into California law, the federal government's limitations on cost sharing for healthcare related to a pandemic.[93] This means even if the federal government stops paying for pandemic-related vaccines, in California

88. *Q&A: Despite pushback, physician lawmaker stands up for vaccines*, *supra* note 1; *'Mob' that temporarily closed Dodger Stadium vaccination site sparks outrage*, KTLA, https://ktla.com/news/local-news/mob-that-temporarily-closed-dodger-stadium-vaccination-site-sparks-outrage/ (last visited Jan. 3, 2023).

89. *Q&A: Despite pushback, physician lawmaker stands up for vaccines*, *supra* note 1; *Bill Text—SB-742 Vaccination sites: unlawful activities: obstructing, intimidating, or harassing*, https://leginfo.legislature.ca.gov/faces/billNavClient.xhtml?bill_id=202120220SB742 (last visited Dec. 29, 2022).

90. *Bill Text—SB-742 Vaccination sites: unlawful activities: obstructing, intimidating, or harassing*, *supra* note 90.

91. *Bill History—SB-742 Vaccination sites: unlawful activities: obstructing, intimidating, or harassing*, CALIFORNIA LEGISLATIVE INFORMATION, https://leginfo.legislature.ca.gov/faces/billHistoryClient.xhtml?bill_id=202120220SB742 (last visited Jan. 4, 2023).

92. *Billing and Cost Sharing Overview for COVID-19 Vaccination, Testing, and Treatment*, BUREAU OF PRIMARY HEALTH CARE, https://bphc.hrsa.gov/initiatives/billing-cost-sharing-covid-19 (last visited Apr. 7, 2023).

93. *Bill Text—SB-510 Health care coverage: COVID-19 cost sharing*, CALIFORNIA LEGISLATIVE INFORMATION, https://leginfo.legislature.ca.gov/faces/billTextClient.xhtml?bill_id=202120220SB510 (last visited Jan. 3, 2023); *Bill Analysis—SB-510 Health care coverage: COVID-19 cost sharing*, CALIFORNIA LEGISLATIVE INFORMATION, https://leginfo.legislature.ca.gov/faces/billAnalysisClient.xhtml?bill_id=202120220SB510 (last visited Jan. 3, 2023).

COVID-19 and future pandemic vaccinations will be free.[94] In codifying this policy as Chapter 729, Statues of 2021, the California legislature ensured the future safety of Californians from preventable diseases during outbreaks.

Future of California Vaccination Law

Prior to leaving office, Dr. Pan and colleagues sought to add COVID-19 vaccines to school mandated vaccinations.[95] Ultimately the measure failed to progress (SB 871, 2021–2022 Legislative Session).[64] Recently, the CDC added the COVID-19 vaccine to their recommended list of vaccines for school-aged children, but California will likely not see action on this recommendation during this legislative session.[96] California's legislature now has a Vaccine Work Group, formed in 2021, to combat COVID-19 vaccine misinformation and ensure Californian's public health.[97] Science and facts will continue to push forward vaccination policy in California.[98]

Conclusion

California's progressive politics did not make for an easy route in forming more stringent vaccination laws.[99] Dr. Pan, as a champion for vaccine legislation, spent over a decade in the California legislature, working with like-minded associations, politicians, and citizens to form the strongest

---

94. *Bill Text—SB-510 Health care coverage: COVID-19 cost sharing*, *supra* note 94.

95. Kevin Yamamura, *California lawmaker proposes Covid vaccine mandate for all schoolchildren*, POLITICO, https://www.politico.com/news/2022/01/24/california-school-covid-vaccine-mandate-proposal-00001261 (last visited Dec. 29, 2022).

96. Elizabeth Aguilera, *CDC paves way for California to require school COVID vaccines—but lawmakers have given up for now*, CalMatters, Oct. 26, 2022, http://calmatters.org/education/2022/10/california-vaccination-requirements/ (last visited Dec. 29, 2022).

97. Legislators form vaccine work group to boost public health policies, California Medical Association, https://www.cmadocs.org/newsroom/news/view/ArticleId/49638/Legislators-form-vaccine-work-group-to-boost-public-health-policies (last visited Dec. 29, 2022).

98. *Q&A: Despite pushback, physician lawmaker stands up for vaccines*, *supra* note 1.

99. Kingkade et al., *supra* note 31.

state-level vaccine policies in the United States.[100] During this time, those supporting stringent vaccine standards that curb infection spread saw legislation pass that was successful in eliminating personal belief exemptions and religious exemptions, and ensuring a clear medical reason for medical exemptions from school mandated vaccinations.[101] Further, legislation that ensures access to future vaccines—during a disease outbreak—was codified.[102]

100. Hart, *supra* note 1; *U.S. vaccine mandates in schools, state by state*, *supra* note 47.

101. SB-277 Public health: vaccinations, *supra* note 68; Bill Text—SB-276 Immunizations: medical exemptions, *supra* note 79; Bill Text—SB-714 Immunizations, *supra* note 86. Delete 103–205 106 should be Bill Text—SB-742 Vaccination sites: unlawful activities: obstructing, intimidating, or harassing, *supra* note 90; Bill Text—SB-510 Health care coverage: COVID-19 cost sharing, *supra* note 94.

102. *Bill Text—SB-714 Immunizations, supra* note 86; *Bill Text—SB-510 Health care coverage: COVID-19 cost sharing, supra* note 94.

Chapter 10

Patient Privacy, Health Information Confidentiality, and Vaccine Information

Stacey A. Tovino

Introduction

Vaccine information is requested, collected, used, and disclosed by a wide variety of individuals and entities in a number of different contexts. Many people assume that these activities are highly regulated by patient privacy and health information confidentiality laws. This assumption is not always true. Many privacy and confidentiality laws are limited in application to certain covered entities, leaving a variety of vaccine information requesters, collectors, holders, and disclosers unregulated. Many privacy and confidentiality laws also are limited in the data that they protect, leaving some vaccine information unprotected. Even when a particular privacy or confidentiality law applies to an individual or entity and in theory protects the information at hand, the law may not regulate the initial request for or collection of the information. That is, many privacy and confidentiality laws only regulate subsequent uses and disclosures of information. Finally, many vaccine information uses and disclosures are permitted without prior notification to or authorization of the individual who has been vaccinated. This chapter examines the application of illustrative privacy and confidentiality laws to a variety of activities involving vaccine information, showing when vaccine information is protected by federal and state law and when it is not.

Regulated Entities

To determine whether an activity involving vaccine information is protected by a particular privacy or confidentiality law, the first step is to determine whether the individual or entity engaged in the activity is regulated by the law. The Health Insurance Portability and Accountability Act of 1996 (HIPAA) Privacy Rule may be used as an example. First promogulated by the federal Department of Health and Human Services (HHS) in 2002, the HIPAA Privacy Rule now regulates covered entities[1] and business associates.[2] Covered entities include health plans,[3] healthcare clearinghouses,[4] and certain healthcare providers[5] (i.e., those healthcare providers that transmit health information in electronic form in connection with certain standard transactions).[6] A business associate is a person or organization that provides certain enumerated services to or on behalf of a covered entity, other than in the capacity of a workforce member of the covered entity, and needs access to protected health information (PHI) to perform the service.[7]

Some individuals and entities that engage in activities involving vaccine information do fall within the definition of a HIPAA covered entity or business associate. Consider a person who receives a vaccine at a chain pharmacy. The pharmacy will maintain an identifiable record of

---

1. 45 C.F.R. § 160.103 (defining covered entity); *id.* § 160.102(a) (applying the HIPAA Rules to covered entities).

2. *Id.* § 160.103 (defining business associate); *id.* § 160.102(b) (applying the HIPAA Rules to business associates).

3. *Id.* § 160.103 (defining health plan as an individual or group plan that provides, or pays the cost of, medical care).

4. *Id.* § 160.103 (defining healthcare clearinghouse as a public or private entity, including a billing service, repricing company, community health management information system, or community health information system, and "value-added" networks and switches, that either (1) processes or facilitates the processing of health information received from another entity in a nonstandard format or containing nonstandard data content into standard data elements or a standard transaction or (2) receives a standard transaction from another entity and processes or facilitates the processing of health information into nonstandard format or nonstandard data content for the receiving entity).

5. *Id.* (defining healthcare provider as (1) a provider of services under section 1861(u) of the Social Security Act; (2) a provider of medical or health services under section 1861(s) of the Social Security Act; and (3) any other person or organization who furnishes, bills, or is paid for healthcare in the normal course of business).

6. *Id.* (defining covered entity).

7. *Id.* (defining business associate).

the person's vaccine administration as required by federal and state law.[8] Because pharmacies fall within the definition of a "health care provider,"[9] the pharmacy is regulated by the HIPAA Privacy Rule with respect to its use and disclosure of that vaccine record if the pharmacy transmits health information in electronic form in connection with a standard transaction.[10] The most common standard transaction is the health insurance claim transaction.[11] If the pharmacy takes any form of insurance, public or private, and bills insurance electronically on behalf of even one patient—not necessarily the patient who had the vaccine—the pharmacy is a HIPAA covered entity for all of its patients. CVS Pharmacy, for example, provides a variety of vaccines, including the COVID-19, flu, pneumonia, shingles, hepatitis A and B, cholera, polio, meningitis, varicella, human papillomavirus, typhoid, and rabies vaccines.[12] CVS Pharmacy accepts insurance and bills insurance electronically.[13] The result is that CVS Pharmacy is a HIPAA covered entity and must comply with the HIPAA Privacy Rule when using or disclosing all of its patients' protected health information, including patients' vaccine records.

---

8. For example, the National Childhood Vaccine Injury Act of 1986 requires every healthcare provider who administers a vaccine set forth in the Vaccine Injury Table to record (or ensure that there is recorded) in the person's permanent medical record information regarding the date of vaccine administration, the vaccine manufacturer and lot number, the name and address of the healthcare provider administering the vaccine, and other information required by regulations promogulated by the Secretary of the Department of Health and Human Services. 42 U.S.C. § 300aa-25(a)(1)–(4).

9. The HIPAA Privacy Rule defines a healthcare provider to include any person or organization who furnishes, bills, or gets paid for "health care" in the normal course of business. "Health care" includes, but is not limited to, the sale or dispensing of a drug pursuant to a prescription. 45 C.F.R. § 160.103 (defining healthcare and healthcare provider).

10. 45 C.F.R. § 160.103 (defining covered entity to include only those health care providers who "transmit[] any health information in electronic form in connection with a [standard] transaction").

11. *Id.* § 160.103 (defining transaction to include "health care claims").

12. CVS, *The Vaccines You Need, All in One Place* ("We offer the following vaccinations"), https://www.cvs.com/immunizations/get-vaccinated?cid=ps_imm&gclid=Cj0KCQiAkMGcBhCSARIsAIW6d0BTc79GYR4j_YMHFiEdX_1eAxJQmtC2wEZt2K-bXXYGD8Xujr6Ldq8aAodbEALw_wcB&gclsrc=aw.ds (last visited Dec. 5, 2022).

13. CVS Pharmacy, *Prices, Insurance and Payment, available at* https://www.cvs.com/help/help_subtopic_details.jsp?subtopicName=Prices%2C+Insurance+and+Payments&topicid=400021 (last visited Dec. 5, 2022) ("We accept most prescription insurance").

Other entities that engage in activities involving vaccine information do not fall within the definition of a HIPAA covered entity or business associate, however. For example, the typical elementary or secondary school will not meet the definition of a covered entity because the school is not a health plan, healthcare clearinghouse, healthcare provider, or business associate thereof. Even if the school employs a nurse or counselor who falls within the definition of a healthcare provider,[14] the nurse or counselor will typically receive a salary from the school rather than reimbursement from third-party insurers for providing healthcare to students. The lack of a standard transaction conducted on the nurse's or counselor's behalf results in the inapplicability of the HIPAA Privacy Rule.[15] This is true even in states that require elementary and secondary schools to collect proof of their students' vaccination.[16]

A variety of other individuals and institutions that engage in activities involving vaccine information also will not fall within the definition of a HIPAA covered entity or business associate. For example, a local restaurant will not meet the definition of a health plan, healthcare clearinghouse, healthcare provider, or business associate thereof. The result is that the restaurant will not be regulated by the HIPAA Privacy Rule, even if the restaurant requests vaccine information from individuals who wish to dine at the restaurant. The same is true of other businesses, including hair salons, clothing boutiques, and grocery stores. Because these businesses do not meet the definition of a health plan, healthcare clearinghouse, healthcare provider, or business associate thereof, they are not regulated by the HIPAA Privacy Rule, even if they ask their shoppers to provide proof of vaccination. The same result holds true for community members who host private events, such as christenings, weddings, and holiday parties, at their homes or other venues. These individuals do not fall within the definition of a covered entity or business associate, even

---

14. *See supra* note 9 (discussing the definition of healthcare provider).

15. *See* U.S. Dep't Health & Human Servs., *Does the HIPAA Privacy Rule Apply to an Elementary or Secondary School?*, *available at* https://www.hhs.gov/hipaa/for-professionals/faq/513/does-hipaa-apply-to-an-elementary-school/index.html (last visited Dec. 10, 2022) ("Thus, even though a school employs school nurses, physicians, psychologists, or other health care providers, the school is not generally a HIPAA covered entity because the providers do not engage in any of the covered transactions, such as billing a health plan electronically for their services. It is expected that most elementary and secondary schools fall into this category.").

16. *See, e.g.*, D.C. Code § 8-502.01(a)(2) (District of Columbia statute requiring K–12 schools to collect a student's certification of COVID-19 immunization (or documentation satisfying an exemption) before admitting the student to school).

if they require guests to provide proof of vaccination before attending an event. Newspaper reporters and other members of the media also are not HIPAA covered entities, even when they are reporting on the vaccination status of a named person. Along the same lines, airlines and transportation agencies that request vaccine information prior to passenger boarding or travel also are not HIPAA covered entities. Again, they do not fall within the definition of a health plan, healthcare clearinghouse, healthcare provider, or business associate thereof. As a final illustrative example of the nonapplication of the HIPAA Privacy Rule, many individuals post photos on social media showing themselves receiving a vaccine or holding a completed vaccination card. Private individuals generally are not covered entities. Even if a particular individual happens to be a healthcare provider who takes insurance and bills insurance electronically in his or her normal course of business, individuals are free to share their own vaccination status. That is, privacy and confidentiality laws only regulate individuals who wish to disclose *other* persons' health information. Privacy and confidentiality do not prohibit individuals from sharing their own information.

Whether and how the HIPAA Privacy Rule applies to universities, employers, and other larger institutions depends on the different functions performed by the institution and whether the institution has designated itself as a "hybrid entity." As background, the HIPAA Privacy Rule defines a hybrid entity as a single legal entity (1) that is a covered entity, (2) whose business activities include both covered and noncovered functions, and (3) that designates its healthcare components.[17] For example, if a university has a student health center, medical school clinic, teaching hospital, or other healthcare provider component that electronically transmits health information in connection with healthcare claims, or if the university has a group health plan that provides health insurance to its employees, the university does engage in HIPAA covered functions.[18] However, most universities also engage in non-covered functions, including operating a law school, business school, music department, or coffee shop. To the extent a university with both types of functions designates its HIPAA covered components, the university will meet the definition of a hybrid entity and the HIPAA Privacy Rule will only apply to the

17. 45 C.F.R. § 164.103.

18. See text accompanying notes 1–6 (defining covered entity and referencing the entities that fall within the definition of covered entity).

university's covered (but not non-covered) components.[19] For example, the HIPAA Privacy Rule would apply to a university-operated student health center (if the health center takes insurance and bills insurance electronically) and to the university's group health plan. However, the HIPAA Privacy Rule would not apply to the university's law school or music department if the university did not designate these components as healthcare components. This is true even if the law school or music department requires its students to be vaccinated and to provide proof of vaccination.[20]

Although the HIPAA Privacy Rule is limited in application to covered entities and business associates, other privacy and confidentiality laws have broader application. The Texas Medical Records Privacy Act, for example, applies to any person who "comes into possession of protected health information," any person who "obtains or stores protected health information," and any "employee, agent, or contractor" of a person described in the previous two clauses to the extent the employee, agent, or contractor "creates, receives, obtains, maintains, uses, or transmits protected health information."[21] The Texas Medical Records Privacy Act would apply to many individuals and institutions that are not regulated by the HIPAA Privacy Rule, such as healthcare providers that administer vaccines but do not take insurance as well as a wide variety of other entities, including restaurants, hair salons, grocery stores, news reporters, and private parties who host events at their homes or other venues. That said, the Texas Medical Records Privacy Act does not apply to everyone. For example, the law does not apply to employee benefit plans or workers' compensation carriers.[22]

A handful of states have new consumer data protection laws that, like the Texas Medical Records Privacy Act, are not limited in application to HIPAA covered entities and business associates. These laws tend to apply to certain persons that conduct business in the state or that produce products or services that are targeted to residents of the state.

19. 45 C.F.R. § 164.103 (defining hybrid entity); *id.* § 164.105(a)(1) (explaining that the HIPAA Privacy Rule only applies to a hybrid entity's covered healthcare components).

20. *See, e.g.*, Loyola University Chicago, *Vaccination Requirement for Faculty and Staff*, July 29, 2021, *available at* https://www.luc.edu/coronavirus/previousmessages/072921-vaccinationrequirementforfacultyandstaff.shtml (last visited Dec. 23, 2022) ("Loyola University Chicago will now require all full-time and part-time faculty and staff, along with students, to be vaccinated from COVID-19").

21. Tex. Health & Safety Code § 181.001(b)(2)(B)-(D)

22. *Id.* §§ 181.054, 181.055

However, these laws usually apply only when the data controlled or processed exceeds certain thresholds or when the data controller or processor derives a certain percentage of gross revenue from the sale of health and other consumer data. For example, the California Consumer Privacy Act (CCPA) regulates certain businesses that collect consumer personal information (including health information such as vaccine information) and that do business in the state of California if the business meets one of three thresholds.[23] The thresholds are (1) having annual gross revenues in excess of $25 million; (2) annually buying, receiving for the business's commercial purposes, selling, or sharing for commercial purposes, alone or in combination, the personal information of 50,000 or more consumers, households, or devices; and (3) deriving 50 percent or more of its annual revenues from selling consumers' personal information.[24] Whether a particular California business that holds vaccine information is regulated by the CCPA would depend on whether one of these thresholds has been satisfied.

Similarly, the Virginia Consumer Data Protection Act (VCDPA), effective January 1, 2023, regulates certain businesses that conduct business in Virginia or that produce products or services that are targeted to residents of Virginia if, during a calendar year, the business controls or processes the personal data (including health data) of (1) at least 100,000 consumers or (2) at least 25,000 consumers and derives over 50 percent of gross revenue from the sale of personal data.[25] Again, whether a particular Virginia business that holds vaccine information is regulated by the VCDPA would depend on whether one of these two thresholds has been satisfied.

Along the same lines, the Colorado Privacy Act (CPA), effective July 1, 2023, regulates certain data controllers (including certain health data controllers) that conduct business in Colorado or that produce or deliver commercial products or services that are intentionally targeted to residents of Colorado if the controller (1) controls or processes the personal data of 100,000 consumers or more during a calendar year or (2) derives revenue or receives a discount on the price of goods or services from the sale of personal data and processes or controls the personal data of

23. California Consumer Privacy Act, codified at Cal. Civ. Code §§ 1798.100–1798.199.35 *et seq.* (latest revisions eff. Jan. 1, 2023).

24. Cal. Civ. Code § 1798.140 (West 2021).

25. Virginia Consumer Data Protection Act, S.B.1392 (Mar. 2, 2021), to be codified at Va. Code Ann. § 59.1-572(A) (eff. Jan. 1, 2023).

25,000 consumers or more.[26] As with the CCPA and the VCDPA, whether a particular Colorado business that holds vaccine information is regulated by the CPA would depend on whether one of these thresholds has been satisfied.

Newer consumer data protection laws also tend to contain laundry lists of businesses that are excepted from regulation even if they satisfy the thresholds described above. For example, the Utah Consumer Privacy Act does not apply to a tribe, an institution of higher education, a non-profit corporation, a financial institution, or an air carrier, among other excluded institutions, even if they hold identifiable health information such as vaccine records.[27]

Protected Health Information

Once a determination has been made that an individual or institution that requests, collects, uses, or discloses vaccine information is regulated by a particular privacy or confidentiality law, the next step is to determine whether the vaccine information that is being requested, collected, used, or disclosed falls within the class of information that is protected by the law. The HIPAA Privacy Rule, for example, only protects a class of information known as PHI. With four exceptions, PHI is defined as individually identifiable health information (IIHI).[28] A record created by a healthcare provider that states, for example, that a named individual has been vaccinated against a particular virus would meet the definition of IIHI. In the hands of most healthcare providers and health insurers, the vaccine record would also meet the definition of PHI and be protected by the HIPAA Privacy Rule.

That said, there are four types of records that meet the definition of IIHI but that are excluded from the definition of PHI—and three of these

---

26. Colorado Privacy Act, S.B. 21-190 (July 7, 2021), to be codified at Colo. Rev. Stat. § 6-1-1304(1) (eff. July 1, 2023).

27. Utah Consumer Privacy Act, S.B. 227 (Mar. 24, 2022), to be codified at Utah Code Ann. § 13-61-102(2)(b), (c), (e), (k), (q) (eff. Dec. 31, 2023).

28. Individually identifiable health information is defined to include information that "(1) Is created or received by a health care provider, health plan, employer, or health care clearinghouse; and (2) Relates to the past, present, or future physical or mental health or condition of an individual; the provision of health care to an individual; or the past, present, or future payment for the provision of health care to an individual; and (i) That identifies the individual; or (ii) With respect to which there is a reasonable basis to believe the information can be used to identify the individual." 45 C.F.R. § 160.103.

exclusions are frequently implicated in the context of vaccine records. The first exclusion relates to education records that are protected by the Family Educational Rights and Privacy Act of 1974 (FERPA). FERPA-protected education records are defined as records that are (1) directly related to a student and (2) maintained by an educational agency or institution, or by a party acting for the agency or institution. For example, if a university maintains information relating to an identifiable undergraduate or graduate student's vaccine status for purposes of determining whether that student may enroll in classes, that information falls within the definition of an education record. FERPA, not HIPAA, protects the information.

The second exclusion involves student treatment records. Student treatment records are records (1) relating to a student who is 18 years of age or older, or is attending an institution of postsecondary education; (2) that are made or maintained by a physician, psychiatrist, psychologist, or other recognized professional or paraprofessional acting in his or her professional or paraprofessional capacity, or assisting in that capacity; (3) that are made, maintained, or used only in connection with the provision of treatment to the student; and (4) that are not available to anyone other than persons providing such treatment, except that such records can be personally reviewed by a physician or other appropriate professional of the student's choice.[29] For example, if a postsecondary student is administered a vaccine at an on-campus student health center and the resulting vaccine record is not available to anyone other than treating professionals at the student health center, the vaccine record would be considered a student treatment record excluded from protection by HIPAA. Congress intended that state law, instead of the HIPAA Privacy Rule and FERPA, would protect the student treatment record. That said, many state laws except both student treatment records and/or education records from the class of information that is protected. The Texas Medical Records Privacy Act, for example, does not apply to FERPA-protected education records or to student treatment records.[30] The Virginia Consumer Data Protection Act also does not apply to FERPA-protected education records.[31]

The third exclusion from the HIPAA Privacy Rule's definition of protected health information relates to employment records held by a

29. 20 U.S.C. § 1232g(a)(4)(B)(iv); 34 C.F.R. § 99.3 (definition of "education records").

30. Tex. Health & Safety Code § 181.058.

31. Va. Code Ann. § 59.1-572(C)(12).

covered entity in its role as an employer. For example, if an employer is a covered entity or hybrid entity under HIPAA and requires an employee to provide proof of vaccination as a condition of employment, the document that provides proof of vaccination would be considered an employment record held by the entity in its role as an employer. That document would not be PHI protected by the HIPAA Privacy Rule. An example of such an employment record would be the vaccine record of a nurse who is employed by a HIPAA covered hospital if the hospital requires its healthcare workers, including the nurse at issue, to provide proof of vaccination as a condition of employment. The reason the hospital has the vaccine record is not to treat the nurse but to make a decision regarding the nurse's continued employment. Employment records—even those that contain identifiable health information about an employee—are simply not protected by HIPAA.

Protection and Regulation

Once a determination has been made that an individual or institution that requests, collects, uses, or discloses vaccine information is regulated by a particular privacy or confidentiality law and that the vaccine information that is being requested, collected, used, or disclosed falls within the class of information protected by the law, the next step is to determine the substantive privacy protections that apply. Most privacy and confidentiality laws establish a default requirement of prior written authorization before the information can be used or disclosed. For example, the HIPAA Privacy Rule generally requires covered entities and business associates to obtain an individual's prior written authorization on a HIPAA-compliant authorization form before using or disclosing the individual's PHI.[32] That said, several exceptions to this authorization requirement exist.[33]

Some of these exceptions are classified as treatment, payment, and operations (TPO) exceptions. For example, a HIPAA covered healthcare provider may use or disclose a patient's protected health information, including vaccine information, to treat the patient[34] or to help

32. 45 C.F.R. § 165.508(a)(1).

33. *Id.* § 164.506(c) (establishing exceptions to the prior written authorization requirement for treatment payment, and healthcare operations (TPO) activities); *id.* § 164.510 (establishing exceptions for disclosures of information to certain persons involved in patients' care); *id.* § 164.512 (establishing public benefit activity (PBA) exceptions).

34. *Id.* § 164.506(c)(1).

another provider treat the patient.[35] By further example, a covered healthcare provider may disclose information regarding a patient's vaccine administration to the patient's health insurer so that the provider can get reimbursed for vaccinating the individual.[36] Likewise, a health plan is permitted to use a completed insurance claim form that references a patient's vaccination to determine whether and how much to pay a participating provider for vaccinating the patient.[37] These and other TPO uses and disclosures may be made without the vaccinated (or even an unvaccinated) patient's prior written authorization.[38]

Other exceptions to the authorization requirement are referred to as public benefit activity (PBA) exceptions. For example, a HIPAA covered healthcare provider may use or disclose protected health information, including vaccine information, pursuant to a court order or in response to a subpoena, discovery request, or other lawful process if certain criteria are satisfied.[39] A covered healthcare provider also may disclose a patient's vaccine information to the Food and Drug Administration (FDA) for purposes of reporting an adverse vaccine event.[40] In certain situations, a covered provider also may disclose a patient's vaccine record to a school if the patient is a student or prospective student of the school and the school is required by state or other law to collect proof of vaccination.[41] In certain situations, a covered provider that is a component of the Department of State also may use protected health information, including vaccine information, to make medical suitability determinations and may disclose whether or not the individual was determined to be medically suitable to the officials in the Department of State who need access to such information for military and other purposes.[42] These and other PBA uses and disclosures may be made without the vaccinated patient's prior written authorization.[43]

Like the HIPAA Privacy Rule, state privacy and confidentiality laws also frequently contain a default requirement of prior written

35. *Id.* § 164.506(c)(2).
36. *Id.* § 164.506(c)(1).
37. *Id.*
38. *Id.* § 164.506(c)(1)–(5) (listing a variety of TPO uses and disclosures that are permitted without a patient's prior written authorization).
39. *Id.* § 164.512(e).
40. *Id.* § 164.512(b)(1)(iii)(A).
41. *Id.* § 164.512(b)(1)(vi).
42. *Id.* § 164.512(k)(4).
43. *Id.* § 164.512(a)–(l) (listing twelve PBA activities for which PHI may be used or disclosed without the patient's prior written authorization).

authorization combined with exceptions to this authorization requirement. For example, the Texas Medical Records Privacy Act generally prohibits a covered entity from electronically disclosing an individual's protected health information without first obtaining an authorization from the individual who is the subject of the information.[44] The Texas law does not require authorization, however, when the information is being electronically disclosed for the purposes of TPO.[45]

Importantly, many privacy and confidentiality laws only regulate the use or disclosure of protected health information, including vaccine information, but not the initial request for or collection of that information. The HIPAA Privacy Rule, for example, applies to subsequent uses and disclosures of protected health information but not to information requests and data collection.[46] Thus, the HIPAA Privacy Rule would not prohibit a covered healthcare provider from asking a patient if the patient has been vaccinated. The HIPAA Privacy Rule also does not regulate the manner in which a covered entity collects vaccine information. However, the HIPAA Privacy Rule would regulate the covered provider if the provider wishes to further use or disclose the gathered vaccine information. For example, if the provider would like to sell the information to an anti-vaccine organization, the provider would have to obtain the patient's prior written authorization on a HIPAA-compliant authorization first, disclosing to the patient that the information is being disclosed in exchange for remuneration. If the provider failed to do this, the provider has violated the HIPAA Privacy Rule.[47]

Many state laws also regulate the use and disclosure of health information, including vaccine information, but not requests for or collection of information. For example, the Texas Medical Records Privacy Act regulates uses of protected health information relating to marketing,[48] the sale of protected health information,[49] and electronic disclosures of protected health information.[50] The Texas Medical Records Privacy Act does not, however, regulate requests for or the collection of protected health information.

44. Tex. Health & Safety Code § 181.154(b).

45. *Id.* § 181.154(c)(1).

46. *See, e.g.*, 45 C.F.R. §§ 164.502–.514 (setting forth the use and disclosure requirements; not regulating information requests or data collection).

47. *Id.* § 164.508(a)(4).

48. Tex. Health & Safety Code § 181.152.

49. *Id.* § 181.153.

50. *Id.* § 181.154.

That said, newer state consumer data protection laws do tend to regulate requests for and the collection of protected health information. For example, the CCPA requires regulated businesses to disclose to consumers the categories and specific pieces of personal information the businesses have collected. In addition, regulated businesses are prohibited by the CCPA from collecting additional categories of personal information or from using personal information collected for additional purposes that are incompatible with the disclosed purpose for which the personal information was collected without providing the consumer with notice consistent with this section.[51]

Individual Rights

In addition to regulating activities involving protected health information, many privacy and confidentiality laws also establish certain rights that individuals have with respect to their protected health information. For example, the HIPAA Privacy Rule gives individuals five rights with respect to their protected health information, including their vaccine information. These rights are the right to receive a notice of privacy practices,[52] the right to request additional privacy protections,[53] the right to obtain a paper or electronic copy of protected health information,[54] the right to request amendment of incorrect protected health information,[55] and the right to receive an accounting of disclosures of protected health information.[56] For example, an individual who has been vaccinated by a healthcare provider has the right to obtain a paper or electronic copy of the individual's vaccine records from that provider.[57] If the provider does not provide the requested records in a timely manner, the provider may be vulnerable to corrective action or civil monetary penalties imposed by the federal Department of Health and Human Services.[58]

51. Cal. Civ. Code § 1798.100.
52. 45 C.F.R. § 164.520.
53. *Id.* § 164.522.
54. *Id.* § 164.524.
55. *Id.* § 164.526.
56. *Id.* § 164.528.
57. *Id.* § 164.524(a)(1), (c)(2).
58. *See, e.g.*, U.S. Dep't Health & Human Servs., *Cignet Health Fined a $4.3M Civil Money Penalty for HIPAA Privacy Rule Violations*, *available at* https://www.hhs.gov/hipaa/for-professionals/compliance-enforcement/examples/cignet-health/index.html (last visited Dec. 11, 2022) (explaining that a covered entity was fined

State privacy and confidentiality laws also give individuals certain rights with respect to their protected health information. For example, the Texas Medical Records Privacy Act gives patients of healthcare providers who use electronic health records systems the right to obtain medical records not later than the fifteenth business day after the date the provider receives a written request for such records.[59] The CCPA, by further example, gives data subjects a wide variety of rights, including the right to know the personal information that the business collects, the right to know how collected information is used and shared, the right to delete some personal information that is collected by the business, the right to correct inaccurate personal information held by the business, the right to opt out of the sale of personal information, and the right to non-discrimination for exercising CCPA rights.[60]

Enforcement and Penalties

If a regulated entity violates a privacy or confidentiality law in the context of an activity involving vaccine information, the law may provide for injunctive relief, civil penalties, criminal penalties, a private cause of action, and/or professional discipline. For example, if a covered entity or business associate violates the HIPAA Privacy Rule, the covered entity or business associate may be subject to technical assistance, corrective action, or civil and criminal penalties. Civil penalties, which are imposed by HHS, are adjusted on an annual basis.[61] In 2022, these civil penalties ranged from (1) $127 to $63,973 (for covered entities that did not know, and by exercising reasonable diligence would not have known, that the HIPAA Privacy Rule was violated), (2) $1,280 to $63,973 (for covered entities and business associates whose violations stemmed from reasonable cause but not willful neglect), (3) $12,794 to $63,973 (for covered entities and business associates whose violations occurred as a result of willful neglect but are remedied within 30 days), and (4) $63,973 to $1,919,173 (for covered entities and business associates whose violations occurred as a result of willful neglect and that are not remedied in a timely manner). Criminal penalties, which are imposed by the federal Department of Justice, range from (1) $50,000, one year in prison, or

$4.3 million in part for failing to give 41 patients copies of their requested medical records).

59. Tex. Health & Safety Code § 181.102(a).

60. Cal. Civ. Code §§ 1798.100–.125

61. 42 U.S.C. § 1320d-5.

both (for covered entities and business associates who knowingly obtain or disclose individually identifiable health information in violation of the HIPAA Privacy Rule); (2) $100,000, five years in prison, or both (for covered entities and business associates whose wrongful conduct involves false pretenses); and (3) $250,000, ten years in prison, or both (for covered entities and business associates whose wrongful conduct involves the intent to sell, transfer, or use individually identifiable health information for commercial advantage, personal gain or malicious harm).[62] At the time of this writing, the HIPAA Privacy Rule neither contains a private right of action nor allows allow injured parties to share in civil settlements or criminal penalties imposed or collected by the federal government. That said, the HIPAA Privacy Rule could be amended to do so in the near future.

Other privacy and confidentiality laws contain different means of enforcement. For example, the Texas Medical Records Privacy Act (TMRPA) permits the Texas Attorney General (AG) to institute an action for injunctive relief to restrain a violation of the Act.[63] The Texas AG also may impose civil penalties against a regulated entity for a violation of the Act. These civil penalties may not exceed (1) $5,000 for each violation that occurs in one year, regardless of how long the violation continues during that year, committed negligently; (2) $25,000 for each violation that occurs in one year, regardless of how long the violation continues during that year, committed knowingly or intentionally; or (3) $250,000 for each violation in which the covered entity knowingly or intentionally used protected health information for financial gain.[64] If an individual or entity that violates the TMRPA is licensed by the state and subject to investigation and disciplinary action, including license probation or suspension, such disciplinary action may be imposed. Illustrative, not exhaustive, examples of individuals and entitles licensed by the state of Texas include attorneys, physicians, psychologists, nurses, social workers, and marriage and family therapists as well as hospitals, nursing homes, home health agencies, and hospices. If there is evidence that the individual's or entity's violations are egregious and constitute a pattern or practice, the individual's or entity's license may be revoked.[65] Finally, TMRPA-regulated individuals and entities may be excluded from participating in state-funded healthcare programs, such as the

62. *Id.* § 1320d-6.
63. Tex. Health & Safety Code § 181.201(a).
64. *Id.* § 181.201(b).
65. *Id.* § 181.202.

Texas Medicaid Program, if a court finds that the regulated individual or entity engaged in a pattern or practice of violating the TMRPA.[66]

Although most state laws do not contain a private right of action that would assist individuals whose vaccine information is breached or otherwise the subject of a privacy violation, the CCPA does contain a very limited private right of action for cases involving negligence with regard to a data breach. In particular, the CCPA provides any consumer whose nonencrypted and nonredacted personal information, including vaccine information, is subject to an unauthorized access and exfiltration, theft, or disclosure as a result of the business's violation of the duty to implement and maintain reasonable security procedures and practices to institute a civil action. The civil action may be to recover (1) damages ranging from $100 to $750 per consumer per incident or actual damages, whichever is greater; (2) injunctive or declaratory relief; and (3) any other relief a court deems proper.[67]

Summary

Vaccine information is requested, collected, used, and disclosed by a wide variety of individuals and institutions in a number of contexts. These activities are not always regulated by patient privacy and health information confidentiality laws. Indeed, many privacy and confidentiality laws are limited in application to certain covered entities and business associates thereof, leaving many vaccine information requesters, collectors, holders, and disclosers unregulated. Many privacy and confidentiality laws also are limited in the data that they protect, leaving some vaccine information unprotected. Even when a particular privacy or confidentiality law applies to an individual or entity and in theory protects the vaccine information at hand, the law may not regulate the initial request for or collection of the vaccine information. That is, many privacy and confidentiality laws only regulate subsequent uses and disclosures of health information, including vaccine information. Finally, many vaccine information uses and disclosures are permitted without prior notification to or authorization of the individual who has been vaccinated. In particular, many privacy and confidentiality laws contain exceptions to authorization for TPO activities as well as PBA activities. Activities involving vaccine information that violate privacy and confidentiality laws may be

66. *Id.* § 181.203.
67. Cal. Civ. Code § 1798.150(a).

subject to a range of enforcement mechanisms, including injunction, civil penalties, criminal penalties, professional discipline, non-participation in public healthcare programs, and, in some states, private rights of action.

About the Contributors

Alexandra Bhatti is a public health attorney and recognized thought leader in vaccine ecosystems, with over a decade of diverse vaccine programmatic and policy experience across the government and private sector. She is currently Director of U.S. Vaccine Public Policy at Merck & Co. Inc, where she leads U.S. state and federal vaccine policy development and research as well as federal vaccine policy advocacy to advance evidence-based policy solutions that can help achieve and sustain high vaccination rates. She concurrently has served as faculty at Arizona State University in the College of Health Solutions over the last eight years. Prior to Merck, Ms. Bhatti was a public health attorney at the Centers for Disease Control and Prevention where she led vaccination law research. Her roots are in state public health where she was previously a manager within the Arizona Department of Health, Immunization Program Office as well as a Senior Scientist within the state health departments laboratory.

Anna Boltyanskiy is an Associate in Patterson Belknap's Litigation department. Prior to joining the firm, Ms. Boltyanskiy served as a Law Clerk to the Hon. Judith C. McCarthy of the U.S. District Court for the Southern District of New York. Previously, she was an Associate at the New York office of an international law firm. Ms. Boltyanskiy earned her JD from Columbia Law School in 2019, where she served as a staff editor for *The Columbia Human Rights Law Review*. She earned her BA, cum laude, from Yale University in 2016.

Matthew Brown graduated from the University of Georgia School of Law and practiced criminal and civil litigation in and around Chattanooga, Tennessee, before relocating with his wife and two children to the Chicago area. He completed an LLM in health law at Loyola University Chicago School of Law; his chapter stems from his LLM thesis. Mr. Brown was looking forward to a career in health law in Chicago, but his career plans are on hold while he and his family care for his son, recently diagnosed with brain cancer. His son's cancer diagnosis and treatment have reinforced his belief in the importance of widespread vaccination to protect the most vulnerable members of society.

Luke Cunniff (U.S. Vaccine Public Policy, Merck & Co., Inc.) is a health policy expert with interests in vaccine policy and advancing and improving health equity in historically underserved communities. He brings experience from service with the U.S. Peace Corps in Togo and working at the Clinton Health Access Initiative. He completed his Master of International Affairs degree at Columbia University preceded by a degree from the University of Michigan. Mr. Cunniff is based in Philadelphia.

Megha Hoon is an Associate in the firm's Litigation department. From 2019 to 2020, she served as a Law Clerk to the Hon. Denis R. Hurley of the U.S. District Court for the Eastern District of New York. Prior to clerking, Ms. Hoon worked as an Associate at an international law firm in New York. She earned her JD from Cornell Law School in 2016 and her BA from Hamilton College in 2011.

Richard Hughes IV, JD, MPH is a professorial lecturer in law at The George Washington University Law School and Partner at Epstein Becker Green, and formerly held leadership positions with Moderna, Avalere Health, and the Association of State and Territorial Health Officials. He also served on the Arkansas State Board of Health and as a professorial lecturer at the GW Milken Institute School of Public Health.

Faith Khalik was the Senior Researcher at the Center for Health Policy and Law at Northeastern University, where she tracked public health authority litigation and worked on a judicial education program on the social determinants of health. Previously, she was the Legal Fellow at Public Health Law Watch, a George Consortium initiative aimed at tracking, analyzing, and responding to public health laws and policies.

Brian Malkin is an Associate General Counsel with Teva Pharmaceutical Industries. He supports Research and Development, Regulatory Affairs, Commercial, Quality, and other client groups by counseling on Food and Drug Administration (FDA) regulatory law and strategy including expedited development pathways, labeling and safety issues, and pre- and post-approval development challenges. Mr. Malkin has more than 30 years of FDA law and policy experience and over 20 years intellectual property law experience, including 9 years at the FDA (Office of the Commissioner and the Center for Drug Evaluation) and a number of boutique

FDA and intellectual property (IP) and international law firms in associate and partner capacities, where his practice focused on innovative and generic/biosimilar pharmaceutical and biologic products, including medical devices and other FDA-regulated products. He is regular adjunct professor or guest lecturer at Katz/Yeshiva University, Georgetown Law University, and American Law University.

Kate Mevis is the Executive Director of U.S. Vaccine Policy at Merck, overseeing federal and state vaccine policy. Prior to her current position, she served in multiple health policy and leadership positions in the White House, the U.S. Department of Health and Human Services, and the U.S. Senate. She holds a Graduate Certificate and a BA from The George Washington University.

Peter Meyers, Professor of Law Emeritus, The George Washington University Law School, created and served as the Supervising Director of the law school's Vaccine Injury Litigation Clinic, as Chairman of the Advisory Commission on Childhood Vaccines Workgroup of the U.S. Department of Health and Human Services, and as a Designated Reviewer of nine publications on vaccines by the National Academy of Sciences' Institute of Medicine. He has published several articles on vaccines, including "The Trump Administration's Flawed Decision on Coronavirus Vaccine Injury Compensation: Recommendations for Changes," *J. Law and the Biosciences*, Vol 7, Issue 1, Isaa082 (Nov. 2020), and "Fixing the Flaws in the Federal Vaccine Injury Compensation Program," 63 *Admin. L. Rev.* 785 (2011).

Bharath Palle is a Law Clerk in Patterson Belknap's Litigation department. Mr. Palle holds a doctorate in legal history from Harvard Law School. Prior to joining the firm, he practiced as a litigator for several years in Chennai, India.

Katherine (Kathy) Pappas is an Associate with McDermott Will & Emery. Ms. Pappas's practice focuses on patent litigation, primarily in the life sciences sector. She handles matters involving a large variety of technologies, ranging from mechanical inventions (e.g., microfluidic devices, injector pens) to pharmaceutical litigation under the Hatch-Waxman Act.

Wendy E. Parmet is the Matthews University Distinguished Professor of Law at Northeastern University, where she is the faculty director of the Center for Health Policy & Law. Her latest book, *Constitutional*

Contagion: COVID, the Courts, and Public Health, was published in 2023 by Cambridge University Press.

Roger Price is a graduate of the University of Chicago Law School and the University of Michigan. Following service as a Law Clerk for federal district court judge Abraham Lincoln Marovitz (N.D. Ill.), he engaged in the private practice of law for almost 40 years, concluding as a partner with the Seyfarth firm. During his career, he authored several legal articles that were published in the *Federal Bar Journal*, the *Illinois Bar Journal*, and *Am. Jur. Trials*. For over a decade, he has been exploring, writing, and teaching about the interrelationship of Judaism and the physical, biological, and social sciences. More recent essays and other materials concerning the interface of Judaism and science can be found at www.judaismandscience.com.

Nicole Strombom, JD, MPH, is a fourth-year doctoral student in the PhD in the Public Health Sciences program at Washington University in St. Louis. She graduated from Saint Louis University with a JD (2019) and MPH (2020). Ms. Strombom is an alumna of the University of California, Davis (2013) and graduated with majors in Anthropology, Psychology, and Communications.

Stacey Tovino, JD, PhD, serves as the William J. Alley Professor of Law and Director of Graduate Healthcare Law Programs at the University of Oklahoma College of Law in Norman, Oklahoma. An elected member of the American Law Institute and an invited fellow of the American Bar Foundation, Professor Tovino's current research focuses on patient privacy and health information confidentiality, mental health law, substance use disorders and the law, and virus and vaccine law. She publishes her interdisciplinary research in textbooks, casebooks, encyclopedias, law reviews, medical and science journals, and ethics and humanities journals.

Jessika A. Tuazon is a Partner in the Los Angeles office of Epstein Becker Green. She advises healthcare, life sciences, and biotechnology clients on the development and commercialization of their products, as well as a broad range of complex legal and regulatory compliance, promotional, risk management, and enforcement matters relating to their products and business operations.

William Walters is an Associate healthcare attorney at Epstein Becker Green. He earned his JD with a concentration in health law from The George Washington University Law School, where he also served as a Kahan Health Law Fellow.

John Winter is a Partner in Patterson Belknap's Litigation department. He has focused his practice on the defense of pharmaceutical and medical device cases. Mr. Winter has tried or argued the appeal of product liability cases in state and federal courts throughout the United States and also has acted as lead counsel for pharmaceutical, consumer product, and medical device manufacturers in consolidated proceedings in state and federal courts. In addition, he has published articles on regulatory and evidentiary issues concerning vaccines, pharmaceuticals, and medical devices. Prior to joining Patterson Belknap, Mr. Winter served as Law Clerk to the Hon. John M. Cannella, U.S. District Judge for the Southern District of New York. He earned his JD from Fordham University School of Law in 1981, where he served as the Editor-in-Chief of the *Fordham Urban Law Journal*. He earned his BA, cum laude, and an MA in Government Affairs from the University of Pennsylvania in 1978.

About the Editors

Alexandra Bhatti is a public health attorney and recognized thought leader in vaccine ecosystem, with over a decade of diverse vaccine programmatic and policy experience across the government and private sector. She is currently Director of U.S. Vaccine Public Policy at Merck & Co. Inc, where she leads U.S. state and federal vaccine policy development and research as well as federal vaccine policy advocacy to advance evidence-based policy solutions that can help achieve and sustain high vaccination rates. She concurrently has served as faculty at Arizona State University in the College of Health Solutions over the last eight years. Prior to Merck, Ms. Bhatti was a public health attorney at the Centers for Disease Control and Prevention, where she led vaccination law research. Her roots are in state public health where she was previously a manager within the Arizona Department of Health, Immunization Program Office as well as a Senior Scientist within the state health departments laboratory.

Montrece McNeill Ransom, JD, MPH, currently serves as the Director of the National Coordinating Center for Public Health Training. Ms. Ransom was appointed as a Presidential Management Fellow and worked at the Centers for Disease Control and Prevention for almost 20 years. For the last 10 years of her service, Ms. Ransom led the CDC's public health law–related training and workforce development efforts. She received her law degree from the University of Alabama, her MPH from Emory University's Rollins School of Public Health, and her Executive Leadership Coaching Certification from Georgetown University. Ms. Ransom is the ABA Health Law Section's 2019 Champion of Diversity and Inclusion Awardee, and the 2017 recipient of the American Public Health Association Jennifer Robbins Award for the Practice of Public Health Law. She is the President of the American Society for Law, Medicine, and Ethics and serves on the Advisory Committee for the Georgia Campaign for Adolescent Power and Potential. Devoted to helping people reach their human potential, Ms. Ransom also spends a lot of time working on career pathing and professional development with new public health practitioners and public health lawyers.

Loren Milliken, MSW, MPH—Epidemiology, is a Program Associate for the National Coordinating Center for Public Health Training at the National Network of Public Health Institutes (NNPHI). In this role, she assists on projects related to performance improvement, workforce development, data modernization, legal epidemiology, and health equity training. Her interest in public health started as a Social Work graduate student at the University of Georgia. Here, she learned about social work principles and practices related to rapport building, community engagement, and social justice, all concepts instrumental in approaching public health concerns. She writes and edits for numerous public health–related publications within NNPHI.

Emely M. Sanchez, JD, MPH. Public health law and policy professional.

Angela K. Shen, ScD, MPH, is a retired Captain from the U.S. Public Health Service, Adjunct Associate Professor in the School of Medicine and Senior Fellow at the Leonard Davis Institute of Health Economics at the University of Pennsylvania, and Visiting Scientist at Children's Hospital of Philadelphia. She is a vaccine policy expert and health services researcher with over 25 years of experience, specializing at the intersection of policy and practice in health disparities, quality measurement, access to immunization services, vaccine confidence, and barriers to innovation. During her 22-year federal career Dr. Shen held leadership roles in the U.S. government health infrastructure at the U.S. Department of Health and Human Services—including the Centers for Disease Control and Prevention, Food and Drug Administration, Administration for Children and Families, and Office of the Assistant Secretary for Health—and the Department of State in the U.S. Agency for International Development.

Table of Cases

E

F

G

H

I

J

K

T

U

W

Z